HEIGHTENED CONSCIOUSNESS

The Mystical Difference

✧   ✧   ✧

by
David Granfield

Paulist Press
New York/Mahwah

To
My Brother
Patrick Granfield
With Great Admiration

Library of Congress Cataloging-in-Publication Data

Granfield, David.
    Heightened consciousness: the mystical difference / by David
Granfield.
        p. cm.
    Includes bibliographical references.
    ISBN 0–8091–3174–9
    1. Mysticism. 2. Trinity. I. Title.
BV5082.2.G74   1991
248.2′2—dc20   90-25505
                                                                      CIP

Published by Paulist Press
997 Macarthur Boulevard
Mahwah, New Jersey 07430

Printed and bound in the United States of America

Contents

✧   ✧   ✧

Preface

✧   ✧   ✧

Our mind is never satisfied: it craves ever more meaning, ever more value. We seek a total apprehension of reality. If we continue the search, opening our minds and hearts, we find ourselves, with the help of grace, knowing and loving the mystery that is the triune God, who comes to us in the person of Jesus Christ, born of the Virgin Mary, and who also comes to us, but much less visibly, through the indwelling Spirit, who lifts us to an intimate sharing in the divine life. This faith experience can become, even in this life, a heightened consciousness of the loving presence of God. Mystical experience is open to all. And everyone and everything, directly or obliquely, positively or negatively, can contribute to the fanning of the spark of this divine love which carries our minds beyond all things into the light of transcendent Mystery.

Over the years, many people have familiarized me with the love of God, especially my parents, Patrick and Mabel Granfield, and my brother, Patrick. The Sisters of St. Joseph at Our Lady of Hope School were my first formal religion teachers. Then come my dear friends and friendly acquaintances, my confessors and professors, my fellow priests and women religious, and in a special way, the Benedictines of St. Anselm's Abbey. A less personal but extremely powerful influence comes from the authors of great books on mysticism, theology, philosophy, law, and all sorts of other subjects, and also from the cohort of mystics and saints who have shown the abundant generosity and mercy of the divine Lover in their own lives. Indeed, the whole world, as a universal theophany, has awakened me to the glory of God.

More proximately, I take great pleasure in thanking, for their careful reading and penetrating suggestions, my colleagues: Avery Dulles, S.J., William Hill, O.P., and James R. Price III. I am grateful, too, to my friend, John Farina, editor-in-chief of the Classics of Western Spirituality, for bringing my book to the Paulist Press. Once again,

I must express my deep appreciation of the painstaking editing and insightful clarifications of Dr. Cathleen Going (Sr. Mary of the Savior, O.P.) of the Farmington Hills Monastery in Michigan, whose efforts have contributed much. Finally, I thank my brother, Patrick Granfield, who as usual has encouraged and assisted me on so many levels, sharing his wisdom and scholarship with me in my formidable task of theologizing about mystical experience. It has been my great privilege to have been able, with the grace of God, to devote myself to such a humbling but inspiring subject.

Introduction

✧   ✧   ✧

Mysticism is sparked by a personal quest: "As the deer longs for the running waters, my soul longs, O God, for you. My soul is searching for God, the God of my life; when can I enter and see the face of God" (Ps 41:2–3). This quest is not an option but a command: "Let hearts rejoice that seek the Lord. Seek the Lord and his strength. Always seek the face of the Lord" (Ps 104:4). This book is my attempt to discover and understand a way to fulfil this longing for intimate union with the divine.

Mysticism is heightened consciousness of the loving presence of God. As simple as that, it still requires a challenging task of self-transcendence. God calls us to himself and expects us to answer that invitation wholeheartedly; mystical experience thus harmonizes a divine gift with a human response. The human role is clearly indicated: "Draw near to God and he will draw near to you" (Jas 4:8). The antecedent action of God must be kept fully in mind: "No one can come to me, except the Father who sent me draw him" (Jn 6:44). God is our destiny, but first he is our origin in the realms of nature and grace. Mysticism is the experience of utter dependence and shared fruition.

The focus here is on the individual person, but the person in context as part of the congregation of Christian believers, as part of the community perfected as the Body of Christ. Nonetheless, there is the clear recognition that God loves all human beings and draws them to him through diverse ways and religions.

We achieve this ever-deepening intimacy with God by doing something that seems simple—the opening of our minds and hearts unrestrictedly to knowing and loving. These actions may be simple, but they are not easy. For they require self-transcendence and the assistance of the Holy Spirit. Since openness to the Holy Spirit makes heightened consciousness possible, openness and consciousness

1

prove to be the twin pillars of the human response; the indwelling Spirit is the proximate principle of divine union.

This book examines mysticism as a progressive consciousness of God: the way that lover and beloved achieve an ever-deepening union through reciprocal love. Chapter 1 describes the potentiality for mysticism that we all have as conscious subjects, embodied spirits, authentic persons, and existential participants. Created with a capacity for God, for unrestricted knowing and loving, we are assisted by grace in its actualization.

Chapter 2 looks at the goal of the mystical life, which is union with God, a theophany or divine manifestation. Theophanies occur on two major levels: the pre-mystical consciousness of God through reason and faith, and the more intense, mystical consciousness of God through the mediated experience of divine immediacy.

Chapters 3 and 4 sketch out the twofold path to mystical union. Chapter 3 discusses the kataphatic way, which is the affirmative use of creatures as created analogies of God, both positively through beauty and other creaturely goods, and negatively through suffering properly understood and accepted. The kataphatic way leads to the apophatic through a growing awareness of the open-ended character of those special analogies called symbols.

Chapter 4 analyzes the apophatic way or the way of denial, by which one experiences the incomprehensible God—more perfectly than in the kataphatic way—by transcending the multiplicity of created forms and inordinate desires. This elimination of all that is not of God—without excluding Jesus—brings, through love, a luminous darkness more divinely revealing than is the whole universe of creatures and leads to an enlightened return.

Chapter 5 looks to the heightening techniques which help remove the obstacles to opening the mind fully to a consciousness of the loving presence of God. It seeks to discover the role of the natural in the realm of grace and what graced nature can do in the normal development of the spiritual life.

Chapter 6 moves beyond techniques to the first principle of mysticism, which works with power to open the mind and heart to God. This revealed principle is found in the Gospel of John with its sequence of law, love, and light: "He that has my commandments and keeps them, he it is that loves me. And he that loves me shall be loved of my Father, and *I will love him and will manifest myself to him*" (Jn 14:21). This principle leads us beyond physiological and psychological techniques to the heart of the Trinity, the Spirit of Truth.

Chapter 7 describes finally the fulfillment of mystical consciousness in the Spirit, who is the mutual love of Father and Son. This union with the Trinity through the divine missions is rooted in exemplarity, facilitated by connaturality, and maximized by epectasy. The latter is the continuing expansion of mind and heart to heights of consciousness that transcend the normal operations of a life of loving faith. Mystical experience does not substitute for faith; it is the phenomenon of enlightened faith perfected by charity. Finally, in surveying the growth of heightened consciousness, we examine the major stages of mysticism and their culmination in the transforming union. The mystics of the Western and Eastern churches call that union a kind of deification—a unity of consciousness despite the plurality of natures.

In short, the book involves these major topics: (1) The potentiality in the conscious subject for mystical openness; (2) The theophanies, pre-mystical and mystical, as the goal and actualization of these potentialities; (3) The affirmative means through created analogies in the kataphatic way; (4) The negative means through transcending created forms and inordinate desires in the apophatic way; (5) The natural techniques, aided by grace, to remove the impediments to those two ways; (6) The revealed first principle for completely opening the mind and heart to God; and (7) The culminating fulfillment by participation in Triune consciousness through the indwelling Spirit of Jesus.

As an attempt at an integrated understanding of mysticism from the perspective of conscious intentionality, the book brings the whole question of mysticism into a new light: how body and soul, nature and grace work together in that fulfillment through the Spirit which is a heightened consciousness of the loving presence of the Trinity. This glorious gift and compelling goal is only a dim foretaste of the eternal vision of God, but it is for us on earth what life in the Spirit should be: it is the mystical difference that love can make.

1

The Openness to Mystical Experience

✧   ✧   ✧

*The sun has one kind of glory, the moon another, the stars
another, for star differs from star in glory.*

I Cor 15:41

In the town of Cassiciacum, near Milan, the thirty-two-year-old
Augustine gathered together a few intellectual friends. He had been
converted to Christianity the preceding year, and now in this secluded
place he found the opportunity to talk over with like-minded persons
many problems of philosophy and religion. He later recounted that
their daily discussions regularly led him to spend the first half of the
night pondering over the questions raised and that sometimes his
reflections continued until dawn.

In the quiet of this country estate, he wrote some short works;
one of them, composed just before his baptism in 387, was an unfin-
ished piece called *Soliloquies*, which took the form of a dialogue between Augustine and Reason. In it, he uttered the now famous words:
"O God, ever the same, let me know myself, let me know you."[1] This
prayer of the Doctor of Grace has beautifully foreshadowed his life-
long quest for interiority and transcendence. The word order here is
especially significant: one must first know oneself, before one can
know God. Augustine's insight sets the theme for this chapter and,
in fact, for this book, that of self-consciousness leading to God-
consciousness.

What is this creature who dares hope for intimate knowledge of
God? To begin answering that question, I shall discuss the potential
mystic as a conscious subject, as an embodied spirit, as an authentic
person, and as an existential participant. These four aspects enable us
to comprehend more perfectly the dynamic character of that being
about which Augustine wrote: "You have made us for yourself, O
Lord, and our heart is restless until it rests in you."[2]

This ultimate rest and fruition in the Lord occurs only if we are truly *capax Dei,* capable of opening our minds and hearts to God, capable of being one with God. We look first at the potential mystic in terms of subjectivity, duality, individuality, and participation. These notions enable us to understand our God-given openness to heightened consciousness of his loving presence. In later chapters, we learn how to actualize fully this marvelous potentiality.

The Conscious Subject

Over a thousand years after Augustine, this same focus on the inner life was reflected by the first woman doctor of the church, St. Teresa of Avila (1515–1582), in a book entitled *The Interior Castle* (1577). "I began to think of the soul as if it were a castle made of a single diamond or of very clear crystal, in which there are many rooms just as in heaven there are many mansions."[3] This was no oversimplified, psychological blueprint of the encounter with God. Acutely aware of the complexities of the spiritual life, she divided her work into seven parts, each of which is itself a series of mansions, *moradas.* The soul in the state of grace, still fighting temptations, enters the first set of mansions and seeks with the help of grace to reach the seventh set of mansions, where God dwells and the mystical marriage occurs.

Always acknowledging grace as a gift of God, which no one can wholly deserve, Teresa of Avila repeatedly assured her sisters that through a life of humility and loving interiority, they could achieve full union with God. "If you consider yourselves unworthy of entering even the third Mansions, you will more quickly earn from him the will to reach the fifth, and thenceforward you may serve Him by going to these Mansions again and again, till he brings you into the Mansion which he reserves as his own."[4] Note that at the core of her search, there was always self-consciousness. She considered the experience of interiority to be absolutely necessary: "It is absurd to think that we can enter into heaven without first entering our own souls—without getting to know ourselves."[5]

In pursuit of this mystical interiority, we look at its two major components: we shall speak briefly here of self-consciousness, distinguishing it from intentionality; and we shall discuss more fully the two forms of intentionality, meaning and feeling.

Self-consciousness

Getting to know ourselves is one of the most natural things in the world; to do so perfectly is one of the most difficult. Yet as potential subjects of mystical experience, we all have the call to full self-consciousness as part of our destiny. The term "subject" gives us a clue, for it means a conscious being; to use the adjective "conscious" to qualify subject is redundant, unless used epexegetically, that is, used to bring out the precise meaning of a shopworn word. Incidentally, it helps to think of oneself first of all in cognitional rather than metaphysical terms, that is, as a conscious subject rather than an immortal soul or rational being, though of course we are all three. The reason is that we best understand our spiritual life if we begin with personal experiences rather than with abstract theories.

A subject is conscious when operating minimally in the dream state, normally in the waking state, or optimally in the mystic state. Whether religiously oriented or not, a subject is more or less aware of its various levels of consciousness: experiencing, understanding, and knowing, as well as feeling, deliberating, and choosing with freedom and responsibility. From this subjective viewpoint, we begin to examine the mystical life in the same way that we look at the rest of our life—with differentiated consciousness. By that term, we mean the awareness and self-appropriation of our various mental operations.

We differentiate not only the levels of conscious intentionality in knowing and doing but, more broadly, consciousness and intentionality themselves. The latter two notions involve the types of presence known through one's mental operations: "Just as operations by their intentionality make objects present to the subject, so also by consciousness they make the operating subject present to himself."[6] Thus by our mental operations we bring to mind our friends, our home, and our thoughts, and we also become aware of ourselves in so doing. The mental operations which bring us into contact with the world of our experience have an intrinsic function which also brings us into contact with ourselves—and not just through introspection, which is a mode of intentionality. Self-consciousness is not an operation in addition to intentionality, but an extension of one's awareness. And, as we shall discover, intentionality and consciousness complement one another in enabling us to know ourselves and by so doing to know God.

Forgoing a purely conceptual and theoretical approach, we begin the discussion of mysticism on more familiar and less abstract grounds—the levels of consciousness. We begin by trying to understand the continuous influx of data from our senses and our consciousness—that is, to get an insight. We are forever asking questions: What do the data mean? Is our understanding of them adequate and verified? How do we act responsibly on what we know? These same questions must be asked about mystics and by mystics, actual or potential.

The subjective perspective helps us appreciate our present stance before God. We come face to face with the immediacy of our experiences as we struggle to make sense out of them. We put to the test whatever in our lives we label religious or spiritual, in order to see what it is that we actually experience, question, know, feel, and value; we seek to determine whether a religious element is present, whether it is real to us, whether it is meaningful and worthwhile.

Looking at spirituality from a subjective viewpoint keeps us in contact with the concrete data of our own lives, data which are all too often overlooked, ill-understood, or deliberately dismissed. Without such insights, we may fall into religious formalism which gives us merely the illusion of security, a security without roots in the concrete realities of our existence. Generalities by themselves afford no guarantee that our thinking is grounded in the insights that correspond to our existential uniqueness and to the singular circumstances of our spiritual life. We can confront the mystery of the Transcendent intimately only in the immediacy of personal experience.

Meaning and Feelings

Intentionality, in making things present to us, fosters our concern with God's presence and directs us to him through meanings and feelings (positive and negative). In this way, we mediate created reality, becoming aware of its truth and value. Indeed, from created things we are able to move to an awareness of the uncreated God, whose providential disposition of our lives uses these natural effects to communicate his divine presence and will. Intimacy with God depends on our listening attentively and with openness as he manifests himself through the complexus of meanings and feelings that we daily experience.

The possibility of mystical experience does not render unnecessary or valueless those experiences that seem to arise naturally; for there are no purely natural experiences. God's eternal decree, his loving providence, our graced nature, and the gifts of the Spirit are ever working to bring us into conformity with God and to full participation in his trinitarian life.

Before getting more theoretical, let us take a concrete example of the complex blend of meanings and feelings that occur when the soul interacts with God: the life of Blessed Marie de l'Incarnation (1599–1672) as described in her *Relation autobiographique de 1654*. At twenty, already a widow with a young son, she experienced an intellectual vision of the Trinity which, despite long and sometimes painful interruptions, remained throughout her life. When thirty, she joined the Ursulines; ten years later, she was sent from France to Canada where she spent her last thirty-two years in missionary work with the Indians. Her contemplative experiences were extraordinary.

Marie de l'Incarnation spoke of a mystical marriage characterized by love, joy, and intimate communications, yet she noted that, during her first eight years after coming to Canada at the age of thirty-nine, she experienced revolts of the passions, temptations of aversion, a tendency to scruples, and anguish at God's absence. About the latter she wrote: "It sometimes happens that God who is the Master of this depth [of the soul] seems to hide himself and to leave it for a little while, and then it remains like a void, which is something unbearable. And it is there that the despair is born, which would throw the soul and body into hell."[7] Finally, on August 15, 1647, she seemed to emerge from this ordeal to experience the transforming union differently—this time with the uninterrupted presence of God. It was for her the thirteenth and last "state of prayer."

Not all mystics evidence the rich diversity of Marie's feelings and the intensity of her constant struggle to discern their significance, but like her they all try to attune themselves lovingly to God through these sometimes ambiguous and often painful intermediaries. Discernment thus remains necessary in appreciating God's presence and discovering his will. Unfortunately, one may all too readily develop an inordinate and egoistic concern about determining the stage of prayer one has reached: Is this the dark night of the senses or the spirit? Has the prayer of quiet been attained? Has one at last become a true mystic?

Nevertheless, there still remains the need to be most attentive to these experiences, for without meaning and feelings, we would not be conscious of God. Even when the meaning is found only in the darkness of faith and the feelings are arid and empty, there can be consciousness of a divine and loving presence. Keeping in mind the complex, imprecise, and overlapping experiences of meaning and feeling so vividly manifested in Marie de l'Incarnation, but found also in the lives of all of us, I shall consider briefly: (1) the connection between meaning and feelings; (2) their proportionate interaction; and (3) the need for discernment.

(1) *Meanings and feelings complement one another in an integrated response to reality.* The mind is unitary; of itself it tends to move from the intelligible to the true to the good; that is, from understanding to knowing to loving. It does that naturally: when we understand something we usually have a feeling and ideally have an appropriate one, for the vital thrust of our mind is to move integrally to the

real as both knowable and lovable. We mediate immediacy in this twofold way. To the extent that we understand things, we tend to respond to them affectively. Of course, biases or other flaws may inhibit or deform our responses but, in a properly functioning subject, feelings follow insight or understanding. I use the two latter terms interchangeably.

We can appreciate more precisely what feelings are by recourse to scholastic thought—still current when Carmelite and Ignatian spirituality began—which contrasted animals and angels. For example, a dog, having what are called concupiscible and irascible appetites, clearly manifests different feelings or emotions in the presence of his master than in the presence of an intruder. On the other hand, according to Aquinas, who wrote about angels (mentioned in the Bible) and about separated substances (discussed by Aristotle), angels have no senses, no sense appetency, no emotions. Aquinas concluded that angels experience neither concupiscence nor irascibility, but they can desire and will the good, for they do have intellectual appetites and can respond to value.[8]

Humans rank between beasts and angels, combining both a sensitive and an intellectual appetite. Because of their bodily component, they share physical responses with the other animals; because of their spiritual component, they share an intellectual response with the angels. Human feelings reflect the two components of our nature, primarily our spiritual appetite, and secondarily the sensible.

Feelings, even religious ones, do not happen merely by chance or by choice but rather occur spontaneously and normally together with insights. The "eros of the human spirit" is an exigency for truth and for goodness. An insight is an act of meaning which, if verified, enables us to make a judgment of fact. But we do not live by truth alone; we are not detached intelligences content with meaning. We also naturally seek goodness. Indeed, awareness of values is prerequisite to fulfilling ourselves through responsible actions. Feelings orient us in a world of good and evil. We crave values as we do meaning, and we must have both to function as human persons, whether religious or not. To become fully human we need not only intelligibility but affectivity; we need to be attuned to the truth of things and to their goodness. Feelings reveal to us a universe of values.

(2) *Feelings tend to be proportioned to the value and concreteness of the apprehended good.* The affective response that is a feeling normally follows an insight or understanding that is rooted in concrete data. Responses to concepts and other abstract formulations, however, are not as strong as the response to an insight, since they are

proportionately diminished by distance from the concrete. In the abstract realm, we may love an act of understanding; however, since the good is always concrete, we may find a concept to be so minimally concrete that we have no solid basis or motivation for further affective response. In Newman's terms, we might say that feelings result more from "real" than from "notional" assent.[9]

Not only the concreteness of the good but the degree of fullness of meaning proportionately determine the strength of feelings. Feelings pass through progressive stages: just as the mind goes from insight to judgment to decision and at each step perceives a deeper meaning or more profoundly affirms its initial understanding, so too the mind experiences a parallel gradation of feelings, which at each step are clarified and strengthened. The initial understanding gives a tentative feeling; verification heightens it; decision further intensifies it; and, finally, the successfully completed action brings that feeling to fruition.

Consider, for example, one's feelings during the various stages of making a visit to someone in a hospital or nursing home. When one first thinks of doing so, a sense of obligation may predominate; on making up one's mind one may feel reluctant but virtuous; during the visit, one becomes warm and caring; at the end of the visit, one rejoices lovingly at being able to comfort some sick and lonely person, but wonders perhaps at how weak one's feelings were in the beginning and how close one came to postponing what now seems patently and incontrovertibly to have been the right thing to do.

Throughout any such scenario, especially long-lasting ones, meaning and feelings develop interrelatedly. Both of them have their ups and downs, their furtherances and setbacks. The low periods may include meaninglessness and aridity; the peak experiences, both light and joy. There are also periods of ambiguity, imbalance, or alienation, where commitment brings little satisfaction or where enthusiasm seems to lack meaningful roots. At such a time, the struggle is for psychic integration in the face of challenges from within and without. Indeed, the mystical life with its contrasting experiences of dark nights and illuminations of faith, is a vivid manifestation of what happens on different levels and intensities in all phases of life.

Feelings in spiritual matters are generally an intentional response to a perceived object. Moreover, feelings differ from emotions in that the latter manifest a greater and more obvious physical resonance. For example, Teresa of Avila, who revealed a variety of profound feelings, insisted: "I am not in the least emotional; on the contrary, my hardness of heart sometimes worries me; though when the fire within my soul is strong, however hard my heart may be, it distils as if in an alembic."[10]

We have to interpret her remark as conditioned by the style of affectivity customary in sixteenth-century Spain, but she illustrates an important consideration: feelings can be powerful and persistent without being "emotional." Everyone must have feelings or there can be no apprehension of values. But these feelings need not reach the intensity experienced by Ignatius. His *Spiritual Diary,* as A.T. de Nicolás observed, reveals that in a period of forty days, "Ignatius had tears over 125 times, an average of four times a day, and 26 times tears with sobbing," as well as other signs of feelings and emotions such as joy, spiritual rest, intense consolation, and spiritual flavor and relish.[11]

Disordered feelings and uncontrolled emotions disrupt the spiritual life, so the refining of feelings remains a lifetime task. Right feelings must be strengthened; wrong feelings, rejected. A problem arises from the fact that there may be dysfunctional feelings that are operative but hidden. Often called unconscious, they are more properly thought of as being conscious but not yet objectified and articulated. There are many ways of bringing the "unconscious" into the light—for example, dream analysis, journal keeping, or psychotherapy—and thereby appropriating and normalizing one's feelings.

A major benefit on the affective level of the Dark Nights, as explained by John of the Cross, is to purify the mind so that through the Night of the Senses, we learn to subordinate our feelings to intelligence and through the Night of the Spirit to subordinate our intelligence to God. In the process, mind and heart are perfected by the virtues of faith, hope and, especially, charity with its unitive function. Aquinas wrote: "Charity is that which, by loving, joins the soul immediately to God in a bond of spiritual union."[12] No longer then do the feelings dominate or distort the soul, but rather, liberated from bias, crudeness, and disproportion, they foster through love the integrity needed for heightened consciousness of God.

(3) *Discernment is necessary for properly assessing the meanings and feelings experienced in the spiritual life.* Knowing abstractly about the role of meaning and value in one's interaction with God is inadequate without knowing also how to discern and decide in the practical realm of the singular. All mystics have had to confront the mystery of divine providence in working out their ongoing response to God, in what Jean-Pierre de Caussade, an eighteenth-century French spiritual writer, called, "the sacrament of the present moment."[13] This task involves living one's daily life attuned to the law

of divine providence, as stated by Paul: "To those who love God all things work together for good" (Rom 8:28).

Both good things and bad things happen to all; everyone experiences pain and suffering as well as joy. It takes strong faith to insist through all the changes, "The Lord is good to all and merciful toward all his works" (Ps 145:9). Whatever happens, our response is crucial. How do we interpret events and feelings and how do we respond to them as coming from the God who is love? Let us look briefly at how two great mystics have handled this problem.

John Ruusbroec (1293–1381), the great Flemish mystic, was keenly aware of intensity of feelings in the ebb and flow of one's spiritual life. He summarized memorably the way to discern the meaning of feelings, whether pleasant or painful. "The most profitable stirrings which such a man can feel, and for which he is best fitted, are heavenly weal and hellish woe, and the ability to respond to these two with fit and proper works." His advice is straightforward: realize that you belong to God and not to yourself, do his will and not your own, and let him work in you in time and eternity, for that is what brings "heaven into hell and hell into heaven." The result is not only spiritual health with an untroubled heart but also the ability "to feel unmediated union with God."[14]

Ignatius of Loyola, born about 200 years after Ruusbroec, developed discernment into a more systematic process. In the first week of the *Exercises,* he established: "Rules for perceiving and understanding to some degree the different movements that are produced in the soul: the good, that they may be accepted; the bad, that they may be rejected."[15] He, too, began with the extremes of feeling—consolation and desolation—but scrutinized both in trying to determine precisely the will of God. He called consolation the interior movements which cause the soul to be inflamed with love of its creator, to shed tears of love, to increase faith, hope, and charity, to have joy and peace and attraction to spiritual things (Rule 3).[16] He called desolation all that is contrary to consolation, namely, darkness, turmoil in the soul, attraction to the low and earthy, moods of laziness, tepidity, and alienation from God (Rule 4).[17]

The battle is between God and the enemy, with angels and devils in the midst of the fray. In his rules for the second week, Ignatius showed that discernment was even more complicated, because: "Both the good and bad angels may console the soul but for different purposes" (Rule 3)[18] and indeed "the evil spirit . . . transforms himself into an angel of light" (Rule 4).[19] Since the combatants use meanings and feelings in the battle over the soul, the *Exercises* proposed a system of decision making based on the discernment of spirits, the key to which was cryptically formulated as "consolation without previous cause" (*consolación sin causa precedente*) (Rule 2).[20]

Since this "consolation" is at the core of Ignatian spirituality and since it involves both meaning and feeling, we shall examine it further. "Consolation without previous cause" is a touchstone for discernment since it can come only from God. Erich Przywara, S.J., explained that, for Ignatius, desolation was a motion from the exterior to the interior, but that consolation was "an inner motion."[21] Of course, the consolation that brings certainty to the soul is not a face-to-face vision nor a mere concept of God, but stems from an experience of unrestricted openness to transcendence. Karl Rahner described the ground of this certainty:

> Pure openness and receptivity is always genuine and can miss nothing because it excludes nothing but includes all. It always refers to the true God because it attributes no law to him that would do violence to what he is and expresses no judgment that is finite and so might falsely circumscribe him. Where the whole of a person's being is poured into this movement of receptivity, we have the consolation which cannot deceive because it carries its own evidence with it, presupposes no other, does not stand in contrast to any other that might be preferred to it, and is the foundation of all truth, certainty, and consolation.[22]

Discernment and election can then take place through what Rahner called "the experimental test of consolation, confronting the particular matter with the utter openness towards God."[23] Speaking more fully, he wrote:

> The particular that is met with or that must be chosen, done or undergone, is placed within this pure openness and receptivity of the consciously experienced transcendence toward God, and kept there. No wonder, then, that everything then becomes transparent in relation to God, that everything is found in God and God in everything, for everything is seen in the ever-open transcendence founded on the theological virtues and no longer obstructed by the particular object.[24]

The result of this process is certainty about the will of God, grounded by a "pure harmony in the depth of one's being which is experienced transcendence," but it is certainty about God's operation in us, not about our acceptance of it, not about our state of grace; so "such an experience, if it exists, cannot be transformed into a knowledge that a man can expressly state about himself."[25] This experience enables the subject to recognize, though he is not able to articulate it conceptually, the divine origin of his consolation and his discernment. "He recognizes the will of God which, over and above the general norms of natural and Christian law, disposes of the individual as such. This will come as a summons to him as the precise individual he is, not simply as the general vocation by which anyone is 'drawn wholly into God's love.' "[26]

This grounding of discernment in the transcendent brings a profound participation in the life of God in terms of knowing and loving him. We shall examine this insight more fully when we discuss the fourth aspect of the potential mystic, that of existential participant. Here our main concern has been the role of meanings and feelings in mysticism.

Both Ruusbroec and Ignatius, as we have seen, recognized these two components of the spiritual life, but they wrote about them from different perspectives: Ruusbroec focused on becoming a God-seeing person; Ignatius on doing God's will perfectly. Nevertheless, they were both God-seeing men conformed to the will of God, and they taught a way to moral and mystical union. What is significant here, however, is they both insisted on the need to be open to God through consciousness of one's own subjectivity. On this foundation, they structured their heightened consciousness of the divine presence.

In short, every human subject mediates the world through meaning and feeling. The religious subject, whether mystical or not, acts similarly in becoming open to ultimate reality and conscious of it through the same twofold instrumentality of meaning and feeling, as clarified and corrected by the discernment process. Being conscious of ultimate reality means that we must be open in knowing and loving—unrestrictedly so. The human subject, however, is not a pure consciousness, but is, as we have seen, an embodied spirit. The questions arise: Does the body limit our consciousness so that we cannot be open enough to God to experience him? Or can the spirit transcend those bodily limitations? We next look squarely at the composite nature of human beings, whose destiny it is to seek the face of God.

The Embodied Spirit

Altered states of consciousness, however ethereal their domain, do not totally escape their somatic matrix. For human beings are embodied spirits. Even in spiritual activities, the body with its brain and nervous system plays an indispensable role. Indeed, the words that Thornton Wilder puts on the lips of Caesar apply also to the contemplative: "To deny that one is an animal is to reduce oneself to half a man." In the strict sense, a human being does not *have* a soul and a body; each *is* a soul and body, an individual being: ensouled matter or embodied spirit.

Part of the confusion over human nature in things spiritual comes from mistakenly equating the scriptural references to spirit and flesh with soul and body or even with spiritual and material. In the New Testament, when John said, "The Word became flesh" (Jn 1:14), he certainly did not mean that the Word became just a body, but rather that the Word became an embodied spirit. Raymond E. Brown rightly observed: "For John 'flesh' emphasizes the weakness and mortality of the creature (not the sinfulness as in Paul); Spirit as opposed to flesh is the principle of divine power and life operating in the human sphere."[27]

Paul, well aware that flesh includes body and soul, brought in another issue. To speak of the spirit lusting against the flesh and the flesh against the spirit did not represent for him primarily the conflict between reason and the passions or between the mind and body, but rather the struggles within the person over whether he is to be dominated by human and earthly drives or is to be willingly influenced by God's revelation and grace. Dom Déchanet neatly stated the distinction in a way that sheds light on mystical openness: "The Apostle is concerned with two dynamisms: 'the flesh,' all human realities including the spirit, in so far as they claim to be self-sufficient and are closed to the Spirit of God; 'the spirit,' all human realities, including the body, in so far as they are open to the spirit of God."[28] Both the Johannine and Pauline meanings of "flesh" must be considered in any study of the scriptural dimensions of mysticism.

The body, however, has two effects on human interaction: it acts as both a barrier and a conduit; it makes communication difficult, but it also makes it possible. We do not directly experience other spirits; our awareness is channeled through the senses. As embodied spirits, humans can be the loneliest beings in the world: because they are material they may find themselves isolated; because they are self-conscious they may experience the pain of that isolation.

The Neo-Platonists gave this insight a dramatic but one-sided *soma-sema* formulation—the body as a tomb for the spirit. Spiritual progress meant for them a breaking free of the bodily prison by a rigorous purification from matter. Only then were human fulfillment and mystical union possible. Aquinas countered this failure to grasp the integrity of human nature by explaining the relationship of body and soul in the Aristotelian terms of matter and form, the soul being the substantial form of the body. His grasp of the unity of human nature had far-reaching effects on both ascetical and mystical theology.

The split surfaced again in the psycho-physical parallelism of Descartes, who separated the thinking spirit from quantified matter, the *res cogitans* from the *res extensa,* as if the soul were an oarsman in a boat, the body. Eventually, the Cartesian dichotomy resulted in a role reversal making the material and empirical component the dominant one. Thus, in many modern men and women, the human spirit, ignored and constrained, experiences its own finitude with existential *angst,* as if it were merely the voice of the material universe bemoaning its plight in finding itself devoid of fully intersubjective and truly transcendent experience. In the crowded realm of fragmented matter, the human spirit seems alienated and alone, with a sense of absurdity, even nihilism, undermining its happiness and reducing it to the status of a "ghost in the machine."

Embodied spirits, however, are not Leibnitzian monads without doors or windows to connect them with one another. Senses enable the spirit to become aware of its body as well as of the world outside. The fact that the senses are material might suggest that all we can learn about the external world is what is material, that we must remain ignorant of everything beyond sensible phenomena. We need not become radical empiricists, however, since we have not only the data of sense but the data of consciousness. Spiritual powers enable us to use the body and the senses as a means of understanding, loving, and communicating. The steps to meaning and value may be feeble and halting, but if made perseveringly they can lead to God.

Human beings, however, do not all have the same capabilities, nor can they all follow the same paths. The scope of their mental and physical powers differs widely. Mystics, too, share these human differences, and their profound self-awareness makes their writings vivid portrayals of a diversity of gifts, natural and supernatural, in the one Spirit. As "star differs from star in glory," the saints differ radically from one another in a spectacular display of divine imitability.

To help dispel any monolithic notion of how the mind of a mystic operates, let us examine a concrete variation, which has its roots not in culture and external circumstances, but in the very physiological, if not genetic, makeup of two persons, a man and a woman, to whom we have already referred, Ignatius and Teresa, both wholeheartedly seeking the face of God. Of course, an obvious difference is the sexual one, but I shall bypass that question to speak of something more explicitly cognitional.

These two sixteenth-century Christians had much in common: they were both Spaniards, founders of religious communities, religious geniuses, and profound mystics, yet they differed radically in a way that, despite a certain significance for the life of prayer, has, to my knowledge, been overlooked even in the present era of psychological sophistication.

Ignatius of Loyola, early in his *Spiritual Exercises,* enjoined the use of detailed and repeated visual portrayals of the places, events, and persons in the life of Christ, and even extended that imaginative reconstruction to heaven and hell. One term he used for it was *composición, viendo el lugar,* "composition, seeing the place," which is often oversimplified in English as "composition of place."[29] He had two other terms as well: "application of the senses" and "contemplation";[30] the former is precise if understood in reference to the imagination; the latter is easily confused since it differs from the use that other mystics of his time, such as John of the Cross, made of it. As Joseph Rickaby, S.J., observed, Ignatius was recommending "mind-painting" or the making of a *tableau vivant.*[31] A good way to appreciate what Ignatius actually intended is to read a typical instruction, such as the one for a meditation on hell; he prescribed "a composition to see with the eye of the imagination the length, breadth, and depth of hell."[32] He enumerated the role of each sense:

> The first point will be to see with the eye of the imagination those great fires, and those souls enveloped, as it were, in bodies of fire.
>
> The second, to hear with the ears lamentations, howlings, cries, blasphemies against Christ our Lord and against all his saints.
>
> The third, with the sense of smell to smell smoke, brimstone, refuse, and rottenness.
>
> The fourth to taste with the taste bitter things, as tears, sadness, and the worm of conscience.
>
> The fifth to feel with the sense of touch how those fires do touch and burn souls.[33]

Teresa of Avila was twenty-five years younger than Ignatius of Loyola and apparently never met him. What would have happened had he been her spiritual director early in her vocation and had demanded that she use "the eye of the imagination" as his method of prayer dictated? From her *Life* (1565), we learn what might well have been the tenor of her response.

> I had so little ability for picturing things in my mind that if I did not actually see a thing I could not use my imagination as other people do, who can make pictures to themselves and so become recollected. Of Christ as Man I could only think: however much I read about his beauty and however often I looked at pictures of Him, I could never form any picture of Him myself. I was like a person who is blind, or in the dark: he may be talking to someone, and know that he is with him, because he is quite sure he is there—I mean, he understands and believes he is there—but he cannot see him.[34]

Even had Teresa been a male, she might have experienced some difficulty in becoming a Jesuit. Because of her lack of a visual imagination, she would have failed the first of the *Spiritual Exercises,* in which Ignatius had written:

> In contemplation or visible meditation, as contemplating Christ our Lord, who is visible, the composition will be to see with the eye of the imagination the corporeal place where there is found the object which I wish to contemplate. By corporeal place I mean, for instance, a temple or mountain where Jesus Christ is found.[35]

Teresa's limitation, or more properly difference, is hardly unique. The pioneer French psychologist, Jean Martin Charcot, described this phenomenon in 1883.[36] A recent study by a Harvard psychologist noted that: "About three percent of people cannot seem to get any mental pictures at all, and about three percent are superb at it."[37]

Is Teresa's intelligence to be considered diminished because of her inability at picture-thinking? Not according to the Jesuit thinker, Bernard Lonergan: "Picture-thinking means thinking in visual images. Visual images are incapable of representing or suggesting the normative exigencies of intelligence and reasonableness and, much less, their power to effect the intentional self-transcendence of the subject."[38]

A radical difference in this one function of the mind did not, however, diminish either saint's greatness. We could never say that Ignatius, because of his strong images, was locked into the material realm and thus impeded in his breakthrough to transcendence nor that Teresa, because of her phantasmic limitations, was out of touch with concrete reality and inept in dealing with the practicalities of life.

The reason for comparing these two saints on this one point is to point out the often overlooked fact that not everyone functions mentally in the same way, especially when a bodily or material component is involved. As a consequence, not everyone can profit equally from the same spiritual practices or forms of prayer. Whatever the similarities we share with others and whatever practices we may profitably undertake in common with them, the uniqueness of each person, determined in part by the body, suggests that each one's path to God will inevitably be unique.

In short, human nature has a twofold reality: as spirit, it has an openness and exigency for the transcendent; as embodied, it is bound to the changeability and precariousness of matter. Because we are spirits, we can share in God's life; because we are embodied, we achieve this goal in part through a series of temporal and physical changes. We all share a common destiny in the contingency, vulnerability, and anguish of finite and flawed men and women striving, often mistakenly, for personal salvation and intimate fulfillment, helped visibly and invisibly, willingly and unwillingly by an ever-present love of God. Our spirit has the ability to break through the cloud cover of limitations and face the infinite horizon through our power of unrestricted openness to knowing and loving. We are embodied spirits, but we can transcend the bodily ceiling.

The Authentic Person

Looking at the mystic as a conscious subject and as an embodied spirit might seem to complete the initial description, at least on the natural level. What more do we add by calling the mystic, or anyone else, a person? And yet, the notion of person has remained a rich and important insight for centuries. The term is still used, but its meaning may vary, emphasizing certain aspects of the traditional definition and overlooking others. Currently, person is synonymous with human subject, a center of intelligence and freedom, joined to a human body.

The older and fuller meaning of person is not to be rejected lightly. It marks an historical achievement, an intellectual discovery, a breakthrough in the task of mediating the world through meaning. Even in a period of cultural transition, we may profit from seeing once again the symbols of the past through the eyes of those first grasping these underlying insights. *Anamnesis* or remembering sharpens our awareness of reality; for, even at this late date, we can look afresh with a "second naiveté" at the brilliant perceptions that have helped form Christian thought and spirituality.

The importance given to the idea of person leaps out at us from the pages of the thirteenth-century *Summa* of Aquinas who described it thus: "The person is that which is most perfect in all nature" (*Persona significat id quod perfectissimum in tota natura*).[39] The symbol had already been in use for centuries, and for centuries more would continue to play a major role in philosophical and theological thinking. What precisely then was this insight into the most perfect thing?

The ancients were confronting the obvious. They were fascinated by oneness, by the perennial problem of the one and the many. What did it mean to be one? How could there possibly be many? Pagan philosophers, such as Parmenides and Heraclitus, Plato and Aristotle, puzzled over this question. Christians, however, had their own special problems: How to explain one God and many beings without resorting to pantheism? How to explain one God as three-personed without resorting to polytheism? How to explain Christ as true God and true man without speaking of two persons and two natures, as did the Nestorians, or as one person and one nature, as did the Monophysites? Christian thinkers had to make sense out of both nature and revelation.

Mystics and mystical theologians have faced that same challenge. How can it be that Christians "being many are one Body in Christ" (Rom 12:5)? How can they become "participators in the divine nature" (II Pet 1:4)? How can they be united with the triune God, in fulfillment of the promise "that they may be one, just as you Father in me and I in you . . . that they may be brought to completion as one" (Jn 17:21)?

The idea of person that emerged did much to clarify Christian thought on these questions. Oneness was seen as the chief characteristic of personality. A person was an individual, but an individual with a difference. The fact of individuality is easily grasped by common sense: a being is one, unified, undivided; it is itself, not another. To express this state, the term, subsistence, was used: "Inasmuch as it exists in itself and not in another, we call it 'subsistence,' for we say that entities subsist which exist not in something but in themselves."[40] One might say that the prime value of the term, subsistence, was not that it plumbed the depths of individuality, but that it defined individuality with philosophic nuances and integrated it into theological thought. Even without full understanding of how individuals subsist, it was clear that individuals do subsist; that is, they do exist in themselves and not in another. One could then speak precisely of a universe of unique individuals, the Trinity, angels, mystics, non-mystics, animals, plants, minerals, atoms.

Although human beings are individuals as we said, they are individuals with a difference: they subsist in an intellectual nature. The definition is brief: "a person is a distinct subsistence in an intellectual nature" (*Persona: subsistens distinctum in natura intellectuali*).[41] So the notion of person refers to God, angels, and humans, but it excludes animals, plants, and things as being merely individuals.

Similarly, although humans are persons, they are persons with a difference. They subsist in an intellectual nature, as do all persons, but that nature is not purely spiritual, for they are, as we have seen, embodied spirits. Now we begin to focus on what individuates human beings.

Medieval theologians discussed the distinction that existed between individual angels. These pure spirits, they concluded, would each have to be a separate species, because if they all had the same form with nothing else to distinguish them, they all would be one and the same angel.[42] All human beings, however, do belong to the same species, because what makes them unique is designated matter. That means that the human spirit or soul or substantial form is individuated by the characteristics and the limitations of the matter that embodies it. Humans, whether mystics or not, are individuals precisely because of their bodies, though they are individual persons because they have an intellectual nature.

Biological science illustrates the material aspects of individuation. As members of the same human family, all human beings share the same nature, but clearly each is a different person. The distinguishing characteristics come into being through the material component. Humans can be both genetically and phenotypically distinct; that is, they almost always differ in their genetic makeup, and they always differ phenotypically because of their material makeup and the differences that result from the interaction of the genetic package, its specific matter, and the environment. For example, twins, genetically identical, show the phenotypical differences occasioned by their own material substances, mutations, growth, diet, activities, accidents, illnesses, friends, enemies, education, religion, marriage, jobs, and the rest of life's variables.

Being a person is not a static oneness. A person acts as a dynamic principle in order to fulfil his destiny. All one's human actions, whether deserving of praise or blame, are attributed to the person as a responsible subject. Men and women through their actions bring the potentialities of their nature to actuality and become fully themselves and fully members of the Body of Christ. Christian mystics bring that spiritual becoming to its highest individual and social perfection, so that they realize the ideal, "You are all one in Christ Jesus" (Gal 3:28).

To become an authentic person requires a threefold unity. First, the subject must be fully integrated by bringing into harmony his knowing and doing through intellectual and moral conversions, so that there is a solidly grounded mental unity in his whole being, broken by neither error nor sin.

Second, each person is a unity, but a unity that seeks community. Men and women do not remain shut up in their own uniqueness. Theirs is a concrete goodness, which, like all goodness, is diffusive of itself. Because their nature is intellectual, human persons can transcend themselves by knowing and loving other persons. Through justice and charity, they can realize that intersubjective unity which is ultimately perfected in the Body of Christ.

Third, persons have a self-transcendent exigency for unity and community that finds its fulfillment in recovering concretely something of the unity of its own divine exemplar, which existed from all eternity and which can be realized only in knowing and loving the three-personed God and through the Spirit sharing in this triune community.

In this threefold way, the triple admonition of Christ is fulfilled: the person loves himself; his neighbor as himself; and God more than himself. The goal of this threefold love is that "they may be brought to completion as one" (Jn 17:23). Through this completion the person, essentially "the most perfect thing in all nature," also becomes perfect fully and concretely in the realm of grace. How this oneness with the divine is to be realized and articulated is the burden of this book. Yet in some way the answer has already been suggested by the notion of openness to God.

The Existential Participant

To be a conscious subject, embodied spirit, and human person is not enough for mysticism; one must also be an existential participant in being—one must act responsibly. We shall look at this fourth and subsuming aspect the better to appreciate the human capacity for the divine. A human being is *capax Dei* by nature and by grace, but can actualize that capacity only in the existential order. Mysticism is a matter of doing as well as knowing.

Life presents us with a problem: we balance our desires and our limitations, and they seem to cancel out one another. We seek meaning and value, but do not find an adequate basis for them in ourselves. Indeed, a major insight, individual and communal, is that human beings are not their own ground of being and cannot by themselves account for their origin and destiny.

So we search the whole universe for an answer to what Eric Voegelin (1901–1985) called "the Question," seeking to pierce through the sense of absurdity occasioned by the human craving to know confronted with the apparent opaqueness of the universe. "The Question is not just any question but the quest concerning the mysterious ground of all being."[43]

It is most important to keep in mind that the Question and reality are not separate from one another; we must understand "the Question as a constant structure in the experience of reality and, since the experience is part of reality, in the structure of reality itself."[44] In brief, since to question is to participate in being—for questions, like all other actions, are beings—the more far-reaching they are, the fuller the participation. The Question, with its infinite vectors, implies the human capacity for transcendence.

The human subject, Voegelin insisted, is truly a participant, not a mere spectator nor a detached observer. He is by nature in tension with reality. To understand fully the process involving the Question, we need to consider Voegelin's notion of tension. Tension here, of course, is not the same as stress; it looks rather to the polarities within which we necessarily function. We are familiar with such tensions in most areas of our spiritual life, in the pull between sensuality and spirituality, privacy and community, liturgical prayer and formless prayer, freedom and authority, to name just a few. For authentic human beings, tension is the way of flourishing, not by removing one of the poles to resolve a tension once and for all, but by preserving a flexible, ongoing harmony between enduring poles.

One tension, however, is fundamental. It involves various modalities, the tensions between ignorance and knowledge, between mortality and immortality, but is, at the core the tension between humanity and divinity. This tension looks to the relation between beings and their ultimate ground. To describe this meta-tension, Voegelin used the Platonic term Metaxy (*metaxu*), the In-Between. Through conscious and progressive participation in Being, humans become more than human while remaining less than divine.

The cognitional aspects of this process involve the capacity for that luminosity, the perfection of which is mysticism. Eric Voegelin characterized this new state of consciousness as "the discovery of the human psyche as the sensorium of the divine *aition* [cause] and at the same time as the site of its formative manifestation."[45] He was at pains to show that we are operating in the realm of interiority. The response consists in articulating the experience through appropriate language symbols. Indeed it is an "experience-articulating-itself." In a key passage, Voegelin described the cognitional dimensions of our capacity for the divine.

> When the insight arises, it has the character of the "truth," because it is the exegesis of the erotic tension experienced; but it does arise only when the tension is experienced in such a manner that it breaks forth in its own dialogic exegesis. There is no erotic tension lying around somewhere to be investigated by someone who stumbles on it. The subject-object dichotomy, which is modeled after the cognitive relation between man and things in the external world, does not apply to the event of an "experience-articulating-itself."[46]

In short, the heart of the process is this: "The consciousness of questioning unrest in a state of ignorance becomes luminous to itself as a movement in the *psyche* toward the ground that is present in the *psyche* as its mover."[47] Note the dual aspect of our relation to God as our origin and destiny. He is the beginning (*arche*) and the end (*telos*). In other words, we are drawn by the divine ground to ask about our own existence and ultimate meaning. This questioning unrest is the work of the ground. If open to the tug of the golden cord of reason, one goes from experiencing not being one's own ground to experiencing the divine ground as something necessary to one's existence and fulfillment. Being conscious of the ground means being aware of rising from the ground as well as moving toward the ground, for the ground is both the alpha and the omega.

Voegelin clearly stated the intrinsic character of the capacity for the divine: "The nature of man is openness toward transcendence."[48] Nevertheless, he was all too aware that one can intentionally limit this capacity, though not without doing serious harm to his psyche: "This interdict on the Question is the symptom of a self-contradiction which makes the existentially open participation in the process of reality impossible."[49]

When the mind is open to transcendence, the answer to the Question is not what one might expect. "There is no answer to the Question other than the Mystery as it becomes luminous in the acts of questioning."[50] Consciousness of the transcendent, Voegelin insisted, is diminished by conceptual or propositional formulations. The divine ground is, of course, not a place or even some distant object, but a presence, which one realizes through a *via negativa*, for the ground is the Beyond, *to epekeina*, and is found only by transcending created reality.

In experiencing this ground fully and then articulating the experience with appropriate symbols, one's consciousness becomes luminous, manifesting both the emergence of the divine ground through questioning and simultaneously one's merger with it through participation in the structure of consciousness. To articulate this ongoing experience of "the consubstantiality of the human *nous* with the *aition* it apperceives,"[51] is to make the truth manifest in oneself; it is to become luminous, to shine with something of a divine character. For God reveals himself in humans who become a theophany incarnate.

This capacity for the divine is twofold: in Voegelin's terms, there is a noetic experience and a pneumatic experience, both of which result in a theophany. Since the next chapter is on the theophanic experience, we shall only note the twofold capacity for such existential participation in the divine in order to help integrate his remarks into our discussion on the mystical life.

Of the noetic experience, which we have been discussing, Voegelin wrote: "Philosophy in the classic sense is not a body of 'ideas' or 'opinions' about the divine ground dispensed by a person who calls himself a 'philosopher,' but a man's responsive pursuit of his questioning unrest to the divine source that has aroused it."[52] When we consider these words while recalling that in Christ all nature has been graced, we see how God is working through philosophy to reveal himself. The work of reason is not merely a second-rate concession to those without benefit of Christianity, it is an experience of the divine in knowledge and love that can be a priceless theophany for both Christians and non-Christians.

The complement to the noetic theophany is the pneumatic one. It would not be accurate to equate the two as referring, for Voegelin, to reason and revelation. For Voegelin, both theophanies are revelatory of God. However, he contrasted Plato and Paul, showing the new dimension of consciousness that the latter's "articulated experience" brings: "Paul does not concentrate on the structure of reality that becomes luminous through the noetic theophany, as the philosophers do, but on the divine irruption which constitutes the new existential consciousness without drawing too clear a line between the visionary center of the irruption and the translation of the experience into structural insight."[53]

To sum up, we see from Voegelin how our consciousness can be existentially open to the full dimensions of the divine-human encounter. Moreover, we can be aware of being a conscious subject ourselves as well as being a conscious object of divine consciousness. There are four aspects of this differentiated capacity for openness, so fundamental to mysticism. First, we are conscious of not being our own ground and the need to account for our origin and end. Second, we consciously follow the questioning exigency without closing our minds to the possibility of an ultimate ground. Third, we consciously grasp that there is a divine ground, our source and our fulfillment, and that it draws us to itself through the very questioning that it inspires. And, fourth, we acknowledge that human consciousness, neither fully opaque nor fully luminous, is in the In-Between, as we become progressively aware of participating in the directional movement of the cosmos. "The reality of history is metaleptic [participatory]; it is in the In-Between where man responds to the divine presence and the divine presence evokes the response of man."[54] We are theophanies in progress.

As Eric Voegelin noted about Plato's *Laws*, his own massive five-volume *Order and History* begins with the word, God: "God and man, world and society form a primordial community of being."[55] The culminating significance of this choice is underscored by the fact that his last volume ends with the word, divine. Having spoken of the participatory tension in which we live in this community of being, he concluded: "This experienced ultimacy of the tension becomes luminous in the symbol 'divine.' "[56]

CONCLUSION

Leo the Great said: "Recognize O Christian, your dignity." This admonition is important mystically; to appreciate one's dignity helps fulfil one's destiny. All men and women, owing to their capacity to share in the life of the Trinity are, potentially, mystics. Having been created in the image and likeness of God, they are fitted by nature and grace for conscious union with him.

The means of achieving this fulfillment is openness to God. We have seen the major aspects of this openness. (1) Because we are conscious subjects, we are finitely compatible with the conscious and triune God, for we have the ability to open ourselves unrestrictedly to knowing and loving and there is no intrinsic repugnance to our being elevated to a sharing in divine life. (2) Because we are embodied spirits, however, we find our capacity for full openness to God, though energized by our spirit, both helped and hindered by matter. Not being pure spirits, we must struggle, sometimes painfully, to open our minds and hearts. (3) Because we are persons, we each have our own unity as a center of inner dynamism, but we must learn to transcend even the self in order to be one with God. (4) Because we are existential participants, we can and must act decisively in seeking our divine ground and growing luminous in that participatory quest. Realizing that our whole nature, body and soul, is graced, we can through this openness to God, become conscious of our elevated state in proportion to our participation in the life of the Spirit.

The search for ultimate reality begins experientially with the meanings and feelings that compose our conscious life. Through them, with the help of divine grace, we can move from darkness into the realm of light inaccessible. Rooted in contingency, we seek to emerge into an immortal and divine life, not by forgetting the body but by subordinating it to the spirit. In doing so we learn to appreciate what it means to be a person, a principle of unity subsisting in an intellectual nature. Bringing our powers into harmony with that intellectual and graced nature, we are able, through active openness to participatory events, to attain a conscious union with the divine.

What this union is and how it is accomplished is our subject. So far we have merely indicated our capacity for things divine and the key to divine union—unrestricted openness of graced minds and hearts. We look next at the goal, an emerging theophany, and subsequently at the many stages of realizing that vision of love.

2

The Experience of Theophanies

✧　　✧　　✧

The great originality of Judaeo-Christianity was the transfiguration of history into theophany.

Mircea Eliade*

The human capacity for mystical experience looks to its goal—a theophany. The word "theophany" does not appear in the Bible; but theophany is the main purpose of the Bible: "That they may know you the one true God, and Jesus Christ, the one you sent (Jn 17:3). This Greek word, which originally described any appearance of the gods to mortals and, more concretely, a festival at Delphi at which images of the gods were shown to the people, eventually played a role in Christian thought. Long before Christ's appearance, however, the Jews believed that God manifested himself to Adam, Abraham, and Moses, and—through the Law and the Prophets, through various dreams and visions, through military victory and even defeat, through storms, winds, and earthquakes—to the people of Israel.

Christians, in interpreting and explaining revelation, have used the notion of theophany for myriad manifestations of God. For example, on the feast of the Epiphany (epiphany, hierophany, and theophany are more or less equivalent) three events are recalled which intimate a divine manifestation: the adoration of the Magi, the marriage feast at Cana, and the baptism of Jesus. Indeed, the teaching and miracles of Jesus, his transfiguration and resurrection, and the coming of his Spirit—all converged in one supreme theophany: Jesus, as true God and true man, the self-revelation of the Father. John Paul II indicated the focal point of this theophany: "The Father's love was revealed in the Son as redeeming love."[1]

For theophanies to occur, human beings must become conscious

---

* Mircea Eliade, *Images and Symbols* (New York: Sheed and Ward, 1961), p. 164.

of God. The heavens may proclaim the glory of God, but not without a conscious subject to respond with praise. No true theophany, neither the burning bush nor the tongues of fire, occurs without an intelligent reception by a conscious human subject. However God may manifest himself, human intentionality forms one pole of that communication. Hence, theophanies differ one from another—not only because of what God wills to reveal but because of what man is ready to receive.

One may, of course, reserve the precise term, theophany, to a rare and extraordinary experience or even to an exclusively biblical one. But in a true sense any consciousness of God is a theophany. On this earth, the peak is mystical experience; in heaven, the beatific vision. In both it is consciousness, rooted in nature and elevated by grace, of the presence of God. I shall use theophany broadly as consciousness of the presence of God, "in whom we live and move and are" (Acts 17:28).[2] This chapter is a discussion of the theophanic experience, first as pre-mystical consciousness and then as mystical consciousness. I shall consider the distinction between these two theophanies as well as their integral continuity.

Pre-mystical Consciousness

To raise the God question is part of one's intellectual and moral growth. Whatever the answer, the question is inevitable in one who experiences reality intelligently. A Christian mystic takes for granted the existence of a knowing and loving God, but must still keep the question alive in order fully and continuously to appreciate the answer.

To label the sources of the pre-mystical theophany, I shall use two parallel expressions: Karl Rahner's "the original experience";[3] and Bernard Lonergan's "the original message."[4] The first denotes the way that the mind, helped by grace, discovers God and the second, the way that God communicates additional truths about himself. In short, graced nature becomes conscious of the Holy Mystery, which is God, and becomes further enlightened by what God has chosen to reveal about that Holy Mystery. These two aspects of God-consciousness— the basic experience with its reflective thematization and the super- natural unveiling with its further thematization—constitute the uni- fied, pre-mystical theophany that God makes to all people: "For this is good and acceptable to God our Savior who will have all saved and come to a knowledge of the truth" (I Tim 2:4–5).

Mystery: The Original Experience

Religion, widespread geographically and historically, appears, even at first glance, to be based on a shared experience of the transcendent. It is possible, however, to speak of God—Yahweh, Allah, Brahman, the Divinity, the Supreme Being, the Transcendent—without adequately noting or describing the character of that experience. We must turn to our own subjectivity to discover how we become aware of the divine presence. So we reverse directions; instead of looking for God, we pause a moment to look at ourselves. Desiring to know, we wonder at the world around us and are flooded with questions. Sooner or later, we begin to ask: Where do the questions come from? Why do we desire to know at all?

Plato and Aristotle faced this problem as they moved from compact to differentiated consciousness. For them, the answer came in the discovery of the *Nous* (divine reason), the ground of human knowing and being. Culturally, this discovery has been made once and for all, but each person must recapitulate that differentiation in his own mental life. Eric Voegelin, as we have noted, made an exhaustive analysis of this historical achievement, and he affirmed its continuing personal validity: "The wondering and the questioning is sensed as the beginning of a theophanic event that can become fully luminous to itself if it finds the proper response in the psyche of concrete human beings—as it does in the classic philosophers."[5]

Voegelin made much use of Plato's puppet myth to explain the pull and the counterpulls on our psyche: we are pulled by the golden cord of reason and by the steel cords of the passions.[6] Lonergan noted that the resulting confusion traditionally occasioned the making of rules for the discernment of spirits to help distinguish "between being drawn by the Father to the Son and, on the other hand, the myriad other attractions that distract the human spirit."[7]

Both the antecedence and the gratuity of the pull of the golden cord underlie the words of Christ: "No one can come to me except the Father who sent me draw him" (Jn 6:44). Although the drawing of the Father is usually interpreted to mean the attraction of grace, the natural drawing also comes from God, who empowers us to seek him as our end. The God-given inclination of our mind prompts us to ask and answer questions; this process leads to consciousness of God, who alone can fully actualize our capacity to know and love. Even without knowing about God explicitly, we nonetheless wonder over this open-ended power that we possess, this inner dynamism that characterizes human life. That wondering, if seriously pursued, will eventually lead to the God question: Does an ultimate ground exist?

A major goal of Karl Rahner's theology was to describe the "original experience" of God and to work out its implications. This experience is rooted in what he called human transcendence; that is, the openness and indeterminancy of men and women, their minds being intrinsically compatible with an unlimited universe of being. He wrote: "Man is transcendent being insofar as all of his knowledge and all of his conscious activity is grounded in a *Vorgriff*, a pre-apprehension of 'being' as such, in an authentic but ever present knowledge of the infinity of reality (as we put it provisionally and somewhat boldly)."[8]

This pre-apprehension of total reality takes the form of an ever-expanding horizon, for every answer leads to more and more questions. Finally, we arrive at a conviction of the incomprehensibility of reality—the mystery. This mystery is not mere nothingness or emptiness, but a positive reality. Indeed, since our questioning mind seeks both meaning and value, part of the conviction about the mystery involves, although still incomprehensibly, infinite meaning and infinite value. Rahner thus called this answer the "Holy Mystery."[9]

Bernard Lonergan, in a way that paralleled Rahner's efforts, spoke of the "mystery of love and awe."[10] His emphasis on the "gift of love" and on "being-in-love with God" ensured that his discussion would focus on consciousness rather than metaphysics, that he would be in the realm of interiority rather than theory. Thus, he spoke of the gift of God's love rather than of sanctifying grace, though he admitted that the two ideas differed only notionally.[11] This equating of the gift of love with the gift of grace suggests the role of mystical experience; it is not merely falling in love with God, for grace achieves that, but it is rather a differentiated and intensified experience of that state of being in love with God.

Prescinding for the moment from the heightening, we still find that the gift of love or grace produces an awareness. A distinction is necessary: "To say that this dynamic state is conscious is not to say that it is known."[12] The human mind experiences something that transcends all finite being. Through this Lonerganian insight, we can understand how Rahner's "original experience" can be original (conscious) without being interpreted (understood and judged, i.e., known). There is an awareness that God is, that he is infinite meaning and value. We cannot grasp that meaning conceptually, though we can totally open ourselves to it; we cannot possess that value though we can surrender ourselves to it unreservedly. We know about infinite meaning and love but do not know them directly. By means of this divine gift, however, we become conscious of seeking this "mystery of love and awe."

The conscious state of being in love with God explains itself. We cannot justify it directly through our knowledge for we are dealing with a mystery. But being in love is, Lonergan insisted, its own justification.

> Being in love is a fact, and it's what you are, it's existential and your living flows from it. It's the first principle as long as it lasts. . . . But if you are in love it doesn't need any justification. It's the justification beyond anything else. Just as you don't explain God, God is the ultimate explanation.[13]

The gift of God's love is self-justifying because it involves a conversion, grounding further conversions, moral, intellectual, and psychic.[14] This reception of the gift of love is a religious conversion because it is the opening of a new horizon of ultimate concern or infinite meaning and value. As a consequence, we tend morally to choose value over pleasure, intellectually to verify our understanding of data, and psychically to rectify the flow of images and feelings. These conversions bring our consciousness to integral perfection. "Being in love with God is the basic fulfilment of our conscious intentionality."[15]

Lonergan further objectified this consciousness of God by explaining how the mental operations of inquiry, reflection, and deliberation lead to consciousness of God's existence and how this process is a movement through self-transcendence to the Transcendent. We shall take these two aspects separately.

The first aspect of the process involves the questions: Can anything be intelligible without an ultimate intelligible ground? Can anything be judged to exist without an ultimate necessary ground? Can anything be considered worthwhile or valuable without an ultimate moral ground? Thus the God question arises inevitably, when one questions one's understanding, judging, or deciding. Just phrasing the question does not give the answer, but it points out where to look for the answer, namely, the realm of meaning, existence, and value. For if there is no ultimate ground for these aspects of the world of our experience, that world is ultimately meaningless, valueless, and—non-existent.

Let us consider how to answer one of the questions: Can anything exist without having a necessary ground? Subjectively, our judgments—probable or certain affirmations or denials about the existence of anything—ultimately entail this question. Lonergan reasoned from the virtually unconditioned beings of our experience (contingent beings) to the absolutely unconditioned being (necessary being). His argument was that existing beings exist because all conditions for their existence are fulfilled; they exist in virtue of that fulfillment. No further conditions are outstanding, so the beings are virtually unconditioned; their existence, however, remains essentially conditioned; they do not exist absolutely; they do not exist of their very nature. To account for their existence, they require an absolutely unconditioned being, one which exists necessarily.

An understanding of theophanies presupposes an ultimate ground of being. Because this conviction of the divine presence is so critical to our thinking here, we do well to consider the implications of our experience of the existential poverty of all the beings of our experience, ourselves included. A distinction long operative in philosophy finds easy acceptance in the compact realm of common sense—the distinction between knowing *what* something is and *that* something is or, more technically, the distinction between essence and existence.

Early in life, unfulfilled hopes and baseless fears as well as ventures into the realm of fiction and fancy, make clear that not everything conceivable actually exists. In time, most people arrive at the unsettling insight that they themselves need never have existed, that their precious and unique being was once so problematic, statistically and humanly, that the odds were overwhelmingly against its biological conception. What if their parents had never met?

The grudging realization emerges that human beings do not have within themselves the sufficient reason for their existence. Men and women cannot account for themselves. They are clearly limited, contingent, and finite beings. Nevertheless, despite existential insufficiency, they do actually exist, so they necessarily depend on some other being or beings. Dependence on another contingent being or on a series of such limited beings does not suffice; the sum of an infinite series of negative numbers still adds up to a negative number. There must be dependence on a being who necessarily exists, one whose essence is to exist, on a being whose essence and existence are not distinct, on a being who is subsistent existence itself. We call that existential source, God.

The second aspect of the process of asking and answering the God-question is the movement from self-transcendence to the Transcendent itself. The first was becoming conscious of God's existence. We can formulate the structure of this development as a twofold opening of ourselves to the Transcendent. Lonergan stated this precisely: "Just as unrestricted questioning is our capacity for self-transcendence, so being in love in an unrestricted fashion is the proper fulfillment of that capacity."[16]

In practice, this fulfilling self-transcendence is a progression from the experiencing of data of sense and consciousness to a consciousness of God. We have already noted in the operations of the mind—the experiencing, understanding, judging, and deciding—a growing transcendence. In both knowing and doing we seek objectivity. We seek to know things as they are, not just as we would like them to be; we seek to choose what is truly valuable, not just what gives us pleasure. Finally, since we have an open-ended capacity for knowing and loving, we seek to fill that capacity, so we seek transcendent Truth and Goodness itself. In this search for reality, the fullness of meaning and value, we come to realize that we can achieve it only through a converted and authentic subjectivity.

The complexus of questions and answers, however, may cause us to overlook a critical fact: the gift of God's love is meant for all as the way of total self-transcendence. By consciously appropriating our operations, we develop a differentiated consciousness which, through attention and verification, helps us love God. In turn, our loving God in an unrestricted way perfects this differentiation. Note that the gift of love or sanctifying grace is a normal condition, not an exceptional one. We may or may not explicitly identify or remember occasions of spiritual experience; they are, however, hardly rare or even infrequent. Virtually everyone has experienced at various times such passing moments of spiritual clarity or loving presence. Usually they involve neither dramatic conversions or feelings of being "born again," but are more simply an awareness of need and gift, a temporary enhancing of what most of the time is taken for granted.

Speaking more concretely, I remember an experience, dating back to my youth, of what I would now call a differentiating of my own commonsense awareness of dependence on God. Walking through the woods one early spring, I stopped by a low-hanging branch and noticed the tiny new leaves that had just unfurled. Touching one of them, I thought of the many circumstances that over the years could have prevented that particular leaf from ever existing: a forest fire, a blight, a bulldozer, a drought, a winter ice storm. But looking at it then, I knew that, despite the probabilities that it would never be, it was there, it was real, it existed: a small, delicate, pale green leaf.

I could switch my mind back and forth, conceiving of it as existing and conceiving of it as not existing: now it is; now it is not. Focusing on the reality of its existence, I knew this tiny leaf, that I could pluck off the twig and mash between my fingers, could never be the sufficient reason for its own existence. There had to be something else, something that was sheer existence, an overwhelming and majestic and self-sufficient being to account for the brief tenure of this speck of life.

By playing the same game with myself, alternately confronting my nothingness and asserting my existence, I brought the experience of the desperate need of a necessary being, an infinite ground, into the inner realm of my own uniqueness. I, too, exist. I, too, am one who cannot account for his own existence. I, too, need the infinite support of the Being who must exist, else I perish. Contemplating my own conceivable nothingness snatches me from the ivory tower of concepts and sweeps me into moment-to-moment actuality. The divine ground is not merely through creation an historical beginning for me, it remains an indispensable presence and an infinitely desirable good. This abiding awareness crowns security with gratitude, humility with love.

Once such an experience has happened, it can be easily repeated. As long as one preserves an open and attentive relationship with God, one can rise to a certain level of self-transcendence and love. Even after one sins against this experience, sincere repentance may bring with it a similar awareness of need and gift, since God is always ready to give his love. These are common religious experiences, not mystical ones, but since our consciousness of God is part of a continuum, they enable us to surmise what that special heightening, we call mysticism, might actually encompass. God is generous with hints.

Revelation: The Original Message

The experience of mystery and its thematization are not the only conceivable source of consciousness of God. Indeed, though God is a mystery, he can, if he chooses, reveal what would otherwise remain hidden. Jews and Christians hold: "There is a God in heaven who reveals mysteries" (Dan 2:28); more specifically, Christians add: "He has let us know the mystery of his purpose, the hidden plan he so kindly made in Christ . . . that he would bring everything together under Christ as head, everything in the heavens and everything on earth" (Eph 1:9–10). Christ is the self-revelation of the Father; he is the God-man, the Savior who will bring human beings to a share in divine life. A theophany is clearly a privileged revelation.

An infinite ground of existence, truth, and goodness having been acknowledged, the major problem is not the possibility of revelation, but the proof that it actually occurred. Indeed, the mysteries revealed, although we might not have thought of them independently and certainly could not have adequately verified them, are in theory conceivable. Otherwise, they could not truly constitute a revelation, since they would not be understandable at all. An atheist might entertain the possibility that, if God exists, he could enable men and women to share in his divine life. But even a theist has no way to verify that possibility and affirm it to be a fact, without divine revelation and the gift of faith.

Throughout history, many have asserted that the content of the Bible does not surpass natural human abilities. Even its beauty and emotional appeal, its profound wisdom and practical sense, do not show conclusively that human beings could never have thought, desired, and expressed such things without revelation. More specifically, some say that the claims of Israel concerning God's love of humankind, the prevenience of his grace, and his providential care, together with the claims of the church concerning the incarnation and resurrection of Christ and the trinitarian character of God are but fictive expressions of the human response to a transcendent experience. Note a remark of Charles Davis: "Christology was a remarkable achievement of the creative imagination as it strove to express the experience of the transcendent as felt overwhelmingly in the first Christian communities."[17] By itself, this statement could mean Christianity was only that or was more than that; there are people on both sides of the question.

An apparent denial that the content of revelation can be antecedently conceivable is found in a statement of Vatican II reaffirming a Vatican I statement on revelation: "He [God] chose to share those divine treasures which totally transcend the understanding of the human mind."[18] What seems to be meant here is that some truths can never be the fruit of self-generated knowledge: we can never know with certitude based on natural reason that these statements are true or how they are true. We affirm their reality only through faith. Here the distinction between understanding and knowing reflects one between possibility and verification. If revealed mysteries were completely unintelligible, they would not be communicable at all. But even if partially intelligible, they must be verified before they can be known. Faith's verification is the authority of God revealing.

Anyone can proclaim a message from God, but not everyone should be believed. "Allah is Allah, and Mohammed is his prophet." The problem is in determining whether the second part is true, whether Mohammed or Moses, Isaiah, Paul, John the Evangelist, or Jesus himself speaks for the Father, and in fact whether the Father has spoken at all.

Every age illustrates how ready people are to follow self-styled prophets. Perhaps human communities are instinct with an exigency to accept as self-validating whatever makes the most sense in terms of a human thirst for the Transcendent. Nevertheless, the critical component of revelation is not that it is intelligible but that it is verifiable. We truly know the reality of whatever we understand only if we can verify that understanding. The problem is: How can we believe something on the authority of God revealing when his message is mediated through human beings, individually and communally? When the voice is the voice of a man or woman, how can we be sure that the words are the words of God?

At issue is the historicity, the factual authenticity, of the receptions of the self-communication of God. That a tradition goes back to time immemorial does not by itself validate its content—for example, the ancient tradition that the earth was flat. A religious tradition may show merely that generation after generation have held that through certain experiences, events, myths, propositions, or symbols, God has revealed his mysteries. The real question remains: Did God actually do so?

Consider briefly what revelation has traditionally meant to Christians. First of all, God does not reveal himself directly. He works through created beings and events (technically, through created existents and the occurrence of their properties) to communicate truth about himself. These beings and events are signs, either simple and indicative signs or, and this is a more recent perspective, symbolic ones—signs with manifold and multileveled meanings. This symbolic realism, as Avery Dulles has made clear, is important since revelation is not to be equated exclusively with propositions, historical events, inner experiences, dialectical positions, or personal responses.[19] Moreover, revelation has cognitive truth, a real content; its symbolic character does not minimize God's self-communication but makes it richer. Indeed, the necessity of symbols arises from the fact of God's ultimate incomprehensibility; for as Dulles said: "Symbols are indeed the only vehicle by which the absolute and the ultimate can make itself present in realities that are provisional and relative."[20]

Revelation does not exist by itself; it is always a divine-human communication, complicated by the use of inspired middlemen and the medium of symbolic signs. God reveals himself mediately but in some way directly, too, through these symbols which are constituted in revelation as his own self-realization. So the question of the reliability of the transmission of this revelation to the rest of us becomes crucial. We rely on those divinely chosen witnesses for the authentic message, whatever its form, that they channel to us.

The credentials of these witnesses to revelation—and tradition forges a chain of witnesses—are their knowledge and truthfulness, as accepted by the community. The community determines the acceptability of the proclamation by the witnesses and takes responsibility for safeguarding, interpreting, and handing down the message. A public revelation goes through four stages: the initial communication, the community acceptance, the faithful transmission, and the personal reception. In each, consciousness plays an essential role. There is the consciousness of the prophet or prophets, the shared consciousness of the first community, the consciousness of the transmitting community, and always the consciousness of the ultimate beneficiary, the current believer. This process is complicated by an ongoing interpretative function necessitated by the symbolic character of the revelation with its fullness of meaning, much of it tacit, which, under the guidance of the Spirit, is gradually objectified and made explicit.

For the prophet and for the current believer, however, the word of God is radically the same: the revelation of a mystery, otherwise inaccessible to human beings. Changes in cultural and other circumstances occasion hermeneutical problems and developments, but the church rejects radical historicism and its assertion of the unknowability of the original intent. At the same time, the church recognizes that, though the substance of the revelation perdures, the formulations tend to change with the times.[21]

Clearly, the fact of revelation poses many questions concerning cognition and many concrete questions of fact. Consequently, a sensitive and nuanced appreciation of the role of linguistics and hermeneutics is indispensable to any sound understanding of God and his revelation.[22] The primary question of course is: How do any of us know that revelations from God have occurred? Going back to the first divine irruptions or revelatory events, we ask: Where does the insight or understanding come from? May the insight ever be naturally imagined or conceived, requiring divine inspiration only for the verification? How does the verification process work? If the community makes a determination, is there just one such community, for example, the Jews, Christians, Moslems, or Hindus, and by what standards can each determine whether it is a channel of revelation? How does the Christian community know how to rank a writing as one of the canonical books of the Bible? What precise meaning is divinely revealed: the first understanding of the message by the recipient? the meaning given by the author of the work at the time of the original writing or compilation? or the meaning given to it by the community when the work is generally accepted as true? or when it is determined to be canonical?

In contrasting the original experience and the original message, we distinguish the Mystery, the revelation, and the mysteries: the Mystery is detected in the original experience; the mysteries constitute the revelation in the original message. The incomprehensible God has chosen to make himself comprehensible, to a limited extent; he is not yet known immediately, but he is known. Remaining ultimately ineffable, he has spoken about himself. Rahner conflated the two ideas of Mystery and revelation into the term "transcendental revelation," using it broadly as we have used the term theophany. To know God as "Holy Mystery" is to have received a divine self-communication. Rahner called any further divine self-communication, "predicamental revelation"; it gives content to the mystery, even though it remains knowledge *about* God and not direct knowledge *of* God.[23]

A further consideration of the relation of mystical consciousness to revelation is appropriate here. Neither inspiration nor belief necessarily entails mystical consciousness.[24] In the initial reception of revelation by the inspired recipients, there may well be a heightened state of consciousness of God through which a supernatural understanding is communicated; it is also quite possible for this understanding to be arrived at without any mystical consciousness. However mixed these experiences may be in a concrete prophetic experience, inspiration and mysticism are notionally distinct. Faith and belief are responses to revelation; they do not require mystical consciousness, though they may act as its foundation and may be enhanced by it. Dulles noted the role that the apophatic character of mysticism plays in the analysis of revelation:

> The mystical component is particularly important for bringing out the negative factor in all thematizations of revelation. The mystic, aware of God as immediately present, is keenly sensitive to the inadequacies of all created images and analogies. More conscious than others that we know God only as

one who escapes all categorization, the mystic celebrates the fact that we are conjoined with him in the utter darkness of Faith. The mystical and the symbolical dimension of the divine human encounter are complementary yet opposed.[25]

Without going any further into the problem of divine inspiration and revelation, we can sum up their connection with mystical consciousness thus: the Holy Mystery has chosen to reveal aspects of itself, supernatural mysteries, to human beings. This new light does not replace the natural exigency toward infinite meaning and value but enhances it immeasurably. In fact, the exigency itself is not purely natural but divinely graced. The light of revelation enlightens and guides the subject in responding to this ultimately ineffable mystery of love and awe, even to that point of heightened consciousness which we call mysticism.

Mystical Consciousness

The radical theophany which is consciousness of the Holy Mystery and the communal theophany which is consciousness of divine revelation are not the only theophanies; there remains also our specific concern, the mystical theophany, the flowering of the other two. We must remind ourselves that even in this mystical consciousness, faith remains necessary. We do not during this life pierce the veil and get a direct vision of God, who "dwells in light inaccessible, whom no one has seen nor can see" (1 Tim 6:16).

To help us focus on this peak spiritual experience, let us consider some preliminary formulations. William James spoke broadly of its noetic quality: "Consciousness of illumination is for us the essential mark of 'mystical' states,"[26] and yet he observed that they are "more like states of feeling than states of the intellect."[27] Joseph Maréchal brought content into the notion: "[Mysticism is] the feeling of immediate presence of a Transcendent Being."[28] Reginald Garrigou-LaGrange made the content more specific: "The mystical life is Christian life, which has, so to speak, become conscious of itself."[29]

To identify this special spiritual experience, I shall describe it thus: Mysticism is a heightened consciousness of a loving union with the transcendent and triune God, a many-leveled awareness of the divine presence, more intimate than usually afforded by graced reason and revelation. In this section, I shall first examine the core of mysticism, which is mediated immediacy, with an objective pole in divine immediacy and a subjective one in human mediation. Then I shall discuss the problems of interpreting the testimony of the mystics, our sole witnesses to the mystical experience itself. In subsequent chapters, especially the fifth, I shall further examine the psychological process involved in the experience of the mediated immediacy of God. In this chapter, I consider mainly the notion itself and its theological basis.

Mediated Immediacy

1. The "original experience" and "original message" show that God's presence, from his perspective, is immediate. For God exists in all his creatures, according to Aquinas, "as an operative cause" (*per modum causae agentis*), that is, *per essentiam, presentiam, et potentiam.*"[30] Let us look further at these three ways: God is in us, first, through his *essence* as our ground, as the sheer existence upon which all other existents depend; second, he is in us through his *presence,* in that for all eternity all things are cognitionally present to him; and third, he is in us through his *power,* in that all beings are ever subject to his will. God then has no need of an intermediary; he exists in us immediately, whether we think about it or not. But we do think about it and from those thoughts mystical experience emerges.

Spiritual writers have drawn heavily but unequally on these three aspects of divine immediacy: that God is our ground is fundamental but is appreciated least; that God knows us and that God has power over us play a more influential role. Moreover, the immediacy engendered by an awareness of God's knowledge and power fosters an abiding reverence for God which is the beginning of wisdom and love. Thus humility was for St. Benedict, Father of Western monasticism, a central virtue; it was not the highest one, for faith and the love of God were admittedly greater, but it was an indispensable basis for all spiritual growth. Today, we might call humility a virtue of existential dimensions: it authenticates our cosmic contextuality as it brings together divine omniscience buttressed by power and human self-consciousness sobered by reverence.

God then has no need of an intermediary; he exists in us immediately, whether we think about it or not. But we do think about it, and this is the second way that God is present in us. The threefold divine immediacy of essence, presence, and power can be mediated as a judgment of fact. From these thoughts lovingly responded to, mystical experience emerges as heightened consciousness of the divine presence.

In this life, human reason cannot know God's essence directly, but only through its created effects. As Aquinas wrote: "We can at least be led from them to know of God that he exists and that he has whatever must belong to the first cause of all things which is beyond all that is caused."[31] It is important to ponder the implications for spirituality our exclusive reliance on created effects, even in the most profound mystical experiences.

Both reason and grace are a sharing in the divine light. But grace, in a special way, intensifies our awareness of God, though he still is known only by his effects on us. We are able to experience God more perfectly than we could through natural reason alone.

> The light of grace strengthens the intellectual light and at the same time prophetic visions provide us with God-given images which are better suited to express divine things than those we receive naturally from the sensible world. Moreover, God has given us sensible signs and spoken words to show us something of the divine.[32]

But grace does more than strengthen, it transforms. "Grace is the only perfection added to the substance of things which makes God exist in them as a known and loved object; grace alone then makes God exist in things in a unique way."[33] Nevertheless, even graced reason, although aided by revelation, does not reveal God's essence immediately. "No one has seen God at any time" (1 Jn 4:12). So mystical consciousness always remains a modality of faith operating through charity.

Consciousness of the immediacy of God's presence becomes perfect in the next life through the *lumen gloriae*, the created light disposing the soul to know the divine essence directly. This light makes the soul deiform, for the divine essence, not any likeness, becomes the form by which the intellect understands. Aquinas made an important distinction about the light: "It is not the medium *in* which God is seen, but the means *by* which he is seen, so it makes the vision of him immediate."[34]

2. To understand how we become fully conscious of God in this life, we can take a term used, though somewhat differently, by many Catholic theologians; for example, Lonergan, Rahner, and Schillebeeckx. They spoke of mystical experience as "mediated immediacy." The term is indeed appropriate, reflecting as it does the way the human mind functions, for our mental life is largely one of mediating immediacy through meaning. The mind begins with the data of sense

and consciousness and proceeds through insight and judgment to the Mystery that we call God, though God remains ultimately incomprehensible. Revelation teaches intimate truths about that Mystery; grace gives us a share in God's life; but neither gives us on earth a direct vision of the divine essence. The question emerges, one crucial to our whole discussion of mysticism, namely: How does one mediate divine immediacy?

God is present to us—through our knowing and loving him. But this knowing and loving must be perfectly attuned to the infinite being that is God. Graced consciousness, in its unrestricted openness in knowing and loving God is the foundation of mystical experience. Divine immediacy is mediated through the mind's consciousness of being fully open to Mystery.

John Ruusbroec made a distinction that is relevant here. He noted that the aspiring contemplative can be united to God through means or without means. The means are obvious: sacraments, virtuous acts, and prayers. Union without means, even for those sufficiently perfected, raises a major question. Is Ruusbroec proposing an unmediated immediacy? Not at all. Actually, his explanation gives all the elements of the mediated immediacy about which we have been speaking: "God is in the being of the soul; and whenever the soul's highest powers are turned inward with active love, they are united with God 'without means,' in a simple knowledge of all truth and in an essential feeling and tasting of all good."[35] Later in the same passage, he repeats the observation substantially: "And so in such an inward man, whom God has adorned with virtues, and, above that, has lifted up into a contemplative life, there is no intermediary between himself and God in his highest introversion but his enlightened reason and his active love. And through these two he has an adherence to God; and this is 'becoming one with God,' says St. Bernard."[36]

In other words, total openness in knowing and loving are for Ruusbroec the means of being united to God without means. Even when he speaks of the highest stage of prayer, where he finds a fusion of consciousness without difference or distinction—the substantial difference between God and man of course continuing—this union without means is still one of mediated immediacy; the mediation is through the operation of unrestricted openness of the mind toward God.

At this point, we must clarify two levels of immediacy. We have been considering the major one, the mediated immediacy of God: he is substantially present to us, but we know him only by means of created effects; that is, through persons (ourselves and others), things and events. The second is the immediacy of the self, which is realized through the operations that we perform. This radical self-consciousness is not a special operation that we perform; it belongs to every operation that we perform. It is not introspection, but expansion. In becoming conscious of ourselves, and of ourselves as an effect of God, we become conscious of God. Because "one who is joined to the Lord is one spirit" (I Cor 6:17), this conscious joining through faith and charity makes God manifest to us.

Being conscious of our mediated immediacy, through our operations, should not obscure God's role in these operations. We learn to recognize that the moving and resting, the seeking and finding are not entirely up to us; we move and rest, we seek and find, because we have a built-in dynamism, a thrust toward reality. God is not only our goal, he is our source.

For example, a Hindu symbol of this divine initiation is the Yogic *pranayama*, breath regulation. By focusing on the involuntary character of their breathing, Yogis soon feel that they are being breathed rather than doing the breathing themselves: the breath goes in and out almost on its own. Furthermore, scrutinizing their mental operations, they notice the continuous flow of their images, thoughts, inner words, and feelings; this stream of consciousness also seems to have a life of its own. The lungs and the brain seem to be the instruments of a principle of life within them, an immanent and energizing power.

As the gift of divine energy operates in us, our expanding consciousness deepens an awareness of the self. In recognizing that this energy is a gift, we gradually realize that we are the objects of another consciousness, indeed that we are the objects of divine consciousness. Despite knowing that truth abstractly, we may not advert to the continuity of God's consciousness of us. Mediating our own immediacy, however, enables us to be conscious that we are subjects of limited consciousness, who at the same time are the objects of a being of infinite consciousness.

Consciously sharing in divine consciousness may well cause a quiet revolution in our attitude toward reality, as we try to respond properly to one who is both our Origin and our End and as we let his power work in us to will and accomplish according to his good will (Phil 2:13). We do so gently, opening ourselves in response to the still voice that tells us: "Be empty and see that I am the Lord" (Ps 45:11). By this detachment, we are able to fulfil the more appealing, complementary command, "Taste and see that the Lord is sweet" (Ps 33:9). The two directives are related because God is love and we know him most fully in the openness of unrestricted love.

3. A continuing debate over matters mystical and religious asks how this mediation affects the credibility of a mystic's testimony. Currently there are three major positions: (a) The perennialists aim at a reductionist commonality, a *philosophia perennis* (a common phrase among Scholastics but used very differently here). This is a longstanding and classicist approach. (b) The radical historicists assert an irreducible plurality based on socio-cultural differences; it is an extreme empiricism. (c) The critical realists preserve the tension between unity and diversity through a gradation of mystical experience, based on cognitional theory.

Most religions hold that their own mystics experienced the truth, but tend to reject or minimize the truth claims of other mystics. As religious tolerance and ecumenical efforts have developed, especially between East and West, a growing number of religious thinkers have affirmed not only the objectivity of religious truth but also its commonality. Aldous Huxley spoke of the *philosophia perennis,* the common truth underlying all the various forms of consciousness of the Ultimate Reality or Divine Ground.[37] For perennialists hold that all religions and all mystics ultimately reach the same reality and that specific doctrinal, moral, ritual differences as well as personal and cultural modalities are secondary epiphenomena, which true saints and sages use but transcend. Huston Smith, for example, gives this principle a narrow reading: "Strictly speaking, this negative, apophatic, *neti-neti* aspect of the Absolute . . . is the only point where perennialists see the traditions converging indistinguishably."[38] Apart from this common consciousness, other experiences, even archetypal ones, are only "correspondences."

The challenge to this radical commonality is a radical historicism or religious positivism. Whereas the perennialists recognize differences but insist on a common ground, the historicists insist on total diversity and brook no exceptions. For example, Steven Katz stated (and the italics and capitals are his): "*There are NO pure (i.e. unmediated) experiences.*"[39] He concluded that all that can be known are particular individual or communal statements: "No veridical propositions can be generated on the basis of mystical experience. As a consequence it appears certain that mystical experience is not and logically cannot be the grounds for any final assertions about the nature or truth of any religious or philosophical position, nor, more particularly for any specific dogmatic or theological belief."[40] His conclusion is that since all experiences are mediated there can be no transcultural, mystical ones; for each person can fulfil only the expectations established by his antecedent personal and social formation and religious tradition.

Obviously, mystical truth cannot be both ecumenically identical and denominationally diverse, objectively provable and irredeemably problematic. Even before the historicist challenge, many found fault with the monolithic character of perennialist truth. R.C. Zaehner, for example, sharply distinguished three kinds of mystical experience, which had as their respective objects: nature, self, or God. He found no commonality between panenhenic nature mysticism, isolative monist mysticism, and integral theistic mysticism. Only the latter, he believed, affords full mystical experience.[41] Moreover, in contrast to Katz, who said "We do not hold one mystical tradition to be superior or 'normative,' "[42] Zaehner recognized a hierarchy of mystical experiences and did not hesitate to evaluate some of them negatively. But Zaehner's critique did not confront the basic issue of mediated immediacy.

The fuller solution lies in an understanding of the cognitional elements at work. Huston Smith spoke of "metaphysical intuitions"[43] and Steven Katz of "the ontological-epistemological interpretations of mystical reports."[44] But neither discussed adequately the cognitional underpinnings of epistemology and metaphysics or ontology. It is necessary, however, to look to the sequence of mental operations as the mind moves from experiencing to understanding to knowing. Understanding is a provisional insight into the meaning of experience; knowing is a verification of that understanding. Each step is important; ignorance and error result from missing or misusing any step.

Drawing on Bernard Lonergan, James R. Price, in an astute response to Steven Katz, effectively revealed from a cognitional point of view the fundamental flaw in both the perennialist and the historicist positions. The perennialists confuse experiencing with knowing.[45] As naive realists they ignore the role of insight and assume that whatever they experience they know directly. They do not appreciate the role that the mind has in interpreting the data that it perceives.

The historicists, however, are hardly naive; they are fully aware of the multitude of experiences and the provisional character of their understanding of the data. Realizing that interpretation by itself is always inadequate, they fail to recognize the role of a further mental operation, judgment, which determines the verification of tentative understandings. Truth is found only in verified insights. In their mistaken identification of understanding with knowing, the historicists have become critical idealists. They have not yet adequately grounded their ideas in reality. They have not self-appropriated the act of judgment.

For a sound theology of mysticism, there is the need for critical realism: critical, because it deals with an assessment of one's knowing: realism, because it roots that knowing in the data of sense and consciousness. Through inquiry, the critical realist attains a provisional understanding; through reflection, he verifies that understanding, so that he can affirm or deny it with probability or certainty. An insight or understanding tells us *what* the data may mean, it takes further weighing and marshalling of data and more back-checking of the insight, to determine *that* it actually is or is not.

Working authentically to understand and to judge his experience of things religious, a critical realist is able to recognize the role of interpretation without being limited by his interpretation, and is able to move validly to knowing without having to make a gratuitous and unverified leap. Through judgment, one transcends the limits of a purely interpretative understanding of experience. The result is, Price concluded, the recognition of a qualified pluralism, of a cross-cultural legitimacy, and of "the foundation of a critically grounded philosophia perennis."[46]

The cognitional approach of critical realism avoids the oversimplification of the perennialists and the reductionism of the historicists. But most important, it affords the means for a hierarchical assessment of the varieties of mystical experience. It does not make this testing of mystic claims easy; sound judgment is never easy, but it may clarify the reliable emergence and nuanced authentication of mystical truth. A fuller elaboration of this process of mediating divine immediacy, we leave to a later chapter.

Mystic Witnesses

The knowledge of mystical experience depends on the reports of the mystics. Their testimony is indispensable. Besides the mystic and God, no one else is fully privy to this consciousness of the divine. The mystic can claim with the prophet Isaiah, "My secret is mine" (Is 24:16). Indeed, Ruusbroec and most other mystics have insisted that their experience goes beyond words; it is incommunicable: "No one can properly or thoroughly understand its meaning through any learning or subtle reflections of his own, for all words and all that can be learned or understood in a creaturely way are alien to and far beneath the truth which I mean."[47]

Nevertheless, mystics often do convey something of their secret inner life. Their testimony affords inspiration and guidance to believers and also supplies raw materials to theologians studying mysticism. The question presents itself: How can believers authenticate and interpret with theological accuracy these personal testimonies, and how does their interpretation comport with reality?

Mystical communication and theological investigation face in two different directions. The mystic starts with the experience, interprets it, and finally tries to communicate it. The theologian starts with the communication, gives it an interpretation, and finally attempts a reconstruction of the experience. The mystic begins with experience; the theologian works back to experience. The theologian seeks first to verify the historicity of mystical events and to achieve their historical reconstruction; he then goes beyond history but does not reject or forget history, for he must ground his theological understanding and verification on solid data. Both the mystic and the theologian have something to interpret; the result is a theological interpretation of a mystical interpretation—a theophany twice-removed from immediacy.

Despite these difficulties, a process for assessing such testimony of the mystics has evolved; the one who judges examines (1) the authenticity of the text, (2) the reliability of the witness, and (3) the meaning of the message. The first is a scholarly determination of the historicity of the document. The second is a screening procedure, impeaching the deceitful or ignorant, suspending judgment about those whose credibility is unclear, and provisionally accepting as believable those deemed truthful and knowledgeable. The third is the task of scrutinizing both the text and its context in order to grasp the meaning of the communication in order to determine its validity.

(1) The *authentication of the text,* as in all historical research, is troublesome. There are many problems. The author, circumstances, and date may be uncertain or even feigned: the influential Dionysius the Areopagite was discovered in the ninth century to be, not an Athenian disciple of St. Paul, but a sixth-century Syrian. Critical parts of the mystic's writings may be lost or withheld: the very important *Spiritual Diary* of St. Ignatius, initially concealed out of fear of the Inquisition, was not published in its entirety until 1934, though the saint died in 1556 and was canonized in 1622.[48] The writings may be distorted by others: the superiors of St. Thérèse of Lisieux after her death edited her work with a pietistic sweetness that tended to conceal her own intellectual clarity and heroic courage.

The communication of a mystical experience demands additional skills in thinking, in speaking, in writing. Not all mystics are so gifted.

Some mystics wrote nothing: the illiterate doctor of the Church, St. Catherine of Siena, had to dictate most of her letters and dialogues, learning to write only in the last three years of her life. Of some mystics, for example, the "desert fathers," there are only reports of what was said; in such circumstances, the objectivity, the expertise, and the accuracy of others become important.

Furthermore, the character of the subject matter does not make the task of communication any easier; human language is largely inadequate, for mystics usually go beyond the sensible and conceptual in their experience. The apophatic aspect of mystical consciousness makes both the knowing and the telling difficult, since created forms veil the Holy Mystery. These considerations highlight the importance of the unending task of scholarship, which is to make sure that the communication is authentic and, if so, to present it accurately, completely, and contextually.

(2) Once the text is clear, the next problem is to assess the *reliability of the author*. The mystic as witness constitutes the central challenge for mystical theology, as it does for empirical psychology in its study of altered states of consciousness. The inability to question acknowledged mystics about important phases of their activity, however, tends to push some conclusions about them toward the problematic. How valuable it would be to have been able to ask the great mystics all the probing questions that the issue demands.

Whether the mystics are present or absent, they are subject to a reliability test, a commonsense one that is appropriate whenever one person communicates with another. It grounds our trust in parents, friends, teachers, priests, doctors, lawyers, scientists, brokers, writers, and mechanics. Finally, it is the basis of our belief in God, as one who can neither deceive nor be deceived. The mystic witness undergoes careful scrutiny, and the test for reliability breaks down into two questions: Is the witness knowledgeable? Is the witness truthful? If we cannot answer both questions affirmatively, we impeach the witness and disregard the testimony, in whole or in part.

The truthfulness test is straightforward; it carefully examines the subject's life and activities in terms of character and holiness, sometimes requiring even heroic virtue in the face of serious difficulties. But even telling what one believes is true is not enough. To be a good witness, actually knowing the truth is equally important. One may have a pure heart but an empty head. Knowledgeability, however, is sometimes more difficult to assess than truthfulness.

Take a secular situation, that of the expert witness at a trial involving the insanity defense. His truthfulness is generally presumed, though of course he may be impeached. His professional credentials, however, will be minutely inspected: what his education was, his clinical experience, his present work, his area of specialization, his professional affiliations, his school of psychiatry, his time with the defendant, his procedures in the examination, and the factual basis for his conclusions.

In comparison, the alleged mystic may manifest nothing more than a simple, uneducated, illiterate mind: "All I know is what I saw in my vision." Obviously, claiming does not make it so, so we are warned: "Believe not every spirit, but try the spirits if they be of God, because many false prophets are gone out into the world" (1 Jn. 4:1). Certain preliminary questions are asked: Is this matter significant enough to bother with at all? Is the message in harmony with the teaching of the church? Even when the answers are positive, the only difference between the content of the mystic claim and the content of a similar statement that any intelligent Christian could make might be the assertion of an extraordinary experience: "I was one with God and had a vision of the Trinity," or the assertion of a divine inspiration: "This is what God told me." Moreover, even if the question is raised only in the inner forum of spiritual direction, the issue is the same: Is the person subjectively reliable?

An historically important instance of an impeached "mystic," or at least an unreliable one, is Margery Kemp, a spiritual figure of the fifteenth century, who claimed to have revelations and locutions, but who, according to David Knowles, Former Regius Professor at Oxford, showed little, in her *Book,* "of deep spiritual wisdom and nothing of true mystical experience."[49] And he concluded: "We may perhaps say that there is nothing in the words themselves that suggest any other origin than the vivid imagination and retentive memory of a sincere and devout, but very hysterical woman."[50]

In this discernment of spirits many commonsense factors are, as we have seen, highly relevant: the subject's education, intelligence, sensitivity to interior matters, mental health, balance and prudence, good works, orthodoxy, and, once again, holiness. In practice, to the extent that the content is unexceptionable, the decisive factor seems ultimately to be the level of personal holiness.

(3) After the authentication of the text and the verification of the witness, there remains the *interpretation of the communication.* Here hermeneutic problems abound. The core of the solution is found in a fundamental scholastic maxim: Whatever is received is received after the manner of the recipient. In hermeneutic terms, it suggests that circumstances affect understanding, the understanding of the

mystic and the understanding of the theologian. The question then arises: How objectively meaningful to others can the mystical experience be, after being twice translated into an interpretation? The mystic and the theologian are concrete individuals, with all sorts of mental and physical specificities both positive and negative; each is located in a particular temporal, spatial, and cultural milieu. What experience do these mystics—the hermit Evagrius, the penitent Margaret of Cortona, the youthful Elizabeth of the Trinity, the brilliant Meister Eckhart, the simple Curé of Ars, or the stigmatic Padre Pio—have in common with one another? Not exactly the same thing in the same way, but how similar and how different?

Whatever the experience may be, the experience is always interpreted, and the interpretation will always be in terms of the mystic's personal and cultural circumstances. Speaking cognitionally, data become intelligible only through an insight. To understand an experience is to impose upon it some kind of unity, some possible light; this understanding is the meaning that the circumstanced subject gives to the experience. More data may enable the mystic to reinforce the provisional intelligibility, to change it, or eliminate it. This process of understanding and verifying the data and then deciding how to act in light of the judgment is called discernment of spirits.

These three stages—authenticity, reliability, and interpretation —are clearly manifested in the writings of Julian of Norwich. Her mystical "shewings" all occurred on one day, May 8, 1373, when she was thirty years and some months old. She wrote two accounts of her experiences: the shorter one was written first; the longer, the one usually read, about twenty years later, quite a lapse of time for mnemonic accuracy, though she must have savored her experience and pondered it in her heart.

What is of special pertinence is her reaction immediately after the experience. Initially, she questioned its authenticity: though fifteen showings had been completed in about five hours, she did not believe them. In her own words, "On the very day that it happened, when the vision had passed, I—wretch that I am!—denied it and said openly that I had raved."[51] Only after she had mentioned it to a Franciscan priest, who took her words very seriously, did she begin to reflect on its possible validity. She then had a terrifying dream about the devil. It was closely followed by a sixteenth and final showing during which the Lord "said so sweetly, 'You know well enough that it was no raving that you saw today. But take it: believe it: hold on to it: comfort yourself with it and trust it. You will not be overcome.' "[52] This almost self-validating vision led to a sleep in which she had another dream of the devil: "This was calculated to drive me to despair or so I thought."[53] Finally she accepted the truthfulness of her earlier visions of the Lord, saying: "I am bound to it and to his interpretation of it. . . . I am bound therefore to keep believing in it."[54] Restored health and deep peace reinforced this conviction.

However we assess the adequacy of her interpretation and judgment, we see that she first distinguished the experience from reality and interpreted it as raving. Only later, after some religious support, some reflection on the visions, a dream of diabolical opposition, the restoration of physical and mental well-being, a final vision specifically confirming the authenticity of the earlier ones, and another dream of the devil, did she accept it fully and with certainty. The various cognitional levels are apparent: the experience, the insight into it at first as false, then as possibly valid, and finally as adequately verified. She then decided to believe it. For the mystic herself, such as Julian of Norwich, the experience may all but compel assent; others learning about it may also believe it and find spiritual reinforcement in it. Some may reject it outright.

Looking over the three stages again, we recall the number of operations to be sorted out, often without fully adequate empirical evidence: the mystic's experience of the data, understanding of the data, verification of the understanding by further recourse to data and, finally, communication of that verified understanding. The mystic must perform four separate, concrete activities before anyone else knows what has occurred. Each stage may make other persons less certain what actually did occur, not because the witness may lie but because at each stage the witness may fail in accuracy, in part because of human fallibility but in part, too, from the effect of culture and language on mediation. Yet the verification remains a key factor in assessing with certainty the transcendent basis of a mystical experience. This understanding, though personally convincing to the mystic, can be assented to by others only on the basis of the mystic's reliability in being knowledgeable and truthful.

Assuming the reliability of the report, what precisely has been proved? The more particular and concrete the experience, the greater the number of cultural forms that may be involved in the mediation process; for example, the extraordinary visions, sensible, imaginative, and intellectual visions of a saint such as Bridget of Sweden, visions that may or may not accompany mystical contemplation. What has been proved? The ineffable or the peripheral? What about the affirmation that there has been an experience of the Transcendent? of the mediated immediacy of the divine? Is this proof to the world of the existence of a transcendent being? It is inspirational and motivational: "If others can, why not I"? (*Si illi, cur non ego?*) of Augustine. It may be persuasive, if substantiated by similar accounts. But is it anything more than anecdotal proof?

Frederick Copleston attempted to assess "the value of mystical experience as evidence of transcendental reality."[55] By transcendental, he meant that it cannot be identified with the physical world around us or with the individual self, but is a One irreducible to the Many.[56]

A major difficulty for Copleston was the ineffability of the experience, which, by definition, mystics have and non-mystics do not. He realized that such experiences can be distinguished from their interpretation or, in his terms, that one can distinguish experiencing (the actual awareness) and experiencing *as* (e.g., as the Father, as the world soul, as the void). He did not, however, advert to the role of verification. He concluded that at best mystical experience forms part of a cumulative argument; it cannot carry the burden of proof by itself.

In view of such considerations, both from within the church and from outside, it is well to recall that proof of the transcendent does not depend essentially on mystical experience. Non-mystics do not need the testimony of mystics to affirm God's existence and his revelation. Moreover, mystics usually have already grounded their relationship with God on reason and faith. Indeed, on this earth they never can transcend their faith in God, although that faith does become for them illuminated.

A more contextual and satisfactory way of describing the function of mystical experience is to see it as a heightened consciousness of what the person has already affirmed at least implicitly to be transcendent reality. Non-mystical theophanies, both the original experience of graced nature and the original message of divine revelation with their subsequent thematizations, do give certainty about God. Mysticism brings to these antecedently held truths an emerging glow which can burst into "a living flame of love."

CONCLUSION

To appreciate fully the divine theophanies, pre-mystical and mystical, which are possible for all human beings, we note first that nature is graced and that consciousness of God on any level is fundamentally a gift offered to all. In analyzing the mind's ascent to God, we see God first as "Holy Mystery," then as "Redeeming Love." We are immediately present to God, but God is only mediately present to us. His grace ultimately ensures the full realization of the already established mutuality, so that we can say, "I shall know even as I am known" (I Cor 13:12). The depth and intimacy of this shared consciousness, of course, are not equal on both sides. It depends on the harmony of divine grace and human efforts for working out in a providential universe the full implications, individual and communal, of the "good news" of revelation. Mystical consciousness is the fruit of the enlightened faith in the "original experience" of the Holy Mystery and the "original message" of divine revelation, both heightened by unrestricted openness to the presence of God whom they reveal.

3

The Kataphatic Prelude

❖   ❖   ❖

I see his blood upon the rose
And in the stars the glory of his eyes.
                    Joseph Mary Plunkett*

Those seeking profound consciousness of God's presence find
two roads stretched out before them: the one passes through more or
less familiar landscapes filled with recognizable objects; the other
through what threatens to be a barren desert.

These traditional approaches to theophany rest on different perceptions about the similarity between the Creator and his creatures.
The way of affirmation—the Greeks called it kataphatic (from *kata-
phemi,* to say yes, to assent)—means that the things that God has
made resemble their maker, so we do well to pray iconically by using,
as analogues of the divine, these created images and forms. On the
other hand, the way of negation or denial—the Greeks called it apophatic (from *apophemi,* to say no, to refuse)—means that God differs
so radically from all other beings that we should pray aniconically by
becoming as free of creatures and creaturely forms as possible.

Each way has a function at some stage in every spiritual life. Their
relationship, however, is not one of parity but of process. In principle,
the kataphatic leads to the apophatic, as the subject finally transcends
creaturely finitude and bows before the Holy Mystery in all its simplicity. But afterwards, in the mediating of this experience, the apophatic
depends on the kataphatic in order to articulate and communicate the
Holy Mystery through finite forms.

In this chapter, we shall discuss the kataphatic way of affirma-

---

* Joseph Mary Plunkett, "I See His Blood," *The Poems* (Dublin: Talbot Press,
1919), p. 50.

56

tion, the way that is initially most congenial to our minds. We are comfortable with images and concepts of creatures. Seeing their perfections in some way contained in God, we gradually turn our minds to him. "For from him and through him and in him are all things, to him be glory forever. Amen" (Rom 11:36). Earlier in the letter to the Romans, Paul used a kataphatic argument against the pagans: "For the invisible things of him, from the creation of the world are clearly seen, being understood by the things that are made, his eternal power also and his divinity; so that they are inexcusable" (Rom 1:20).

The perfections of creatures attributed to God are of two kinds: simply simple or absolute perfections; and mixed or relative perfections.

(1) Absolute perfections, such as knowledge, goodness, beauty, power, imply no limitations. Essentially compatible with God's essence, they seem to be declarative of the divine, though in a more sublime and eminent way than is found in the world of our experience. We must not overlook the fact, which is the justification of the apophatic approach to God, that we can know perfections of whatever type, only in their limited, finite, created mode. So we cannot fully predicate of God even the most perfect of them. They may not contradict his essence, but neither are they adequately declarative of it.

(2) Relative perfections are perfections after a fashion; they involve qualities that are essentially limited and thus not found in the divine essence—for example, bodily strength, visual imagery, fleshiness, sense perceptions, discursive reason. Such limited creaturely perfections are in God only virtually, by reason of his creative power; they are the effects or vestiges of divine causality. Since that power is creative and thus unique, it transcends that of created causes with their finite efficacy. Yet all divine effects reveal something about God, his intelligence and power and love. Most significantly, they can help lift the mind to a sense of presence and appreciation.

All creatures, if they are to exist at all, must reflect divine ideas —ways that the divine essence or perfection can be imitated. There is nothing for created beings to be patterned after other than the all-perfect God with his fullness of being. Divine exemplarism, which grounds all creaturely perfections in God, provides for both the kataphatic and the apophatic—but, as we shall see, very differently. Hence, creaturely perfections, limited though they may be, do speak of God: "The heavens proclaim the glory of God, and the sky shows forth the work of his hands" (Ps 19:1). But God utterly transcends them all.

The kataphatic approach to God, which is the subject matter of this chapter, should not be overly simplified by narrowly focusing only on the positive aspects of creatures as stepping stones to theophany. Kataphatics has two modalities: it takes into account both good and evil in enabling the subject to lift mind and heart to God. It thus specifies that programed thrust to happiness, which has a normative formulation as the primary principle of natural law: good is to be done and pursued, evil is to be avoided. Growth in holiness and mystical consciousness are the fruit of graced actions in response to the variety of events, permitted by "the Father, who is in heaven, who makes his sun to rise upon the good and the bad, and rains upon the just and the unjust" (Mt 5:45).

The response to the dualities of life kataphatically is, on the one hand, that God's creatures are essentially good, so all the more must God be good and, on the other hand, that God's creatures are sometimes evil, but that, nonetheless, God is still good. The positive kataphatic approach moves us to appreciate God's goodness, but we do not always achieve self-transcendence when events match our desires; the negative kataphatic approach, however, moves us to affirm God's wisdom and benevolence in the face of the non-being that seems to frustrate our desires. We learn to transcend our constricted horizon for a higher viewpoint and thus to see all events, even tragic ones, through the eyes of God, *sub specie deitatis.*

We shall consider first the positive modality for raising our minds liltingly to God through created beauty; then we shall consider the negative modality for forcing our minds agonizingly to God through human suffering.[1] In both, by confronting authentically the world of our experience we become conscious of the unseen God. "For the things which are seen are temporal, but the things which are not seen are eternal" (II Cor 4:18). Finally, we shall examine the affirmations that we give to those symbols, which, by their obvious dissimilarity to God, open the mind to an apophatic approach to transcendence.

Beauty and Sadness

To call sadness a child of beauty is to point out a relationship not usually acknowledged, since pleasure rather than grief is supposed to be the only legitimate fruit of that union between humans and loveliness which is called aesthetic experience. "It should bring forth grapes and it has brought forth wild grapes" (Is 5:4) and "the teeth of the children are set on edge" (Jer 13:29). Our task, then, is to distill this tartness, to identify and perhaps even to justify it. We shall consider: first, the psychological experience, which at times impresses us so painfully; then the philosophical basis, which gives us a partial insight; and finally the theological dimension, which brings the answer into full perspective.

The Empirical Fact

Edgar Allan Poe, in an essay entitled "The Poetic Principle," wrote a sensitive account of the full reaction to created beauty, with special emphasis on its unexpected by-product, melancholy. In his own words, "The impression left is one of pleasurable sadness"; for he insisted: "This certain taint of sadness is inseparably connected with all the higher manifestations of true beauty."[2] It was for him, in the words of Longfellow:

> A feeling of sadness and longing
> That is not akin to pain,
> And resembles sorrow only
> As the mist resembles the rain.[3]

The subtle emotions that blend so delicately in aesthetic intuition are, however, strangely elusive. The total effect is both something "pleasurable" and something that "resembles sorrow." But the clue to the mystery of this mixed response may well be found in the word "longing," for there is, indeed, frustration and disappointment in that grasp of created beauty which, albeit pleasantly, distresses the soul.

> We weep, then, not through excess of pleasure but through a certain petulant, impatient sorrow, at our inability to grasp now, wholly, here on earth, once and forever, those divine and rapturous joys of which through the power or the music we attain to but brief and indeterminate glimpses.[4]

Poe's explanation was that "This thirst belongs to the immortality of Man. . . . It is no mere appreciation of the beauty before us but a wild effort to reach the beauty above."[5] He justified his conclusions by a reason similar to the one, as we have seen, Augustine formulated with profounder vision many years earlier: "You have made us for yourself, O Lord, and our heart is restless until it rests in you."[6] Thus Poe wrote:

Inspired by an ecstatic prescience of the glories beyond the grave, we struggle by multiform combinations among the things and thoughts of time to attain a portion of that loveliness whose very elements perhaps appertain to eternity alone.[7]

These words explain the bittersweet reaction and the incessant searching that characterize a soul touched by a deep love of beauty. It is not a hunger for sensation that is easily satiated, but a hunger of the spirit, a hunger for reality. Obviously, the major harmony in aesthetic appreciation is not sadness or impatience or petulance; yet, very often, an echo of these feelings sounds the note of precariousness in our possession of created loveliness. Our soul reverberates with the realization that earthbound beauty must suffer the fate of its antecedents. In our hearts we keep hearing, like background music for the love feast, plaintive strains reminiscent of Rossetti's "Ballad of Dead Ladies," with its oft-recurring and plaintive cry, "But where are the snows of yester-year?"

The Philosophic Basis

To appreciate the significance of Poe's observations, we look briefly at the aesthetic experience itself, specifically at the fundamental distinction between transcendental and aesthetic beauty, a distinction important only for humans, since for God everything has as much beauty as it has being.

Beauty, as an attribute of being, is called transcendental because it is found in all things, yet surpasses their limitations and imperfections. Our minds, however, do not respond easily to beauty in its transcendental form. Embodied spirits that we are, we depend partly on sense powers for aesthetic experience, so the ambit of the soul is narrowed by the limitations of a body "troubled about many things" (Lk 10:41). Jacques Maritain spelled out this distinction clearly:

I would say that aesthetic beauty, which is not all beauty for man but which is the beauty most naturally proportioned to the human mind, is a particular determination of transcendental beauty: it is transcendental beauty as confronting not simply the intellect, but the intellect and the sense acting together in one single act: say, it is transcendental beauty

confronting the sense as imbued with intelligence or intellec-
tion as engaged in sense perception.[8]

Transcendental beauty is hidden as a universal attribute; aesthetic beauty is on display as something unusual and unique. Beauty
thus comes either plain or fancy, in a housedress or in a party dress. It
is aesthetic beauty, however, that evokes in us the response which all
reality demands but which we are not always able to give. What is
more, when we do perceive the loveliness of creatures, our reaction,
though joyous, is not without shadows. "For all flesh is as grass; and all
the glory thereof as the flower of grass. The grass is withered, and the
flower thereof is fallen away, but the word of God endures forever" (1
Pet 1:24–25).

Søren Kierkegaard, in his aesthetical work *Either/Or*, imaginatively analyzed the fleeting satisfaction that the objects of our experience afford us.[9] As Judge Williams, he speaks to a "young friend,"
who portrays him as he was in his student days, and who like him, is
"through with finiteness altogether." The youth is "superbly proud"
of his detached attitude to pleasure, though he cannot do without it.
As for the glories of the world, "Well, one might devote to them a
whole day." Or if he could be a millionaire, "Well, it might be quite
interesting to have been that, and one might well spend a month at it."
Or if he had won the love of a most beautiful woman, "Well, for a half a
year that would not be so bad." Even the things that tempt him most,
dignity, honor, and the admiration of contemporaries, are met with a
"Well, for a short time that would be pretty good." Kierkegaard ap-
praised this apparently blasé system of rejections with understanding
and sympathy.

> I will not here join in the cry of complaint often raised against
> you that you are insatiable, I would say rather that in a cer-
> tain sense you are right, for nothing finite, not the whole
> world can satisfy the soul of a man who feels the need of the
> eternal.[10]

Penetrating more deeply than the "melancholy Dane," Thomas
Aquinas discovered why even the comeliest of creatures is insufficient for man. "Happiness," he declared, "is a perfect good, which
quiets the appetite totally; otherwise, if something remained to be
desired, it would not be the ultimate end."[11] Then he considered the
nature of man and the object of his will, which is the "universal good,"

which alone can quiet man's appetite; it "is not found in any created thing but in God alone because every creature has only a participated goodness."[12] Like goodness, beauty, as we have seen, is a transcendental: "For the beauty of creatures is nothing else than the likeness of divine beauty shared by things."[13] How understandable then is the cry that was wrung from the heart of Augustine:

> Late have I loved Thee, O Beauty, so ancient and so new; late have I loved Thee! For behold Thou were within me, and I outside; and I sought Thee outside and in my unloveliness fell upon those lovely things Thou has made. Thou were with me and I was not with Thee. I was kept from Thee by those things, yet had they not been in Thee, they would not have been at all.[14]

The appetite is never fully quieted, never fully at rest. Ever yearning for something that cannot be found on earth, it is ever disappointed; but its very frustration sparks it to greater efforts. This dynamic aspect of the dissatisfaction with created beauty was touched upon by Jean Mouroux, when he distinguished two key phrases of Aquinas, "repose in the end"[15] and "rest in the good obtained."[16]

> For though man is in motion towards his last end, he needs occasional rests along the way. All real ends are stages in his journey, and inchoate manifestations of the final end; and in this endless dynamic process delectation is the time of rest because it means a state of appeasement in joy. But as the possession is only partial, the flowering is only temporary, and both ultimately insufficient, there is always a resurgence of movement, desire, effort, towards a new joy.[17]

"We have not here a lasting city" (Heb 13:10); but we are not men and women without a country; we are pilgrims, "pilgrims of the absolute," on the way to our true homeland. Like travellers in a Swiss station en route to Rome, we are delighted by the scenic majesty around us, but are unable to quell the impatient cry in our hearts. "Over the Alps—and beauty." Moved by "the desire of the everlasting hills" (Gn 49:26), we seek that Eternal City which is the New Jerusalem.

Sometimes a person may rest content with the gorgeous things that God has made without knowing the dull ache that a full insight into their reality should inspire. Perhaps natural insensitivity is the obstacle. Or perhaps earthiness or sensuality has deadened one's feelings for the more subtle overtones. Even if the ability to respond is flawless, one may lack the holy leisure, the contemplative quiet which lets the fullness of the experience take possession of the soul. "There is no grief of mind," Gregory the Great observed, "when one is head over heels in activity."[18] If, however, a man can free himself for a while from the rush of events, then, though he vibrates to the many-colored splendors of the world, he gradually with growing desire—and with sadness too—learns "how much the Lord of them is more beautiful than they, for the first author of beauty made all those things" (Wis 13:3 [Douay Rheims]).

The Theological Development

The floodlights of faith focus on depths of meaning in the relationship of beauty to sadness that the frail candle of human reason can never reach. Thus the beatitude, "Blessed are they that mourn for they shall be comforted" (Mt 5:5), and the gift of knowledge, which complements it, as habit does act, illumine with a supernatural radiance the whole problem of the sorrow of the saints. First let us examine, with the help of three great Doctors of the Church, what the beatitude really means; and then let us see what is the function of the gift. Though they wrote from a classicist perspective and relied on an unscientific scriptural exegesis on the Gifts and the Beatitudes, their words still manifest an enduring psychological and spiritual reality.

Leo the Great, in a sermon on the steps to happiness, unhesitatingly asserted that sin alone is a justifiable cause of grief.

> The mourning for which everlasting consolation is promised has nothing in common with the affliction of this world; nor do these grievings make anyone blessed, which are poured forth by the violent weeping of the whole human race. There is another reason for the groans of the saints, another cause for the tears of the blessed. Sadness based in devotion grieves for its own or for another's sin. And it does not bewail what is done by divine justice, but it does mourn what is perpetrated by human injustice. There, doing evil is more to be deplored than enduring it, because wickedness plunges

the unjust man into punishment, but endurance leads the just man to glory.[19]

Superficially, Augustine seemed to interpret the words in a much broader light by contrasting two loves, that of the temporal good and that of the eternal good.

Mourning is sadness due to the loss of cherished things. Those who have turned to God lose those things which, in this world, are held dear; for they do not enjoy the things they formerly enjoyed. And until the love of eternal things is formed in them, they are wounded by some sadness. Therefore, they will be comforted by the Holy Spirit who, on that account especially, is called "Paraclete," that is, "Comforter"; so that losing temporal joys they might the more thoroughly rejoice in eternal ones.[20]

On analysis, however, we find that the teaching of Aquinas, by implying the other two explanations, surpasses them as does white light its colored refractions. He said simply, "One is moved to grief, especially by the knowledge through which a man knows his own defects and those of the things of the world; for, according to Ecclesiastes (1:18): 'He who adds knowledge, adds grief also.' "[21]

Deficiency of some kind is, then, the source of sadness, whether it be moral defects or the radical limitations of all creatures. We sorrow because the beings around us cannot satisfy us and because sin, the inordinate love of these same unsatisfying things, only increases the bitterness of our hearts.

Fundamentally, the Leonine and the Augustinian interpretations are consistent with the Thomistic formulation: Leo's emphasis on moral deficiency implies a radical one, since creatures can be loved inordinately, that is sinfully, only because they are not the highest good; conversely, Augustine's emphasis on the latter implies the former, since separation from temporal goods will distress us, only if through sinfulness we fail to love the eternal good well enough.

To try to follow the beatitude of mourning without possessing the gift of knowledge is to do it the hard way, for one cannot respond to reality adequately without a proportionate supernatural perspective.

Before continuing our discussion of the gift of knowledge, I will mention briefly the role of the gifts of the Holy Spirit. A major distinction must be made: the Spirit is uncreated grace; the gifts of the Spirit are created effects making a person docile to the Spirit. Everyone in the state of grace, not just saints or mystics, have these gifts and have them in proportion to their graced state. The gifts differ from the infused cardinal virtues and the supernatural virtues—both kinds are abiding dispositions of the soul perfecting it for specific actions in the supernatural order. The gifts enhance the operation of the virtues by adapting them more perfectly to this new life, which to sinful human nature seems in some way alien. The beatitudes, as norms for members of the Body of Christ, can be followed fully only if Christians through the gifts are sensitive to the promptings of the Spirit. In short, the gifts make the person docile to the Spirit so that his virtuous actions are perfectly attuned to the singular decisions that the beatitudes encompass.

But to return to the gift of knowledge, which renders the soul more sensitive and sure in its appraisal of creatures. Aquinas explained the process thus: "One does not have a right judgment about these things as long as one estimates that the perfect good is in them; hence, one sins by establishing one's end in them, and one loses the perfect good"; the gift, however, helps prevent this, "For right judgment about creatures pertains properly to knowledge."[22] The purpose and function of this gift are described by John of St. Thomas in his commentary on the teaching of the Angelic Doctor. From him we see its ordered purpose which is to lift the mind of man to God and its essential function which is to judge creatures through a connaturality with them rooted in charity. In brief, we learn to judge things rightly, because we begin to see them as God does.

The tremendous scope of the gift of knowledge, which encompasses all truth from human and created causes, is always directed toward God. Thus John of St. Thomas wrote: "An experience and taste of creatures as well as an insight concerning them is given to the soul, not that it may rest in them as its ultimate end, but that it may proceed through them to God with a correct estimate and judgment of its last end."[23]

The gift of knowledge ought not, however, make us regard creation cynically, for it comes to us from God who "saw all the things that he had made and that they were very good" (Gn 1:31). So the judgment we form is a balanced one, springing from charity which sets all things in order. John of St. Thomas expressed the balance thus: "Love has a taste and experience of creatures. It forms a correct judgment of them, both to despise them lest the soul be distracted by them, and to love them moderately ordaining them to God."[24]

Here we face a hermeneutic question: what does it signify to "despise" creatures, however beautiful they are? It seems that John of St. Thomas actually meant that we should be sufficiently detached from them so that all our actions are in accord with the will of God. Thus he added that we must love them, though only "moderately." This word means with due measure and order; it does not mean without energy or intensity. We must love and love wholeheartedly, but always as God's law specifies. For if we did not love, we would lose the gift of knowledge, which dwells only in a soul filled with charity. And the more charity increases, the more perfectly do we share in the gift.

The response that gift of knowledge directs towards a thing of beauty is sparked by a twofold love of creator and creatures. In the first place, "The gift of knowledge comes from a loving union with God, not indeed as He is in himself, but as He is the reason for loving creatures in an orderly way and acting correctly in their regard."[25] In the second place, "Founded upon a motion of the Holy Spirit, it moves the mind not by a pure and naked light manifesting exterior truths, but by a sort of loving and supernatural connaturality to the things that it judges."[26] What happens is this: loving God, we begin to share the love that he has for his creatures, and are thus enabled to attune ourselves to them, to resound in harmony with them. Our union, then, is almost second nature: it is connatural. It gives the intimacy and sympathy which is necessary to lift us to that *perfectio veritatis,* which is an insight into the uniqueness of a thing, a grasp of its beauty.

Aquinas began the first article on the gift of knowledge with the words: "Grace is more perfect than nature; therefore, it does not fail in those things in which man is able by nature to be perfected."[27] He then showed how natural reason is made more effective in its judgment of creatures by the gift, not in a crude, insensitive wielding of the axe of abstract ethics, but in a subtle and delicate appreciation of the great things of God, the *magnalia Dei.* The human mind becomes more perfectly conformed to God, who sees all things in their metaphysical loveliness, a loveliness which inspires in us what Charles Baudelaire called, "an irritated melancholy"; for the person whose soul is athirst for total beauty is, as he points out, "a nature exiled in the imperfect which would fain possess immediately, even on this earth, a paradise revealed."[28] Wait we must but with patience, since we have a promise of comfort. The very gift that whets our appetite by sharpening our judgment strengthens our hope. "I will not," said Jesus, "send them away fasting lest they faint on the way" (Mt 15:32). We grieve because we hunger for supernal loveliness; Jesus will not let us starve.

Parenthetically, it should be noted that this graced connaturality that comes from loving God also accounts for the gift of wisdom which, subject to special impulses of the Spirit, helps the mind to judge about things divine. It is important to see how the gifts of wisdom and knowledge complement one another, for our destiny is not merely to deal with creatures, however properly, but also to move toward the creator. Through this loving experience of God, the gift of wisdom points us beyond creatures to the apophatic way, as we see from John of St. Thomas:

> It is a taste, love, delight, or internal contact of the will with spiritual things. By reason of its union with spiritual truths the soul is, as it were, made connatural to things divine. Through this tasting, wisdom discerns spiritual truths from the sensible and created. In this life wisdom acts only imperfectly, by means of negation, but in heaven it acts quite perfectly through positive evidence.[29]

To sum up, sadness, then, is beauty's child, a child of whom it can be said, "Out of the mouths of infants and sucklings you have perfected praise" (Mt 21:16); for sadness, rightly experienced, leads men and women to acknowledge and to possess the Lord of Loveliness, the Father and creator of beauty itself, who so surpasses his creations that it is written of the vision of his glory, "Eye has not seen, nor ear heard, nor has it entered into the heart of man what God has prepared for those who love him" (1 Cor 2:9). But now, and for a little while longer, they must weep for uncreated Beauty, and yearn for that time of blessed comfort when "God shall wipe away all the tears from their eyes" (Apoc 7:17).

Pain and Suffering

Despite having discussed the kataphatic approach to God-consciousness in terms of beauty, the highest manifestation of divine glory, we still remain uncomfortably aware that not all the things and events of this world are matters of sweetness and light. Darkness and pain also play a major role in our lives. All too familiar with sin and misfortune, we are occasionally shocked, by the personal impact of evil, into an acute awareness of lost beauty and wasted gifts—of thwarted destinies. Then we question shrilly, as did the second-century contemporaries of Tertullian: "Whence comes evil and why?" (*Unde malum et quare?*)

Can the answer possibly be that evil itself may be a masked theophany, in that a true understanding of the role of evil and a proper response to it may heighten our consciousness of God?

The Challenge of Evil

Evil has long been a philosophical and theological problem, but for a much longer time it has been a personal one. We often find ourselves glumly fixed on evil's pervasive ugliness as it touches our lives or as the media continuously depict its corrupting of the world around us. In modern thought, from Kierkegaard's *Concept of Dread* (1844) to Sartre's *Being and Nothingness* (1943) and beyond, fear and anguish have become philosophic catchwords. The case against evil has moved to the existentialist forum of untrammeled choice where suffering and death are discussed in terms of dread, forlornness, and despair.

How should we respond when confronted with this dismal heritage? Do suffering and death have a hidden significance that can lead man to God and preserve him from becoming merely, as Sartre suggested, *une passion inutile*? We chant the age-old refrain: "Whence comes evil and why?"

Too sophisticated to attribute an independent existence to evil, as did Zoroaster and Manes, we are still mystified by its role in our lives. Certainly, one of Augustine's great contributions to philosophy was to point out that evil, though real, is not a real thing, but rather "the privation of a good."[30] As Aquinas phrased this insight: "Evil according as it is evil is not something in things, but is the privation of some particular good, inhering in some particular good."[31] Evil is not a being but is found in a being. Though negative, evil is not a mere negation; rather it is the absence of a good that ought to be present, a *privatio boni debiti*.

Pain clearly illustrates the qualified absence which characterizes evil. It is an excellent example because: "Pain insists on being attended to."[32] Although we recognize it more easily than we define it, "Pain means, I suppose, awareness of some desire or tendency which is frustrated."[33] For a burned finger and a political defeat to be painful, there must be a conscious subject who has a tendency to physical well-being and a hope for public office, both of which fall short of fulfillment: the one because some skin is lacking, the other because the votes are insufficient. The tendency and the desire have been thwarted; consciousness of this thwarting is what we mean by pain.

Of course, pain is not something good in itself, an end to be sought for its own sake. Indeed, evil as such cannot be desired, for it is non-being. The physical evil, which is pain, is not a value but a lack of value, though indirectly it may be a means to something good or an unavoidable accompaniment of good. "It is always better if the good result for which it is normally necessary can be obtained without pain."[34] This point is not always grasped by those of a Manichean, Jansenistic, or Puritanical frame of mind.

Moral evil also manifests a lack of the good that should be present: that good is essentially the consistency between knowing and doing. The subject's unity of consciousness grounds an exigency for psychic integrity. To violate that by going against one's conscience is to bring into the mind a principle of division with its sequelae of guilt and anxiety and even externally imposed punishment—deprivations consequent on fault. In fact, moral evils are both the cause and the occasion of many, many physical evils—evils which, though deprivations of goods that should be present, are morally neutral. A death can be caused by a criminal homicide or a terminal illness. Human beings suffer from their own moral evil and from the physical evils caused by the moral evil of others or from physical evils that occur apart from human wickedness. But evils, whatever their source, bring pain and suffering and death.

Our present concern with evil is not so much what it is or how it can be avoided but how it can lead obliquely to consciousness of God. I shall examine from two positions the challenge that suffering presents to an anguished world: on the humanistic level, I shall analyze a natural response to evil, a value judgment consciously and freely made; on the Christian level, I shall consider the transcendental perfection that God has added to this natural response thereby transmuting the problem of evil into the mystery of divine providence. Together, these two perspectives will reveal how negative kataphatics brings us to a deepening awareness of God's presence.

The Existential Foundation

In response to the unavoidable evils in human life there should be a search for the inner meaning and values that emerge. Whether or not the search explicitly reaches out to the divine, it may contribute something to the foundation of negative kataphatics—the approach to God-consciousness through the proper facing of pain and suffering.

Just such a humanistic response has been formulated with great psychological insight by Viktor Frankl, a Viennese Jew, who had been dragged from a university post to a Nazi concentration camp. His book on existential analysis, *The Doctor and the Soul*,[35] is dedicated "To the Memory of Tillie." This affectionate diminutive gives no hint of the horrors that crushed his young wife, as well as his father and mother and brother. Only he and his sister escaped the gas chambers. Despite the death of those he loved and his own three years in the dreaded Auschwitz, he did survive against odds that were more than twenty to one. Exhausted, starved, frost-bitten, and beaten, he ferreted meaning and value out of his tortured existence. He learned, to use Paul Tillich's phrase, "the courage to be" in the devastating face of non-being, grasping his destiny, when he had seemed merely to have met his fate.

Subsequently, Dr. Frankl became Professor of Neurology and Psychiatry on the Medical Faculty of the University of Vienna and President of the Austrian Society of Medical Psychotherapy. He was the founder of the "Third Viennese School of Psychotherapy." The first was Freudian and emphasized the Will to Pleasure; the second was Adlerian and emphasized the Will to Power. Frankl's contribution, however, centers on the primary role of the Will to Meaning. Frankl considers the human person to be a conscious and responsible being capable of freely establishing ends and taking the means to attain them. His primary goal, personal and therapeutic, is the search for meaning. So logotherapy seeks to realize the "highest possible activation" of life[36] by making it "as meaningful as possible."[37]

This meaningful goal-orientation involves three sets of values.[38] *Creative values* are actualized by doing, by accomplishing tasks; they concern one's capacity for work. *Experiential* values are actualized by the passive receiving of the world (nature or art) in the ego by experiencing the good, the true, and the beautiful or by knowing a single human being through love in all his or her uniqueness. They concern one's capacity to enjoy. *Attitudinal* values are actualized wherever the individual is faced with something unalterable, something imposed by destiny. It looks to the possibility of realizing values by the very attitude with which we face our destined suffering. They concern one's capacity to suffer.

In his book, *Man's Search for Meaning*, Frankl movingly chronicled his experiences in a German prison camp. At one time, it seemed to him that he would die in the near future.

In this critical situation, however, my concern was different from that of most of my comrades. Their question was "Will we survive the camp? For, if not, all this suffering has no meaning." The question which beset me was, "Has all this suffering, this dying around us, a meaning?'' For, if not, then ultimately there is no meaning to survival; for a life whose meaning depends on such happenstance—whether one escapes or not—ultimately would not be worth living at all.[39]

From his own personal confrontation with suffering and death, implemented by profound study of the nature of man's mind and soul, Frankl concluded, not just that suffering has value, but that: "The right kind of suffering—facing your fate without flinching—is the highest achievement that has been granted to man."[40] Although here he seems to have put on the stern mask of Stoicism, his head "bloody but unbowed," he has actually added a new dimension, meaningfulness, which makes his response more truly human. "The right kind of suffering" certainly needs the elaboration which only religion can give, yet Frankl's contribution as a scientist is of immense significance, especially in an era of human vilification.

A number of times, Frankl quoted approvingly the remark of Goethe: "There is no predicament that we cannot ennoble either by doing or enduring."[41] He insisted, however, that for the acceptance of suffering to be a moral achievement, the suffering be such that it cannot rightly be altered by doing or avoided by not doing. This making a virtue of necessity, at first, seems to produce but pale nobility, yet by its very lack of obvious productivity, the tangible fruit of a job well done, it reveals the human person as worthwhile in his own right, as an end and not merely as a means to an end. Men and women can be noble as well as useful, sometimes most noble when apparently least useful.

The inevitablity of death seems to limit drastically the meaning of life. But for Frankl, human finiteness and the temporality and singularity of human destiny give each moment of life a perishable but irreplaceable value. "In the face of death as the absolute finis to our future and boundary to our possibilities, we are under the imperative of utilizing our lifetimes to the utmost not letting the singular opportunities—whose finite sum constitutes the whole of life—pass by unused."[42] The certainty of death and the uncertainty of the hour of death, we must consciously accept "as part of the bargain."[43] All we have is the present moment with its implicit duty to realize values.

The very precariousness of our lives should make us try always to live meaningfully. Frankl formulates the "leading maxim of existential analysis" in this way: "Live as if you were living for the second time and had acted as wrongly the first time as you are about to act now."[44] This consideration highlights our personal responsibility. The system of choices which is our life's work is irreversible. Important though the time factor is, meaningfulness is not measured by length of days. "The heroic life of one who has died young certainly has more content and meaning than the existence of some long-lived dullard."[45] The thought of death, far from enervating the spirit of man, should spark him to shape his destiny with vigor. "Man works the matter which fate has supplied him: now creating, now experiencing or suffering, he attempts to 'hammer out' values in his life—as many as he can of creative or experiential or attitudinal values."[46]

If it were purely humanistic, the logotherapeutic response to misfortune would be incomplete, though in many ways admirable. For unless space in the theory is provided for God, the theory in the end has no adequate ground. Frankl, to preserve his scientific credibility and professional accessibility, does not usually deal specifically with belief in God. He is not a theologian. His theory, however, is fully compatible with such a belief, which belief he in fact shares. In speaking of uniquely human phenomena, he wrote:

Among them, there is one which I regard as the most representative of human reality. I have circumscribed this phenomenon in terms of "man's search for meaning." Now, if this is correct one may also be justified in defining religion as man's search for *ultimate* meaning. It was Albert Einstein who once contended that to be religious is to have found an answer to the question, What is the meaning of life?[47]

He faced the issue of ultimate meaning concretely in terms of God and the "holocaust": "For either belief in God is unconditional or it is not belief at all. If it is unconditional it will stand and face the fact that six million died in the Nazi holocaust; if it is not unconditional it will fall away if only a single innocent child has to die—to resort to an argument once advanced by Dostoievski."[48]

Grace is necessary to perfect this natural foundation. "Unless the Lord build the house, he labors in vain that builds it" (Ps 127:1). Since all nature is graced, man's task is to discover and articulate that new dimension. Only through cooperation with this gift of God, can man bring full meaning and value into a life challenged by non-being. Our next question emerges: What has God revealed about responding to the evil in life, to this "mystery of iniquity," which looms like a dread specter over the human family? The answer to that question will suggest the role that negative kataphatics has in deepening our consciousness of God.

The Christian Implementation

The tension between good and evil affects all human beings; they seek fullness of life, but are destined to die. This tension is exacerbated by the apparent contradiction of the presence of mindless evil in a universe created by a God who defines himself as love. Since God does exist, how does one justify the pain and suffering of the innocent? My purpose here is not to solve the problem of evil but to suggest how a proper response to evil can lead, by the kataphatic path, to mystical experience.

Caught up in the tension of existential ambivalence, we seek to come to terms with reality, to catch a hint of the meaning and value of suffering, so that it does not block the conscious presence of God but augments it. To this end, I shall discuss three aspects of this spiritual challenge: (1) its principle, which is divine providence; (2) its paradigm, which is Jesus Christ; (3) its practice, which is negative kataphatics; that is, the acceptance of the cross of Christ as the mysterious working of divine providence. The subjective core of this victory over evil is an expanding consciousness of God through principle, paradigm, and practice.

First, the resolution in *principle* looks fundamentally to divine providence. The First Vatican Council stated in 1870: "God by his providence protects and governs all the things he has made 'reaching strongly from end to end and ordering all things graciously' (Wis 8:1), for 'all things are naked and open to his eyes' (Heb 4:13) even those which are to occur through the free action of creatures."[49] This is the traditional teaching of the Old and New Testaments, and it implies that there is really no such thing as chance; though evil is in the world, nothing, including pain and suffering, falls outside the scope of divine providence.[50] Centuries before Vatican I, Aquinas, drawing on Augustine, applied these same principles to the problem of evil:

> God is so good that he would never permit there to be any evil, unless he were so powerful that from every evil he is able to draw good. Wherefore it is neither on account of the impotency, nor on account of the ignorance of God that evils appear in the world. But it is from the order of his wisdom and the magnitude of his goodness.[51]

The formulation of this truth which is most often discovered in the works of mystics and spiritual writers goes back to the New Testament and Paul's aphorism: "To those who love God all things work together for good" (Rom 8:28).[52] Joseph A. Fitzmyer has summed up the meaning of this text: "God's purpose and plan are really behind all that happens to Christians. For Paul, God is in control of everything."[53]

That very control could worsen the tension were it not for the fact that the core of the providential resolution of the problem of evil is love: God as love, in effectively ordering all things, provides especially for those who love him. As for the forces of evil? "But in all these things we overcome, because of him that has loved us. I am sure that neither death, nor life, nor angels, nor principalities, nor powers, nor things present, nor things to come, nor might, nor height, nor depth, nor any other creature shall be able to separate us from the love of God" (Rom 8:37–39). The underlying implication is that by loving God we are completely fulfilled. Only our own refusal can prevent or limit that fulfillment. God in his providence takes infinite care of all that he has created; indeed, the initiative is his, as Paul indicated, adding after "work together for good," the phrase "to those who are called according to his purpose" (Rom 8:28). This addition suggests the statement in John: "Not as though we had loved God, but because he has first loved us and sent his Son to be a propitiation for our sins" (1 Jn 4:10).

Love responds to love; the response on our part requires faith and trust with a humble acceptance of his loving will, mysterious though it may be. Paul makes this latter point eloquently: "O the depth of the riches of the wisdom and the knowledge of God. How incomprehensible are his judgments and how unsearchable his ways. For who has known the mind of God? Or who has been his counselor?" (Rom 11:33–34). Indeed we labor against evil in the darkness of faith; if we know how to love, however, we are able in Christ to overcome "the mystery of iniquity."

Second, the unique *paradigm* of this resolution is Jesus Christ, the vital power for transforming evil into good. Because of moral and physical evils, we have need of a savior. It is not enough to know in theory that God has assured those who love him of their victory over death; we seek concrete evidence to that effect. We need to see that promise realized somewhere. In Jesus Christ, who is the self-revelation of the Father, the theory becomes a living reality. "We have not a high priest, who cannot have compassion on our infirmities, but one tempted in all things as we are, without sin" (Heb 4:15). Paul described Christ's kenotic role: "He humbled himself, becoming obedient unto death, even to the death of the cross. For which cause God also has exalted him" (Phil 2:7–8). The vivid memory of the death, resurrection, and glorification of Jesus, gives the Christian a guarantee of personal fulfillment, for the victory has already been won in Christ.

From the perspective of mysticism, it is important to note that in this same passage Paul stated: "Let that mind be in you, which was also in Christ Jesus" (Phil 2:5). This direction is to an expanding consciousness, which comprehends the value of obedience unto death, as it transcends death itself, for sharing in Christ's suffering, we too shall be exalted, "so that, if we suffer with Him, we may be glorified with him" (Rom 8:17). The death and resurrection of Jesus Christ afford both a conclusive proof and a practical paradigm of the Father's promise to those who love him.

Third, the actual *practice* of God's plan manifests ascending levels of God-consciousness. Holiness of life reflective of the will of God brings a deepening union. Mysticism at this stage is a kind of realized eschatology of the kataphatic way, a heightened awareness of the divine dimension of one's positive and negative interaction with creatures.

Each stage of the gradual ascent toward face-to-face vision of God requires faith, but often we are unable to appreciate, especially in matters touching us closely, the greater good that God has directly willed, when it is hidden by limitations of creatures and the trappings of evil. So faith is tempered through concrete events which involve permitted evil but manifest the divine will. This strengthening is necessary, for Christians may readily accept the mysteries of the Trinity and incarnation, but find their faith in divine providence shaken by frustrations and failures, by sicknesses and betrayals, by pain and anguish. It is not easy to have a crucified savior as a role model.

Four observations may help to put faith and suffering into a clearer perspective. (1) Even those who lack faith or even deny God's existence experience the problem of evil: atheists, too, suffer and die. (2) Faith does not pretend to eliminate suffering or trivialize it; faith reveals how evil, though it cannot be escaped, can be overcome. (3) Faith complements nature, so the response to sin and suffering should not overlook the rational and existential clarifications, which show that despite the burden of evil, one's life can still be meaningful and valuable. (4) Faith gives Christians an advantage in knowing that in Christ they are assured of ultimate victory, and that in the person of the crucified and resurrected Savior they have the ultimate pledge from the Father: "He that spared not even his own Son, but delivered him up for us all, how has he not also, with him, given us all things?" (Rom 8:32).

In a word, the meaning and value that the Christian message brings into one's life is love. Faith in divine Providence is a faith that operates through love. The sufferings in this life come from a God who is love. And if the attitudinal response to one's destiny is love, then one is assured by the Spirit of Love that for those who persevere in love, there shall come a time when "Death is swallowed up in victory" (I Cor 15:55).

The Symbols of Transition

The spiritual quest involves moving from the known to the unknown, from the categorical to the transcendental, from the creature to the creator. Kataphatics, using created things and events, leads to God-consciousness. But full consciousness of God is ultimately apophatic, for the creator transcends all the images and ideas that we have of him. Thus kataphatics, if pursued faithfully, leads beyond itself.

The key to understanding this transition from kataphatics to apophatics is the function of religious symbols in opening the mind to reality. In chapter three of his *Mystical Theology,* Dionysius the Areopagite (c. 500) distinguished the kataphatic and apophatic approaches. But in his *Celestial Hierarchy,* he made a further distinction in kataphatics itself between the affirmation of similarities and of dissimilarities, between like symbols (*homoia symbola*) and unlike symbols (*anomoia symbola*), for example, between saying that God is beauty and that God is a fire.[54] About these "unlike symbols," he said paradoxically: "I doubt that anyone would refuse to acknowledge that incongruities are more suitable for lifting our minds into the domain of the spiritual than similarities are."[55] His reason was that God transcends all his creatures, and the clearer we are on that point the better. We shall see how these "unlike symbols" lead smoothly into an apophatic theology.

Since we do not know God directly but only analogously, we must carefully assess the limits of the created analogues, the signs that tell us of God.[56] These signs have a literal meaning, but also a special symbolic meaning. These two levels are exemplified in Paul Ricoeur's definition: "I call symbol every structure of signification in which a direct, primary, literal sense designates by excess another sense, indirect, secondary, figured, which cannot be apprehended except across the first."[57]

An exclusive emphasis on meaning, however, unduly narrows the notion of symbol. Ricoeur did assert with Freud that the creation of symbols was the result of the repression of desire. Nevertheless, he stated explicitly with no mention of the feelings: "That symbols are signs is certain: they are expressions that communicate a meaning; this meaning is declared in an intention of signifying which has speech as its vehicle."[58] In speaking of "the second *naïveté*," he noted the continuing need for interpretation: "Thus it is in hermeneutics that the symbol's gift of meaning and the endeavor to understand by deciphering are knotted together."[59] Throughout his work, references to feelings, emotions, and passions abound, but the affective element does not seem to be adequately incorporated into his system.

For Bernard Lonergan, however, feelings are an essential component of symbols, as his concise definition indicates: "A symbol is an image of a real or imaginary object that evokes a feeling or is evoked by a feeling."[60] This statement is of course consonant with his cognitional theory whereby, in accord with the eros of the spirit toward reality, the mind responds to meanings with feelings. This twofold response to reality helps explain the integrated energy at the core of a true symbol. "It is through symbols that mind and body, mind and heart, heart and body communicate."[61]

By apparently equating symbols with concrete objects, however, Lonergan might seem to have limited the range of symbols, which actually encompass both objects and actions. Historical celebrations, liturgical rituals, courtship practices, are symbolic both in the actions done and the objects used. To understand Lonergan properly, however, it is necessary to note that for him "object" means more than the concrete beings of our experience; he said that "by an object one means anything that is intended in questions and known through correct answers, anything within the world mediated by meaning."[62] So the object with an affect that is a symbol includes things, actions, events.

Moreover, using Ernst Cassirer's phrase, Lonergan spoke of man as "the symbolic animal, whose knowledge is mediated by symbols, whose actions are informed by symbols, whose existence in its most characteristic features is constituted by self-understanding and by commitments specified by symbols."[63] Mircea Eliade, whose work Lonergan said was consonant with his own, specifically spoke of symbolic actions: "The symbolism *adds* new value to an object or an activity without any prejudice whatever to its own immediate value. In application to objects or actions, symbolism renders them open."[64] This element of openness is crucial to my position on the transitional function of kataphatics.

A symbol enables us to become aware of reality, both its meaning and its value. But here is where we note the difference between a symbol and other signs; the symbol transcends other signs by leading to a new realm of meaning, as Ricoeur rightly noted: "The function of a symbol is precisely that of revealing a whole reality inaccessible to other means of knowledge."[65]

Lonergan formulated this cognitive dimension of symbol more neatly than Ricoeur: "As symbol, the image is linked simply with the paradoxical 'known unknown.' "[66] What we know only well enough to ask questions about is the "known unknown"; what we cannot even ask questions about is the "unknown unknown"—it is not even a possibility for us. In time the "known unknown" may become known and something of the "unknown unknown" may emerge sufficiently to prompt a question. Our heuristic endeavors, however, are limited to the "known unknown." Symbols are ways of suggesting answers to questions in this arena. Common sense and theory give us some answers, but we still require symbols for a fuller appreciation of the mystery of reality, of that which remains for us the "known unknown." We should note here that God is for us a "known unknown," hence our need of religious symbols.

The multivalence of symbols, their bringing many levels of meaning and value into an overall unity, underscores their perennial need. They form, Eliade said, "a metaphysic—a whole and coherent conception of Reality."[67] This world pattern or system of symbols always involves the manifestations of human life. "Thanks to symbols, the individual experience is 'awoken' and transmuted into a spiritual act."[68]

Symbols tend to emerge from the common sense realm in which we relate persons and things to ourselves. We seek to make contact with the unknown, a contact perhaps imprecise and mysterious but emotionally vital and personally satisfying. This contact enables us to go beyond the limits of theoretical understanding. For Eliade, the symbol is a natural response of human beings to the world of their experience: "The symbol itself expresses an awakening to the knowledge of a 'limit-situation.' "[69] And this knowledge in turn becomes "an 'opening out' into the transcendent."[70]

The relationship of limit-situations to symbols is profoundly important. By that term, I mean the universal experiences of human contingency and mortality as well as the concern with what is beyond those experiences as their source and their end. Symbols lead to God by raising questions about limit-situations and the known-unknown; these questions are eventually articulated as questions about the ultimate ground of existence, intelligibility, and value—namely God. "The man who understands a symbol," Eliade says, "not only opens himself to the objective world, but at the same time succeeds in emerging from his personal situation and reaching a comprehension of the universal."[71] Through symbols limit-situations open the mind and heart to the limitless divine.

Indeed the universality of the human condition with its limit-situations accounts largely for the ubiquity of archetypal symbols. Cultures may change, but throughout history men and women ever face a common destiny in their temporal vulnerability; they are born, mature, reproduce, grow old, become ill, and die. They sin and seek forgiveness; they are overwhelmed and seek salvation. They look for meaning and value in their daily lives; above all, they hunger for ultimate meaning and value. Through the centuries, most people have experienced and expressed their yearnings in symbols and, most profoundly, in religious symbols. These symbols are affected by circumstances but are not determined by them. They have a transcultural and transhistorical vitality. "The more a consciousness is awakened, the more it transcends its own historicity: we have only to remind ourselves of the mystics and the sages of all time, and primarily those of the Orient."[72]

When human consciousness has been awakened, appropriated, and developed, it becomes possible for it to perceive in its symbols an intrinsic presence of the object symbolized. Karl Rahner, writing on the theology of the symbol, spoke of it as no more than an exegesis of the text, "He that sees me sees the Father" (Jn 14:9). Rahner emphasized the immediacy of symbolic representation: "For a true and proper symbol being an intrinsic moment of the thing itself has a function of mediation which is not at all opposed in reality to the immediacy of what is meant by it, but is a mediation of immediacy, if one may so formulate the actual facts of the matter."[73]

To develop this notion, Rahner, working within a highly developed system, examined the symbolic dimension of creatures as images or vestiges of God. Starting with the doctrine of the Trinity, he showed the continuity of a symbolic but intrinsic self-expression: the Logos is the symbol of the Father, the humanity of Christ is the symbol of the Logos, the church is the symbol of Christ, the sacraments are the symbols making concrete the reality of the church, the graced Christian is the symbol of the church, and the body is the symbol of the soul.

What is critical in his thinking is that the symbol is not "an extrinsic and accidental intermediary, something really outside the reality transmitted through it, so that strictly speaking the thing could be attained even without the symbol."[74] Rather, for him, the symbol is internal and indispensable: "The being is known in this symbol, without which it cannot be known at all: thus it is symbol in the original (transcendental) sense of the word."[75]

Rahner worked out his theory of symbols through an analysis of the theology of the Sacred Heart. For him, the soul, as the substantial form of the body, makes itself present in the body which directly symbolizes it. The key element is presence, so essential for spirituality. His explanation of the symbol of the Sacred Heart makes all theophanies more intrinsically meaningful:

> Reality and its appearance in the flesh are for ever one in Christianity, unconfused and inseparable. The reality of the divine self-communication creates of itself its immediacy by constituting itself present in the symbol, which does not divide as it mediates but unites immediately, because the true symbol is united with the thing symbolized, since the latter constitutes the former as its own self-realization (*Selbstvollzung*).[76]

Be that as it may, there are symbols, very important ones, that are adventitious and conventional. The cross on which Christ died is a very different kind of symbol from the Sacred Heart that was pierced when he hung on that cross. Both are symbols of the crucified God-man, one is extrinsic, the other intrinsic.

To understand how symbols function in our move toward God-consciousness, we shall consolidate what has been discussed thus far. Here is an initial description: A religious symbol is a thing or event functioning analogously as a sign to produce meanings and feelings concerning limit-situations, tending thereby to unite the person with the being symbolized, or conversely to separate the person from the non-being symbolized.

Obviously, things and events are realities in themselves; as signs, however, they refer to something else, to limit-situations when the symbols are religious. It is this subjective reference which makes them symbols. Here is a different but more complete description, formulated from the perspective of interiority: Religious symbolization is an act of the mind using things or events analogously to produce meanings and feelings about limit-situations, thereby tending to unite the person using the symbol with the being symbolized, or conversely to separate the person from the non-being symbolized. The symbol is a bridge between the person and the referent; its function is to open the mind through meaning and feeling to the sought-for reality.

Although we speak of things and events as the mediating factors, we are accustomed to use multivalent and affect-laden images of these things and events in our venture into the unknown through analogical reasoning. Symbols fill the gap in our direct knowledge as we seek religious consciousness. Though not conceptually precise, symbols unify a complexus of meanings and feelings to give a personal approximation of what is, simply speaking, a known-unknown. The known part may be authenticated by revelation or other traditions or it may merely reflect one's own imaginative and emotional convictions. But the symbol also stands for what is unknown, for what escapes full rational consciousness, in that there is no virtually unconditioned judgment about it. Religious symbols rise from questions about limit-situations for which we do not have full answers. We know enough to ask, but the best that we can do is find answers that are only analogously true, answers that express a similarity but not the full reality. Nevertheless, through meanings and feelings, symbols give us the ring of truth and the confidence to make a real assent.

One aspect of symbols needs fuller examination; that is, the function of the symbol to unite the person with the reality signified or to separate the person from the non-being signified. I shall give an example of each: first two positive symbols for rebirth and then a negative symbol for sin.

Whether or not human beings originally grasped the notion or fostered the hope from seeing the phases of the moon or the miracle of spring, death and resurrection have a role to play in most religions.

Benedictines in the past adapted this symbolism to their religious profession of vows. The monk, robed in black with a hood over his head, lies face down upon a rectangular black pall, with three large candlesticks on each side, while the community prays over him. After making his vows, he spends the next few days *incommunicado,* not even reciting aloud in choir. Only on the third day does he rejoin the community. Symbolically, he has died with Christ and has been born anew; now he no longer lives, but Christ lives in him.

By dying to the world, the monk has promised to do God's will faithfully for the rest of his life. Through his symbolic death, he has rejected in principle every temptation. For he is dead and his life is hid with God in Christ Jesus. Mystically, it is a commitment to the apophatic way, the leaving of all things to follow Christ.

Although this symbol may seem to be the heritage of a monastic elite, it is by no means an exclusive one. Indeed, a truism of the monastic life is that it is essentially an intensified version of the ordinary Christian life. The monastic profession is a version of one's baptismal rebirth, where the immersion in water symbolizes a going back to the womb (*regressus ad uterum*), effecting the beginning of a new life; the salt reminds us of the wisdom that faith brings, the oil recalls the anointing by the Spirit. So all Christians have an enduring source of spiritual strength, not only the sacramental grace, but the power of the sacramental signs, which symbolize vividly meaning and feelings of a death and a resurrection into a new life.

A negative religious symbol is seen in the wide use made of the literal notion of stain or blemish to construct the moral symbol for sin, as Paul Ricoeur has shown.[77] The attribution is not univocal: the sinner does not have dirty marks or filthy scum on his soul. Nevertheless, these terms remain a powerful way to imagine the effects of evil choices. Certainly, such a symbol indicates a flawed character and arouses emotional repugnance. But spiritual beings are not polluted *simpliciter* but only *secundum quid*. Strictly speaking they do not actually undergo material corruption, but do so only analogously. The accusation or attribution, however, is none the less forceful or insulting for all of that. The symbol may be a devastating weapon, even though its point is metaphorical; for example, Christ's calling the Pharisees "whited sepulchers" and "a brood of vipers."

This brief sketch of some key symbols indicates concretely the kataphatic approach to God, especially its transitional function. In mediating the world through meaning, we experience data, understand them provisionally, verify our understanding, and act in harmony with that judgment. Symbols are dynamic images which enable us to act strongly with spiritual meaning and value.

We do not, however, usually operate in a logical, abstract, or piecemeal way in moving from creatures to God. Kataphatics affords a much more integral experience, encompassing the major exigencies of our life in terms of limit-situations. The kataphatic way to consciousness of God uses these symbols, these images freighted with feeling, to bring an intensified awareness and love of God. More specifically, the symbols involve us in limit-situations and, in doing so, open our minds to the transcendent. They make us aware of ourselves as contingent beings and suggest our indispensable relationship to the Absolute. The very ambiguity of the symbol reflects the overarching mystery of reality. But our openness to mystery is not yet complete; even symbols tend to translate divine simplicity into created terms however open-ended; and they keep our understanding of the infinite on the level of the finite. Though we are lovingly and even intensely aware of the divine presence, we may yet have to take the step past images and concepts, past symbols but with the help of symbols, into the realm of sheer Being. This is the apophatic challenge.

CONCLUSION

The world of our experience ever confronts us with beauty and suffering, with Tabor and Calvary. We must attend carefully to these dualities so that our responses lead us to consciousness of God without putting a ceiling on our search. No such cloture need occur, for although God transcends all created beings, human beings are created with an openness to transcendence. So we find our experience of beauty and suffering to be instinct with the residual query: Is that all there is to this life? Is there a way even here to know God more truly?

The beings and events that we experience, whether good or bad, can afford us a sense of a presence that transcends everything else. This divine presence is the focus of the kataphatic way and shines forth positively in the hierarchy of creaturely perfections and negatively in the daily crosses of affliction. Both modalities, inspired by a faith which operates through love, lift our minds and hearts to the realm of the transcendent.

Nevertheless, the vision of God that comes through the kataphatic way is not an immediate one nor does it purely and accurately reflect the divine essence. As the Fourth Lateran Council stated: "Between the Creator and the creature no similarity can be expressed without including a greater dissimilarity."[78] The kataphatic way anticipates a spiritual leap beyond every creature, beyond every image and notion of God, a leap that is inspired by the hints of the divine beauty and the providential wisdom and goodness that the things and the happenings of this world reflect. As long as we live in this world, kataphatics remains a foundational function to which the mystical subject frequently returns. Indeed, as von Balthasar said: "The Areopagite and John of the Cross—the two theologians who relied most consistently on the apophatic method—never divorced it from the kataphatic approach. They could exalt the vertical to such a degree only because they never let go of the horizontal."[79]

A religious symbol keeps kataphatics in true proportion. As an open-ended analogy, a symbol, functioning imaginatively and with feeling, takes into account the infinity of God. To think of all created beings and events as symbols of the divine presence preserves the

transcendent character of religious experience. Tapping the archetypal energies of the psyche, symbols direct the searching mind
beyond the symbol to the God symbolized, who is to be found more
perfectly in the apophatic way. Indeed in the emptiness of the apophatic way, the very openness of the soul in knowing and loving becomes functionally through self-consciousness a quasi-symbol of the
divine presence.

4

The Apophatic Venture

✧　　　✧　　　✧

Nothing in all creation is so like God as stillness.
Meister Eckhart*

The only language he hears is the silent language of love.
John of the Cross**

On reaching the outer boundaries of the kataphatic through symbols, the potential mystic, unless transported by a special grace, faces
a checkpoint in the spiritual quest and must decide whether or not to
venture into the forbidding territory of the apophatic, there to confront the apparent sterility and silence of the void, where the promised joys and intimacy of divine love may seem to be discouragingly
distant.

The pressure for such a choice arises from the inadequacy of all
creaturely analogies, which shows the kataphatic stage to be essentially transitional. Not everyone consciously makes this choice, nor is
the apophatic an exclusive path for anyone. The option emerges as
the fruit of a restless search for God, as he really is, by one convinced
that: "Better is one day in your courts than a thousand elsewhere"
(Ps 83:10).

In pointing out the apophatic path to heightened consciousness
of God, we consider five points: first, the stark reality of divine incomprehensibility, as understood by reason and affirmed by revelation;
second, the challenging hope sparked by the principle that nature

* Meister Eckhart, *Meister Eckhart,* trans. R. B. Blakney (New York: Harper and
Row, 1941), p. 243, fragment 29. See also note 29, p. 329.
** John of the Cross, *Collected Works,* trans. K. Kavanaugh and O. Rodriguez
(Washington, D.C.: Institute of Carmelite Studies, 1979), letter no. 7, p. 689.

abhors a vacuum; third, the response to that challenge by analyzing the process of purifying the mind of created forms and inordinate desires; fourth, the last capitulation that must be made for divine consciousness to be complete—the transcending of the self; fifth and finally, the obligatory return of all mystics to the service of the Body of Christ and the whole human family.

The Known Unknown

The focus of our question is, in Lonergan's term, a known-unknown. We have seen how it operates kataphatically through symbols. Here we consider the move toward God as infinite mystery. Christian tradition is blunt about the impossibility of immediate knowledge of God. In this section, we shall consider first what revelation states; next what reason affirms; finally what methodology dictates. In brief, God is an object not a thing. We can know *that* God is. We cannot know *what* God is. But we can know about God, and we can experience his presence.

1. *From revelation* we learn the fundamental unknowability of God during our earthly existence. Even the light of faith does not give us a divine vision. Rather, it confirms the fact that God is the known-unknown: we know only about God, who told Moses: "You cannot see my face, for no one shall see me and live" (Exod 33:20). Paul, having had extraordinary mystical experiences, wrote that God "dwells in inaccessible light, whom no one has seen or can see" (I Tim 6:16). And in one of the last books of the New Testament, we read: "No one has seen God at any time" (I Jn 4:12).

Admittedly, this divine distancing is not to be permanent: "We know that when he shall appear, we shall know him as he is" (I Jn 3:2); and "We see now through a glass in a dark manner, but then face to face. Now I know in part, but then I shall know even as I am known" (I Cor 13:12).

These texts show that graced human reason, even augmented by revelation, cannot experience during this life a direct or immediate vision of God's essence. The First Vatican Council reiterated this point: "The divine mysteries so exceed the created intellect that even when given in revelation and received by faith, they remain covered over by the very veil of faith itself."[1] The strengthening light of grace and the God-given images of revelation are a great help in getting to know God.[2] But they operate within a clear boundary, as Aquinas stated:

Although in this life revelation does not tell us what God is, and so joins us to him as to an unknown, nevertheless it helps us to know him better in that we are shown more and greater works of his and are taught certain things about him that we could never have known through natural reason, as for instance that he is both three and one.[3]

Moreover, as far as knowing "in part" is concerned, there is the proof from effects to cause mentioned by Paul: "The invisible things of him, from the creation of the world, are clearly seen being understood by the things that are made, his eternal power also and divinity" (Rom 1:20). So reason alone—without revelation but not necessarily without grace—can, according to the traditional interpretation, ascertain God's existence and something of his attributes. Vatican I stated: "The same holy Mother Church teaches that God, the origin and end of all things, can be known with certainty by the natural light of reason from the things he created."[4] The Council added the canon: "If anyone says that the one and true God, our creator and lord, cannot be known with certainty by the natural light of reason through the things that have been made: let him be anathema."[5] Here, of course, "with certainty" does not mean by direct vision.

Some Protestant theologians have held that even the existence of God is known only through revelation. For example, Karl Barth wrote, in contradicting the conciliar position: "We have affirmed that God can be known only through God, namely in the event of his self-revelation."[6] He systematically rejected any other analogical basis as an alternate source.

Both sides, however, do agree on a proposition that is at the heart of this chapter, namely, that the essence of God is not directly knowable. A dispute still remains over the value of kataphatic analogies to reveal naturally and inferentially the fact of God's existence and some of his attributes. A denial of the possibility of natural theology, however, makes the apophatic way without revelation a spiritual dead end and limits the kataphatic way to an extrapolation based solely on revealed analogies.

2. *From reason*, we grasp the fundamental explanation as to why the created mind cannot know naturally what God is in his essence. Very simply, it is because God's essence is identified with his existence; he is sheer existence, *ipsum esse subsistens*, and no created form can adequately represent that truth to the human mind. Humans think with limited concepts. Heuristically open-ended though some concepts may be, they are not capable of encompassing the infinite,

divine essence. The Vedantic words, *neti, neti* (not this, not that), catch the gist of Aquinas's explanation of the underlying demands of transcendence.[7]

> The divine essence is beyond description, containing to a transcendent degree every perfection that can be described or understood by the created mind. This could not be represented by any created likeness since *every created form is determinately this rather than that,* whether it be wisdom, power, existence itself or anything else.[8]

A subject seeking to know as perfectly as possible this unknown God confronts the challenge of transcendence. On the one hand, God remains both unknown and disguised. For created images mask his transcendence and communicate his infinitude in the language of limitation. On the other hand, a true lover—even a philosopher or theologian, whose profession is to conceptualize and thematize—may, prompted by love, attempt a breakthrough to the purely existential God, who is described as "He who is."

Aquinas, in his early writings (1252–1256) on the *Sentences* of Peter Lombard, dealt with the frustrating impasse that the mystical subject experiences in seeking the face of the unknown God. Aquinas pointed to the arduous road, the lonely road, the *via remotionis*. In a key passage Aquinas asked whether *Qui est,* "He who is," is appropriately used of God and concluded that it is the most appropriate term of all. He was at pains to point out the thoroughness with which we must purify our notion of being if we are to apply it to God, especially if, as a practical matter, we desire to be "best joined to God." I shall quote his thoughts at some length, since they focus on the heart of the question. First there is the statement of the principle:

> It must be said that all other names mean to be determined according to some other notion; just as "wise" means to be something [particular], but this name, "He who is," means to be absolute and not determined by an added something. And therefore Damascene says that it does not signify what God is, but it signifies a certain infinite sea of substance as indeterminate.[9]

Aquinas then explained the stages of negation through the various levels of being, as the soul seeks to be one with God moving from the sensible to the conceptual to the purely existential to the uncreated.

> So, when we proceed toward God by the way of removal, we first deny of him corporeal things; second even intellectual things as they are found in creatures such as goodness and wisdom, there then remains in our intellects only that he is and nothing further, whence there is a certain confusion about his existence. But finally, we even remove from him this [notion of] being itself as it is in creatures, and then he remains in the darkness of unknowing, and in accord with such unknowing as it pertains to the wayfarer, we are, as Dionysius says, best joined to God; and this is the darkness in which God is said to dwell.[10]

Years later in the *Summa theologiae*, Aquinas took up the same question, concluding again that "He who is" is the most appropriate name for God and this for three reasons: its formlessness, its universality, and its syntactical presentness.[11] First, it has no particular form, but expresses only existence. Second, it excludes all other names which are less general or are restrictive and determinate. (Here he referred again to God as "an infinite sea of being.") Third, it signifies God's being through the use of the present tense, since for him there is no past or future. Here, too, Aquinas underscored, almost shockingly, the limits of the created mind in knowing God: "In this life our minds cannot grasp what God is in himself; whatever way we have of thinking of him is a way of failing to understand him as he really is."[12]

3. *From a methodological perspective,* we question whether we can call God an object at all. Defining an object as "what one knows through a set of true judgments,"[13] we can survey some of the occasions for using the term God as the possible object of philosophy, religion, mysticism, and common sense.[14] By asking questions about the intelligibility, the contingency, and the worthwhileness of the world of our experience, we can reason philosophically to the existence of an ultimate ground, which we can rightly understand as an object called God.

As members of a religion, we ask questions and give answers about the same divine object. As mystics, we experience an orientation toward transcendent mystery, sought as infinitely lovable. This gift of divine love, we distinguish from the personal consciousness of an emergent reality. Only in interpreting and articulating this objectification of consciousness, does God become for the mystic an object, known properly through a judgment.

> Such an orientation, while it is the climax of a self-transcend-ing process of questioning, nonetheless is not properly a matter of raising and answering questions. So far from lying within the world mediated by meaning, it is the principle that can draw people out of that world and into the cloud of unknowing.[15]

Moreover, questioning from the viewpoint of common sense, we might tend to conclude that God is a thing, "a unity-identity-whole which insight grasps, some identical unity that is comprehended of a whole in individual data."[16] Actually, God surpasses all things; he is no thing. To get closer to his reality, we must radically transcend the data of our experience, if only by means of religious belief when our consciousness is neither philosophically grounded nor mystically ele-vated. While still in the realm of common sense, however, we might, through false judgments based on a naive realism, think of God as a body, invisible perhaps, but nevertheless "the already-out-there-now real."[17]

Of course, we do not quantify or materialize or reify God. God is no-body as well as no-thing; God is neither kind of object, though many pious imaginations have faithfully and anthropomorphically so pictured him. Indeed, philosophic minds have sometimes relied so strongly on analogous concepts—which are also created forms—that they do not fully conceive of God as transcending being itself. God is not a being, if we understand being as it is in creatures. We may conceive of God as a being, only if our notion of being is purified, for this unique case, of all created limitations. Truly a rigorous task.

In properly understanding God as an object—as known by a judg-ment—we can affirm his existence, pre-mystically or mystically, but we cannot comprehend his essence either way; we know that he is, but not what he is. We use created analogies, but we transcend these analogies. The answer to our questions about what is God is that God is positive nothingness; he is no-thing, but he is not nothing. We can-not know God's essence in itself, but we can know it to be real.

So far, we have brought some precision into our way of thinking about God. We thus arrive at a crucial point of spiritual conscious-ness, when it becomes clear to us personally and experientially that: "Man reaches the peak of his knowledge of God when he realizes that he does not know him, understanding that the divine reality surpasses all human conceptions of it."[18] These are the words, we should remind ourselves, not of Karl Barth, who would agree with them, but of Thomas Aquinas.

When we reach that stage in our spiritual quest, we have to make a choice: either we try to content ourselves with analogies, ultimately unsatisfying, or we strive, without counting the cost, toward the inconceivable, the ineffable, the inexpressible, the divine nothingness. This latter alternative, seemingly futile, is not the curse of radical skepticism, but the challenge of *kairos,* the opportune moment, that has its roots in revelation and its fruit in apophatics.

To summarize, during this life we do not know God, the known-unknown, immediately. Although we are immediately present to God, God is only mediately present to us through his effects. Hence all our knowledge of God is mediated. This mediation has, as we have seen, two modes: the kataphatic looks to forms, analogous ones; the apophatic looks to formlessness. Both involve divine effects: the forms are obviously created effects; the formlessness is also a created effect, though less obviously in that it results from unrestricted knowing and loving. Since God as sheer existence is incomprehensible to natural reason, we find created forms radically inadequate and are left with formlessness infused with love as our closest approximation to divine union but still an approximation since it looks to the capacity of a finite mind opening itself to the infinite.

Spiritual writers—Augustine, Dionysius the Areopagite, Aquinas, Eckhart, John of the Cross, Teresa of Avila, and countless others —have acknowledged this call to utter transcendence. And yet the abundant literature on visions, touches, locutions, raptures, and mystical heights belies the starkness of the fact that God exceeds the capacities of the natural mind, that even with grace and revelation human beings do not know God immediately in this life, and that only in the light of glory is face-to-face vision realized. From this fact, we can understand how prayer soon tends to become formless contemplation of an incomprehensible but present God of pure existence. We thus appreciate what trust and courage the apophatic way demands.

The Vacuum Principle

The black and white clarity of the apophatic way has inspired a fascinating but easily oversimplified analogy based on the scientific principle that nature abhors a vacuum. In the *Ascent,* John of the Cross formulated the principle in spiritual terms: "As soon as natural things are driven out of the enamoured soul, the divine are naturally and supernaturally infused, since there can be no void in nature."[19]

This formulation of God's response to the apophatic soul was not a sixteenth-century insight. The vacuum analogy was a commonplace of Hindu spirituality.[20] It also goes back to the beginnings of Christian mystical theology when Neo-Platonism was the major philosophic vehicle for understanding revelation.[21] Plato and Plotinus were the pagan sources; Augustine and Dionysius the Areopagite articulated this position in Christian terms. Much later, the vacuum analogy was used by Bonaventure and Albert the Great. By that time it had become normative in the Eastern and the Western churches, reaching its high point during the fourteenth century in the works of Eckhart, Tauler, Suso, and Ruusbroec. By the sixteenth century, the analogy had found its way into the writings of John of the Cross, who quoted from the *Mystical Theology* and *Divine Names* of Dionysius.

Some formulations of the vacuum principle seemed almost to depersonalize the relationship between God and man; for example, Meister Eckhart wrote with forthright daring:

> Do not imagine that God is like a carpenter who works or not, just as he pleases, suiting his own convenience. It is not so with God, for when he finds you ready he must act and pour into you, just as when the air is clear and pure the sun must pour into it and may not hold back.[22]

His contemporary, the gentler and more practical John Tauler, who was influenced by Eckhart, summed up the matter similarly: "If you go out, he will most surely come in, no more, no less."[23] Elaborating on this point, he said:

> If a man would prepare an empty place in the depths of his soul there can be no doubt that God must fill it at once. If there were a void on earth the heavens would fall to fill it. God will not allow anything to be void. That would be contrary to his nature and his just utterance.[24]

Dangers persist, however, for the subject may put undue reliance on human efforts in the spirit of Pelagian activism or may put total reliance on a divine agency in the spirit of Quietistic passivism. The application of the *horror vacui* analogy to the spiritual life might seem to make the divine response too automatic and mechanical. The fault may be that, in stating the main point aphoristically, mystical theologians have given the impression that other important components are irrelevant.

Scripture, of course, is equally aphoristic in teaching of divine reciprocity and promptitude. Note, for example, the words from the epistle of James: "Draw near to God and he will draw near to you" (4:8) and from the book of Revelation: "Behold I stand at the gate and knock. If anyone hear my voice and open to me the door, I will come in to him and will dine with him and he with me" (3:20). In commenting on this second text, Eckhart concluded: "The opening [of the door] and the entry are simultaneous."[25]

The theological justification of this simultaneity rests on the gratuity of divine grace, both the antecedent *gratia operans,* "The love of God is poured forth in our hearts from the Holy Spirit who is given to us" (Rom 5:5) and the concomitant *gratia cooperans*: "No man comes to me unless the Father who sent me draw him" (Jn 6:44). A loving response to the freely given grace of God makes us capable of receiving what God from all eternity has resolved to give us.

Piercing through the metaphor, we find that the so-called vacuum is actually the loving openness of the human spirit, which has it roots in the obediential potency—the nonrepugnance of the creature to the work of the creator—and its fullness in the response to grace, operative and cooperative.

In the Song of Songs, the bride said: "Draw me, we will run after you" (1:3). John of the Cross suggested the twofold role of grace suggested in that cry of the heart: "So the movement toward goodness must come from God, and from God alone as here declared; but the writer says not that he alone will run, or she alone, but that they will run together—that is that God and the soul will work together."[26] God gives us the first grace; if the soul then cooperates with divine grace in achieving detachment and emptiness of sense and spirit, God does the rest and fills the soul with himself. Clearly without God's help there would be no vacuum, no loving openness for him to fill.

Augustine was keenly conscious of the dispositive role of prayer; in fact, he found in prayer the perfection of the emptying that he strived for in other areas of life.

> God does not hear us because he seeks the favor of our prayers, he who is always ready to give us his light, not that which strikes the eye, but that of the intellect and spirit. But we are not always prepared to receive, attracted as we are to other things and benighted by our desire for temporal things. Hence there takes place in prayer a turning of the heart to

him who is ever ready to give if we will but accept what he gives. And in this turning there is effected a cleansing of the inner eye consisting in the exclusion of those things which filled our earth-bound desires so that the vision of a pure heart may be able to bear the pure light, radiating from God without any diminution or setting; and not only bear it but also to remain in it, not merely without discomfort but with the unspeakable joy whereby truly and unequivocally a blessed life is perfected.[27]

The Process of Purification

The hope prompted by the vacuum principle inspires efforts to open the mind lovingly toward God. The mystic subject seeks to be in harmony with a personal but incomprehensible God through unrestricted openness to knowing and loving. To understand what this goal involves, we shall consider the two major impediments, the two stages of detachment from them, and finally the two roles of memory perfected by openness to the divine presence.

The Obstacles to Simplicity

The simplicity needed for mystical consciousness requires one to overcome two sets of obstacles: created forms and inordinate desires. Both bring multiplicity into the soul; both can be eliminated by detachment. But to eliminate them totally, one must first recognize them. Since we must live full and productive lives in conformity to the will of God, we cannot simplistically empty our minds. True simplicity is enhancement of life, not its impoverishment. Our handling of forms and desires must be nuanced by an ongoing discernment of spirits.

1. *Created forms* are the obvious threat to simplicity, because they distract one from God and because they distort one's knowledge of God. Speaking broadly, we refer to the images and ideas in the mind of real or possible objects whether or not anything is present. To understand form more properly, however, we must view it in context; that is, in relation to potency and act.[28] The three constitute a unity— the known object. We would naively simplify reality if we regarded an object as something already out there now. We do better to think of an object as whatever is known by experiencing, understanding, and judging. Hence, potency is the experiencing of the data of sense and consciousness; form is the understanding of the data; and act is the

judgment affirming or denying the understanding as verified by the data.

Aquinas, as we have seen, in speaking of God as "He who is" (*Qui est*) explained the need to proceed to God by way of removal; that is, by denying him corporeal attributes, intellectual attributes as they are found in creatures, and even being itself as it as found in creatures. In knowing God as a cognitive object, a person tries to remove created objects from his consciousness. This subjective endeavor involves purifying the notion of God of all created potencies (the experiencing of creatures), all created forms (the understanding of creatures), and all created acts (the judging of creatures). Thus stripped of creaturely veils, the mind can expand with unimpeded openness in knowing and loving the infinite Being. John of the Cross phrased the requirement succinctly: "In order to arrive at knowing everything, desire to know nothing."[29]

The term "created forms" is often used without referring to potency, act, or object. The reason for these omissions is that form is intelligible in itself and that form implies both potency and act. Understanding involves form, so when we wish to understand God, we eliminate from our consciousness the understanding of other objects; we purify our minds of created forms by rejecting them in themselves and especially as descriptive of God. To empty the mind of forms is not to gather up a dozen or a hundred or a thousand forms, all to be tossed out, but rather to transcend all particular and categorical and creaturely modes of being by opening the mind to the fullness of God and to the exclusion of everything else, thus to be informed by the infinite.

Our prayers to God need not always be apophatically free of creaturely knowledge, for, as the kataphatic way illustrates, we can, with the help of creatures, lift our minds to God, who we remain aware, transcends creatures. The kataphatic is clearly convinced that God is an underlying or overarching presence, but has not adequately emptied his knowledge of all creaturely potencies, forms, and acts. So the kataphatic lacks the perfection of God-consciousness on the purely intellectual level that the apophatic has achieved. Of course, ultimately, love engendered connaturality gives the most intimate awareness of divine presence. So the truest measure of God-consciousness is always love.

The interface between the kataphatic and the apophatic consists in the moment of moving normally beyond created objects. The kataphatic way ends and the apophatic begins with the removal of all created attributes from our knowledge of God in totally unrestricted openness of mind. The kataphatic knows well that God transcends all creatures; the apophatic is conscious of this transcendence. The difference is not in the engendering love but in the heightened consciousness.

To know God most perfectly we try to bypass consciousness of created objects to live in the darkness of faith. That seems a straightforward directive, but it has its own complexity. It is sometimes difficult for us to think specifically about what God is, as contrasted with what he has done for us; that is, the many effects of his love seen in creation, revelation, world history, and our own personal lives. We are familiar with the stream of our ceaseless imagining and thinking. We appreciate the price that must be paid for profound silence and peace. John of the Cross abundantly detailed in his *Ascent* and *Dark Night* what this purification of the mind and heart involves.

Often in prayer, even in contemplative prayer, familiar images and ideas emerge and with ghostly bonds constrict the sought-for openness of the soul. Let us examine in some detail an example of a subtle but widespread distortion in our thoughts about the indwelling presence of God, namely, our tendency to use spatio-temporal language and images. Meister Eckhart took this failing very seriously and gave a stern warning:

> Nothing hinders the soul's knowledge of God as much as time and space, for time and space are fragments, whereas God is one. And therefore, if the soul is to know God, it must know him above time and outside space, for God is neither this or that, as are these manifold things. God is one.[30]

To say that "He who is" is here and now does not necessarily mislead; to detail what we mean by here and now, however, may occasion certain errors about the divine presence. Time, superficially at least, is easier to deal with than is space. We understand enough to think of eternity as an ever-present now, that in God there is no past or future, that our triple division of the temporal continuum describes human duration, not the divine. The present tense, according to Aquinas, most fittingly describes God's subsisting existence. We respond comfortably to this aspect of immediacy. Though we experience past, present and future, we live in the present and we are ever temporally present to a God who is eternal.

The spatial problem is more difficult to resolve psychologically, for even in the present moment there are a variety of different places in which to imagine the divine presence: God is up in heaven, in the universe, in the believing community, in the parish church, by one's side, in one's mind, or deep within the heart. An ancient definition of prayer, that of John Damascene, was a lifting up of the mind to God, *ascensus mentis ad Deum*.[31]

Currently, physical imagery is still used, but the recommended movement is not up but down, a sinking into silence. The popular term, centering, conveys this sense. Such terms are acceptable, as the author of *The Cloud of Unknowing* would agree, yet he added a caveat against literalness: "Take care not to interpret physically what is intended spiritually, even though material expressions are used, like 'up, down, in, out, behind, before, this side, that side.' "[32] Admitting that someone may be right in advising you "to withdraw all your powers and thoughts within yourself and worship God there," the anonymous author worried about a literal interpretation even of these words and so reversed himself: "See that in no sense you withdraw into yourself. And briefly, I do not want you to be outside, above, behind, or beside yourself either." Of course, as he then noted, that would leave a person nowhere, but that is as it should be: "When you are nowhere physically, you are everywhere spiritually." The reason for his conclusion is that "wherever that thing is that you are giving your mind to, there you are in spirit."[33] God is not in space as material things are; to localize him is to diminish him. The human mind is likewise constricted and thus unable to open itself fully to receive God.

John Ruusbroec deconditioned the spatial sense of God's presence in a different way. Instead of thinking of the spiritual subject as nowhere, he thought of God as everywhere.

> And therefore we must all found our lives upon a fathomless abyss, that we may eternally plunge into Love and sink down into the fathomless Depth. And with that same Love, we shall ascend and transcend ourselves in the incomprehensible Height. And in that Love which is wayless, we shall wander and stray and it shall lead us and lose us in the immeasurable Breadth of the Love of God.[34]

As we have seen in the second chapter, God acts always and everywhere, not through a body but through his essence (as grounding all beings), through his presence (as knowing all beings), and through his power (as controlling all beings). Spatial images help one focus on God, but they should not distort the focus by limiting God. What is signified in all such images is a qualitative change in the spiritual subject: God is wherever he acts and he is continuously acting on us, and thus he is for us a living presence.

Thinking of union with God as a sharing of the life of God through nature and grace, we escape from the material confines of our limited minds. Although we may still use spatial imagery—it would be difficult to think without it—we can affirm, in terms of participation: "I no longer live, but Christ lives in me" (Gal 2:20). Here is the perfection of presence that enables spiritual subjects to experience the truth of the words, "We are alive to God in Christ Jesus our Lord" (Rom 6:11). Let us examine the notion of life further. "To live is the 'to be' (*esse*) of a living being" (*Vivere dicitur esse viventis*).[35] In other words, life is the concrete and dynamic actuality of a living being.

To the extent that we live—that is, exist as principles of self-movement—God is present to us. God is not here or there but rather is present as the ground of our life both naturally and supernaturally. Vitality rather than locality more accurately conveys the presence of God. To think of God in terms of life rather than of time and space gives a truer appreciation of the God who still dwells in incomprehensible light. The perfection of our consciousness of God transcends sensible or intelligible forms; we are conscious of his loving presence; we are not just imagining it or conceptualizing it. Be that as it may, we must recognize that our notion of life is a created one and that it cannot describe divine life adequately. We must try to decondition his living presence from the creaturely analogues, both spatio-temporal and vital, which we ordinarily use. Of course, even contemplatives occasionally need to go back to meditation and the concrete images of the kataphatic way, but for perfect consciousness of God, they must transcend all creaturely experiencing, understanding, and judging lest they impede unrestricted openness.

2. *Inordinate desires* are obstacles at once more subtle and more deleterious than created forms. These feelings undercut the pure love that is essential for union with God and for heightened consciousness of his loving presence. The function of the "dark nights" of sense and spirit, which John of the Cross analyzed so carefully, is to purify the soul; but as he often repeated, it is not desire but inordinate desire that is the enemy. Inordinate desires, whether of sense or spirit, cause positive evils in the soul; John of the Cross in the *Ascent* marshaled a worrisome list: weariness and fatigue, torment, darkness and blindness, defilement, and weakness and lukewarmness. Even venial sins and imperfections are impediments to growth in the contemplative life.

God sets the norm for judging desires or, to use a different phrase, for discerning spirits. His will is either declared or determined; that is, it is sometimes clear from reason, revelation, or tradition what is right for us to do; but more often it is not, and we must decide for ourselves how to order our actions in doubtful situations. What is important here is not to examine specific rules for discernment or for the formation of a right conscience, but rather to appreciate the paramount need for openness to the will of God in our whole spiritual life.

God's directions for our decision making are partly hidden in a cloud of unknowing. We do not understand in advance the precise details of our way to God. Indeed the vain attempt to get the terms spelled out in black and white is called legalism. Based on spiritual insecurity, limited generosity, or diminished confidence in God, legalism wants no surprises; it demands the game plan in advance: what God commands, what he permits, what we can get away with, what we must not do under pain of grave sin or under pain of venial sin. For the legalist, mystical experiences may be problematic, but moral obligations are to be clear cut.

Legalism does not treat God as a lover but as a party to a binding contract. To discover ahead of time all that God wants of us might be comforting. It might be troubling too. We do know, however, that human affairs, especially loving and romantic ones, are not regularly so scheduled. At any rate, in spiritual matters, we are to be led by the Spirit of love, who through his gifts and his graces guides us tenderly and lovingly into full union with the Trinity.

Our response to God must be, in Eckhart's term, "a wandering love"—we follow the Spirit who directs us as he chooses. Universal willingness characterizes a true love of God. We are not yet aware of all that unrestricted love may require of us, what heroism it may demand, what light it may bestow. To be open to God in knowing or doing is necessarily to be open to mystery, the mystery of divine love.

Why should the eternal law be a mystery? The technical answer is that God's will is identified with his essence, and like that essence, it is infinite and incomprehensible. We do not know his essence fully; we do not know his will fully. But if we love him, we submit in advance to his will, surrendering ourselves to him totally, for in his love is our happiness.

The apophatic way leads along a path of twofold darkness: we leave created light behind us but have not yet arrived at the fullness of divine light, the mind being blinded by infinite truth and the heart consumed by infinite love. We follow God's directives step-by-step, following a path that is strange and unpredictable, for we cannot totally comprehend his eternal law. But guided by faith and inspired by love, our steps are true. Openness of mind and heart work together. A mind empty of forms needs a heart filled with love to focus its attention on the divine presence.

The Stages of Detachment

The proximate goal of apophatics is to bring knowing and loving to perfect simplicity, as the mind moves to the reality which is supremely meaningful and worthwhile. This goal can be realized only by a thoroughgoing detachment. Detachment, however, is not a rejection of all things—that would make life impossible. Rather it is radical ordering of one's life, subordinating everything to God, so that he can be known and loved perfectly.

Detachment is a forbidding term implying the sacrifice of many good actions and many good things. Admittedly, the road of detachment is hard, but it is the royal road, a necessary ingredient of all great achievements. In writing of Francis of Assisi, who spoke so eloquently of Lady Poverty, G. K. Chesterton said: "Asceticism, in the religious sense, is the repudiation of the great mass of human joys for the supreme joyfulness of the one joy, the religious joy."[36] Apophatics is asceticism or detachment for the sake of union with God. In finding God, Francis realized, one finds everything. Frequently he used a simple mantra-like prayer, saying for hours only the words: *Deus meus et omnia*, "My God and my all." He impressed upon himself the infinite riches of God by articulating his own heartfelt rejoicing over that overwhelming truth.

Because detachment is necessary yet may be painful, it must be understood precisely. Meister Eckhart distinguished two terms, "letting go" and "letting be." Together they complete the liberation of the person for union with God. Actually they are the two stages of the purification of the soul: *Abgeschiedenheit* is a letting go or cutting off—detachment in the narrow sense; and *Gelassenheit* is a letting be or releasement—detachment in the fullest sense.[37] They structure the proper stance of the soul in its relationship to other creatures and to God. We let go of things and renounce them in order to turn to God (our attitude is one of abnegation, sacrifice, emptying), and we let things be themselves, acknowledging that they belong to God (our attitude is one of resignation, acceptance, reverence, serenity).

Eckhart succinctly pointed out the secret of both forms of detachment: it is the rectifying of our desires by turning them from creatures to God:

> Whatever you choose not to long for, you have wholly for-saken and renounced for the love of God. That is why our Lord said, "Blessed are the poor in spirit" (Mt 5:3), that is, in the will. . . . For whatever a person would gladly have that he relinquishes and goes without for God's love, be it something material or spiritual, he will find all of it in God, just as if he had possessed it and willingly abandoned it; for a person ought gladly be robbed of all that he has for the love of God, and out of love he should wholly abandon and deny love's consolations.[38]

Detachment does not mean that we reject or abandon all persons or things; we do not cease to love and to appreciate beings that are true and beautiful. We do not become diminished but fulfilled and perfected. We cut off only those things that impede our union with God and his will, but we let all things be as creatures of God without trying to own or possess or dominate them. And we let God be God in determining our destiny through his gifts and his providence. We thus bring it about that the openness, begun by letting go and perfected by letting be, is gradually filled with the divine presence, and we are at rest.

These two operations facilitate the opening of the mind to full reality, without demeaning the things God's love has brought into existence and without allowing them to compete with him in the slightest way. Both *Abgeschiedenheit* and *Gelassenheit* affirm the dignity of creatures and the sublime glory of their Creator. Detach-ment makes living in the world a means of living in the presence of a loving God.

By letting go of inordinate longings, the subject is able to be himself fully, for human nature is openness to transcendence, an openness which only God can fill. Eckhart related detachment and union: "Rid yourself of all that is your own, then God will properly be yours as he is his own."[39] Moreover, we realize that we must even let God be God and not try to force him into our souls. After letting go of created forms and inordinate desires, a final letting be fulfills the potency of our graced nature for union with God.

We have been speaking of acts of detachment, but mysticism is not built on acts alone. Habits of detachment are necessary. Before going further, we should note that habits are not rote, mechanical actions, but rather they are skills freely acquired so that certain kinds of actions become second nature to us, easily performed with efficiency and joy.

These habits of detachment make possible the complex action that is heightened consciousness. Habits do this in three ways: first, they help bring the subject into a state of spiritual integrity; second, they give the subject a stable base from which to rise higher; and third, they energize the mind in that habitual loving makes possible habitual attention to the divine presence. Progress in the spiritual life is not the fruit of a momentary *tour de force,* a spiritual rising to the occasion. It is a gradual development in knowing and loving that attunes the soul to the Transcendent. The need for such habits explains the disconcerting remark of John of the Cross about the duration of the dark night of the spirit: "If it is to be truly efficacious, it will last for some years, no matter how intense it may be."[40]

The Role of Memory

Memory operates paradoxically in apophatic persons as they try to forget the past and remember the present. St. Paul's phrase, "forgetting the things that are behind and stretching forth to those that are before" (Phil 3:13), has long characterized the mystic way, which requires a purified memory to ensure that the past foster and not hinder present consciousness of God. Forgetting is obviously important, since the apophatic state is one of openness through the rejection of created forms and inordinate desires. But remembering the divine presence is central.

Before we examine the forgetting, let us note briefly that for the Greek Fathers, the perfection of memory consisted in being continuously mindful of the presence of God; the memory of God, *mneme theou,* is to be guarded by *nepsis,* watchfulness or vigilance.[41] Without this living memory, the spiritual life is sterile and true mysticism impossible.

The memory is purged and healed to make room for God. To achieve this openness, drastic measures must be taken, measures that seem to cut the roots of a fully human life. So much of our activity is contingent on remembering our experiences and accumulating insights, that to treat memory as more of a liability than an asset seems ridiculous. But John of the Cross insisted that we should act spiritually as if we had no memory. Is this a rhetorical exaggeration? Consider his advice for the potential mystic:

All the things that he hears, sees, smells, tastes or touches, he must be careful not to store up or collect in his memory, but he must allow himself to forget them immediately, and this he must accomplish, if need be, with the same efficacy as that with which others contrive to remember them, so that there remains no knowledge or image of them whatsoever in his memory. It must be with him as if they existed not in the world . . . as if he had no faculty of memory.[42]

His basic principle was: "Everything that is natural, if one attempts to make use of it in supernatural matters, is a hindrance rather than a help."[43] Yet John of the Cross, in his writings, manifested a prodigious memory. He was said to know the Bible by heart; he had a thorough grasp of Thomistic philosophy and a fund of empirical data about psychological types and practices; his poems showed a keen perception of natural beauty and a sophisticated knowledge of literary forms. The scope and preciseness of his memory were extraordinary, yet he was an apophatic who insisted that one's memory of creatures must be emptied, if the mind is to be filled with the awareness of God. But John of the Cross was practical: he subordinated the rejection of multiplicity to the overriding exigency of doing God's will.

It [the soul] must neither think of these things nor consider them beyond the degree which is necessary for the understanding and the performing of its obligations, if they have any concern with these. And this it must do without setting any affection or inclination upon them, so that they may produce no effects in the soul. And thus a man must not fail to think and recall that which he ought to know and do, for, provided he preserve no affection or attachments, this will do him no harm.[44]

From this passage we see the prudent balance required in the apophatic life: if one avoids inordinate desires for created things, any necessary involvement with multiplicity in doing God's will does not impede mystical union. Success, however, depends on fidelity to the general principle: "The more the soul dispossesses the memory of forms and things which may be recalled by it, which are not God, the more will it set its memory upon God and the emptier will its memory become, so that it may hope for him who shall fill it."[45] The directives are clear: remove all inordinate desires; and remove all created forms that are not necessary for doing the will of God. A problem in discernment remains: what desires are inordinate? What forms are unnecessary?

Through detachment the subject clears out all that is not suitable and keeps out everything that is not clearly and necessarily God-related. This purification of the memory enables the mind to actuate its potency for unrestricted openness. It sheds the habits of unauthenticity and the clutter of curiosity by pulling away the inordinate desires and the created forms that darken the soul and imprison it in the nether world of multiplicity. A purified memory stabilizes the soul in the presence of God and remains undiminished by the creatures that surround it. When called to think exclusively of God, a detached lover easily transcends all that is not God.

The Last Capitulation

The promise, "To be empty of all things is to be full of God, and to be full of all things is to be empty of God," seems to ensure swift and complete access to mystical experience.[46] Thorough emptying should enable the mind to go beyond multiplicity, to simplify and unify the psyche, and finally to experience divine life.

True, the removal of created forms and inordinate desires is necessary and fruitful. But is it sufficient? Three observations are relevant: first, the mystical process is not psychic mechanics but a personal relation to God; second, the mystical process is not purely cognitional but also involves feeling and choosing; third, the mystical process requires that the citadel of the soul capitulate to God, if mystical consciousness is to be authentic and divine union complete. Indeed, this last barrier can be breached only if the mystical subject reaches out wholeheartedly to God with a pure and profound love.

Carl Jung, while working on the *Answer to Job*, had a series of dreams, one of which forced him to relive Job's trial. That dream revealed, as had the earlier ones in the series, his own shadow—the personification of those traits or tendencies which are incompatible with one's consciously chosen attitude.[47] Here in striking imagery is a dream parable of the testing which every potential mystic must ultimately face if he is to leap the shadow barrier that keeps him from full consciousness of God.

At the top of the stairs was a small door, and my father said, "Now I will lead you into the highest presence." Then he

knelt down and touched his forehead to the floor. I imitated
him, likewise kneeling, with great emotion. For some reason
I could not bring my forehead quite down to the floor—there
was perhaps a millimeter to spare. But I had made the
gesture.[48]

The millimeter that distanced Jung from unrestricted openness
marks an infinitesimal but infinite separation. It is like the coveted
gold thread that remains after all other bonds have been cut; it still
ties the soul to creatures and keeps it from winging its way to God.

Total emptiness liberates the subject from multiplicity. But for
the subject to be filled by God, that emptiness must be positive, not
merely a saying no to creatures but a saying yes to God and only then,
in a God-like return, saying yes to creatures. In his dream, Jung had
turned his back on creatures but the totality of his homage to God
remained a gesture. He had progressed so far, but his shadow came
between him and the light.

In examining this touchstone of true mysticism, the final renun-
ciation of self, I discuss first the negative apophatics of the mistaken
mystic, who prematurely terminates the search for God-consciousness with natural rest in his own being. Then I move to the positive
apophatics of the true mystic, who combines self-consciousness and
self-transcendence to orientate his whole being to God, and for whom
natural rest is a stepping stone not a terminal point in the mystical
journey. The final capitulation is not an empty gesture but a genuine
gift; it is the habitual state of a total giving of oneself to God. Only then
does God give himself in the mystical embrace of transforming love.

Negative Apophatics

Detachment, freeing the subject from the many evils and imperfections that had plagued it previously, now brings it a calm silence
and a deep peace: "My house being now at rest."[49]

But rest is neutral; it may, as John of the Cross noted, consist
merely in "the natural rest which the soul obtains when it is free from
images and forms."[50] John Ruusbroec had given a fuller description of
this type of acquired contemplation: "When a man is bare and imageless in his senses, and empty and idle in his higher powers, he enters
into rest through mere nature; and this rest may be found and pos-
sessed within themselves in mere nature by all creatures without the
grace of God whenever they can strip themselves of all images and all
activity."[51]

A purified peacefulness is normally a condition for heightened consciousness of God. As something pleasant, however, this natural rest can be overprized. Through inordinate attempts to foster it and justify it, practical and intellectual derailments may occur. Ruusbroec criticized this barren emptiness: "But now mark the way in which this natural rest is practised. It is sitting still without either outward or inward acts, in vacancy, in order that rest may be found and may remain untroubled."[52] So he called it unlawful and idle as well as forgetful of God, the self, and all that involves activity. In a marvelous phrase worthy of modern cognitional theory, he described this flawed experience as "vacant introversion in quietude."[53]

Those fixed on the plateau of natural rest find this addiction strengthened by a presumption of mystical success and superior holiness. Their option for complete passivity and the elimination of further spiritual decision making seeks to preserve the abiding peace of self-awareness. Ruusbroec wrote in detail of this inordinate attachment to self and its disordered sequelae.

> Behold these men have gone astray into the vacant and blind simplicity of their own being, and they seek for blessedness in bare nature; for they are so simply and so idly united with the bare essence of their souls, and with that wherein God always is, that they have neither zeal, nor cleaving to God, neither from without nor from within. For in the highest part into which they have entered, they feel nothing but the simplicity of their own proper being, depending on the being of God. And the onefold simplicity which they there possess they take to be God because they find a natural rest therein. And so they think themselves to be God in their simple ground; for they lack true faith, hope, and charity. And because of the naked emptiness which they feel and possess, they say that they are without knowledge and without love, and are exempt from the virtues. And so they endeavor to live without heeding their conscience, what wickedness soever they commit.[54]

This progressive derailment of the eros of the mind brings the mystical life to a premature cloture. John Tauler, a German contemporary of Ruusbroec, said bluntly, "These people have come to a dead end."[55] His own description of the unraveling process parallels that of Ruusbroeck; he traced out the path from natural emptiness to antinomianism (a bypassing of moral norms):

They have unified themselves in a blind and dark vacancy of
their own being; and there they think that they are one with
God, and they take this for the Eternal Blessedness. And they
have entered into this, and have taken possession of it,
through self-will and their natural tendency; and therefore
they imagine themselves to be set above the law and above
the commandments of God and the Holy Church.[56]

Tauler did not censure these false mystics for eliminating
"images and forms" but for "doing so before they are ready for this";
nor does he censure them for passivity, but "for their own false passivity, false because it is not combined with active charity, interior and
exterior."[57] He understood charity as conformity to the will of God:
"Even at the highest peak of holiness, he must always say and mean:
'Your will be done.' "[58]

The doctrine of passivity preached by the false mystics of the
fourteenth century is a recurrent one. For example, the controversy
over Quietism in the seventeenth and eighteenth centuries caused a
thoroughgoing ecclesiastical repudiation of this kind of spiritual response. Note, for example, one of the condemned propositions of
Molinos, its main advocate: "To want to work actively is to offend
God, who wishes himself to be the sole agent; and thus one must lose
oneself in God wholly and absolutely and thenceforward remain as a
dead body."[59]

Long before Molinos, Ruusbroec had realized that the greatest
danger of this false passivity was its tendency to still the soul's dynamic thrust to reality. He observed perceptively: "But in this the
loving man cannot find his rest, for charity and the inward touch of
God's grace will not be still: and so the inward man cannot remain long
in natural rest within himself."[60] This restlessness occurs because
human beings naturally tend to transcendence and their nature is
unfulfilled without God. The residual uneasiness in those seeking con-
tentment in negative emptiness results from the half-smothered cry of
the spirit for the fullness of reality. Through pride or other sinful or
mistaken motives, however, many are able to stifle this urge to move
beyond the self and so manage to remain content, lifeless souls in
solitary repose.

Let us summarize our assessment of negative apophatics. The
attaining of natural rest through the elimination of images and concepts together with inordinate desires may be good as far as it goes.
But it presents a real possibility of stunting true spiritual growth. This
misfortune occurs when the mystic subject decides to rest passively in

the awareness of his nature, mistakenly identifying it with his divine ground. Flawed simplicity thus puts a ceiling on progress, for it renders decision making expendable. To justify their refusal to change, false mystics plead perfectionism or antinomianism and assert that their complete and permanent oneness with God ensures their inability to sin whatever they may do. In thus escaping from the bondage of multiplicity, they have locked themselves in the inner sanctum of the self, the last barrier to true consciousness of God, but they will not capitulate.

Positive Apophatics

Apophatics, though a way of negation, is eminently positive. Since God is a positive nothingness, the mystic must be a positive emptiness. God is full reality, infinitely meaningful and worthwhile, but he is incomprehensibly no-thing; the mystic is a limited reality and must be positively and unrestrictedly open to knowing and loving the no-thing thereby transcending everything.

To understand the character and function of positive apophatics we use two major distinctions: the first between self-knowledge and self-consciousness; and the second between self-completion and self-transcendence. Reluctance to make a final capitulation cannot be overcome through either self-knowledge or self-completion. Only through self-consciousness and self-transcendence can the mystical subject achieve the positive emptiness which brings heightened consciousness of union with God.

The *first distinction* centers on the difference between self-knowledge and self-consciousness. In making things present to the mind, we operate through intentionality: experiencing data, understanding it, and then verifying our understanding and finally judging it. This objectification, when directed back at the subject, is self-knowledge or introspection. The self is known as an object.

At the same time, intrinsic to all these operations of intentionality is consciousness, not an additional operation but an expanding awareness of the self that is operating. True self-consciousness is not an act of intentionality, but is a dimension of all mental actions. The operations that make objects present to us also and simultaneously, if we expand our awareness, make us present to ourselves as subjects.[61]

Consequently, positive apophatics eliminates determinate intentionality or introspective self-knowledge, but it enables the subject, by unrestrictedly opening its mind to knowing and loving, to become conscious of itself in its orientation to God. The distinction is important, for introspection radically blocks the achievement of apophatic purity by putting a created form, the self, between the subject and God. On the other hand, self-consciousness is an expanded awareness in the subject, but as we have seen, it is an awareness that does not rest in the subject as does introspection, but opens unrestrictedly toward God.

So can mystical consciousness be said to be a "final self-forget-fulness"?[62] The term is ambiguous: it is correct if it means that we do not intend the self as an object; it is wrong if it means that there is no self-consciousness in the self as subject. Since self-consciousness is intrinsic to all operations, then to know God fully is also to be most fully self-conscious.

In like manner, we would explain the statement of Isaac of Jerusalem as reported by John Cassian: "Prayer is not perfect when the monk is conscious of himself and of the fact that he is actually praying."[63] Certainly, the monk should not be watching himself pray. He should be wholly attentive to God. But in giving all his attention to God, he is more fully alive and self-conscious than ever before. So true is this that mystics sometimes assert that they feel themselves to be one consciousness, one spirit, with God—but as participants in love and not as spectators.

Significantly, Plotinus (205–270), whose opposition to self-consciousness was very influential among the Greek Fathers, implied what, but for his lack of a more fully developed cognitional theory, would approximate what we have been proposing. His major concern seems to have been the impediment that the objectification of self through introspection brings to the life of contemplation. Introspection puts another form between the mind and God; this intermediary prevents the necessary simplification of the soul. This is not the place to attempt to reinterpret the teaching of Plotinus in terms of conscious intentionality, though it would indeed be a profitable exercise.[64] Suffice it to note here that the transcending of introspection does not involve the loss of self-consciousness. As subjects, we are necessarily conscious; as subjects, we can become aware through unrestricted openness of "a presence surpassing all knowledge."[65] And we may find that "the soul cannot distinguish itself from the object of this intuition."[66] In attuning ourselves to God, we transcend the intentionality toward created forms, including our own, yet become aware of his divine presence through its theophanic effect on our minds and hearts which, by being self-consciously and unrestrictedly open, symbolize it.

To understand this process more fully, we look to a *second dis-*

tinction, the one between self-completion and self-transcendence. Superficially, perfection seems to be adequately definable in terms of self-completion. If the subject has all that his nature requires, he is truly happy. Aristotle spoke of self-sufficiency; Jung later spoke of individuation.

To understand the place of self-completion, this notion of Jung's, though limited, is relevant in its focus on the relationship between the ego and self. For him the conscious ego is part of the whole, the self, which encompasses both the conscious and the unconscious. Perfection consists in bringing these two components into harmony, into an undivided state, that is, into in-dividuation.[67]

Unfortunately for the full integrity of Jung's thinking, the process seems to stop prematurely. Beyond individuation is another stage, one essential to human fulfillment. In short, true self-completion is impossible without self-transcendence. The explanation is found in human nature and the actions consonant with it, open as it is to transcendence. Nature is a dynamic principle of action. We achieve our destiny only by acting properly. In Lonergan's words, "Man achieves authenticity in self-transcendence."[68] What does this authenticity involve? As we saw earlier, his answer was: "Just as unrestricted questioning is our capacity for self-transcendence, so being in love in an unrestricted fashion is the proper fulfillment of that capacity."[69]

The subject learns about its transcendent ground by following the perfection of intentionality as it leads beyond the subject and other finite creatures to God. Knowing of God, the subject transcends itself and the rest of creation in seeking union with the divine. Consciousness of an orientation to unrestricted knowing and loving reveals a self-transcending nature.

Neither self-knowledge nor self-completion bring the subject to true mysticism; both are contained within the created realm. Only through self-consciousness and self-transcendence can the breakthrough be achieved. If I remain purely in the realm of intentionality, I cannot totally intend myself and at the same time unrestrictedly intend God. Since intentionality makes things present to me, I would find God and the self in competition for my attention. Self-consciousness as non-intentional reveals its compatibility with self-transcendence; both reach fulfillment together. In a phrase, it is the self-consciousness of the self-transcendent subject. When openness to knowing and loving is truly unrestricted, there is no room for the finite determinations of the self. Yet the self in its unrestricted operations is conscious, precisely through its own unrestricted openness as through a pure symbol, of being conscious of God.

The Anaphatic Return

Radical detachment, in directing us out of this world to be alone with God, seems to conflict with the incarnational character of Christianity, namely, with the role that Christ must play in our lives and with the duty we have to love one another.

But actually, the apophatic way results in a return to the world. We see this requirement prefigured in the familiar story of Elijah (I Kgs 19:9–18). The word came to him: "Go forth and stand on the mount before Yahweh." But Yahweh was not to be found in the great wind or in the earthquake or in the fire. Finally Elijah, hearing the sound of a gentle breeze, covered his face with his mantle. A voice asked him what he was doing there and, after dismissing his complaints, told him: "Go, return." He was being sent back to Israel to anoint kings and to establish the prophetic succession.

This duty to return after one's encounter with the numinous is part not only of the Judaeo-Christian experience but of many others. For example, it is the return to the cave after the vision of the sun in the Platonic parable in Book VII of the *Republic*.[70] One of the prisoners, brought into the light, undergoes a *periagoge,* a turning around of his soul, a conversion; later, in a second turning around, he goes back enlightened to the rest of the prisoners in the cave. By this parable Plato enjoined a civic duty on all who have had the vision of the Good: "Down you must go then."[71] Returning to the *polis,* they are to foster in others through *paideia,* education and governance, "the art of turning around" (*techne tes periagoges*),[72] so that they make the radical turn to the light, to the idea of the Good.

Elsewhere we find this theme repeated in the return to the marketplace after the experience of *satori* or the unity of reality in the Zen journey. It is also captured in the Dominican motto: "To give to others the fruits of one's contemplation" (*Contemplata aliis tradere*). The true rhythm of the human spirit encompasses this twofold turning.

Let us examine its development. The return begins with an attempt to describe to ourselves the experience of divine intimacy. To do so we must use created concepts and images, as did John of the

Cross in the *Spiritual Canticle* when he wrote of his own mystical consciousness:

> My Beloved is the mountains,
> And lonely wooded valleys,
> Strange islands,
> And resounding rivers,
> The whistling of love-stirring breezes,
> The tranquil night
> At the time of the rising dawn,
> Silent music,
> Sounding solitude,
> The supper that refreshes, and deepens love.[73]

It is crucial to understand at the outset that this stanza is not kataphatic: these creatures do not lead the soul to an experience of God. John of the Cross had a very different direction in mind: the images were to help him express what he has already experienced. He spoke from a mystical perspective called the spiritual espousal with the Son of God, "a high state and union of love, in which, after much spiritual exercise, the soul is placed by God."[74] Having become profoundly aware of God, the mystic tried to articulate the experience in concrete terms: "Since God is all things to the soul and the good that is in all things, the communication of this superabundance is explained through its likeness to the good of the things mentioned in these stanzas."[75]

He delicately sketched out similarities: the mountains are vast, beautiful, and bright; the lonely wooded valleys afford recreation, solitude, and rest; the strange islands give new and surprising wonders; the resounding rivers inundate everything, drowning all other actions and passions, filling everything with peace and glory; the love-stirring breezes touch the soul in its substance with knowledge and the most exalted delight that the soul knows. He painted in natural images the effects of God on the soul. He used these created forms because they were the only ones available—open-ended symbols of divine perfection.

Note his progression: having experienced God, he saw God in created things: "Inasmuch as the soul in this case is united to God, she *feels* that all things are God."[76] He was at pains to point out that this is not "an essential or clear vision of God," and he explained: "This experience is nothing but a strong and overflowing communication and glimpse of what God is in himself, in which the soul *feels* the goodness of the things mentioned in these verses."[77]

Let us look at the cognitional underpinnings of these observations of John of the Cross. Using scholastic psychology, he elucidated the events in terms of the agent intellect (which deals with forms) and the possible intellect (which passively receives substantive knowledge without forms), and he spoke of this contemplation as "knowing by unknowing."[78]

Today, we might explain things differently by saying, as we have seen, that the psychological basis for contemplation is the unrestricted openness to God in both knowing and loving, since we know God fully through the effects on the self-conscious soul. In other words, the focus of the experience is consciousness of oneself as a created effect operating self-transcendently with full openness to God. This experience is not an "essential vision of God," but rather an existential knowing without images or concepts. It is a "secret and hidden knowledge": God is glimpsed and felt connaturally through this unrestricted loving. He is not known through created forms other than that of transcending self-consciousness, but the soul must use these other forms to articulate and communicate its experience. The power of this mystical experience is such that the soul continues to feel the presence of God in other creatures.

John of the Cross used a felicitous distinction to describe the two levels of knowledge—morning and evening knowledge of God; that is, the soul seeks to be transformed into the beauty of the divine wisdom of the Word (morning knowledge), and it seeks to be informed with the beauty of the lesser wisdom found in creatures (evening knowledge).[79]

When mystics, after an apophatic experience, encounter other men and women or other creatures, they do not merely take up again the kataphatic way, though of course kataphatics remains valid. They now see things differently. Looking at God's creatures, they see more than resemblances to God; they are aware of God's presence in each person or thing. John of the Cross showed the mutuality of that vision: "Let us rejoice, Beloved, and let us go forth to behold ourselves in your beauty."[80] He explained this line as the participation by adoption through grace. Christ's promise—"All my things are yours and yours mine" (Jn 17:10)—extends this sharing in divine beauty to the whole mystical body, the church. All mystics—indeed, all Christians —married or single, religious or lay, are called to this sublime life. All the faithful should behold themselves and one another in the beauty of the Word.

If, in seeking divine beauty, mystics start up the mountain by the kataphatic path in the ascent to the apophatic peak, they do not come down the same way. The experience of presence makes everything different. The world is now full of God. The experience is a spiral: things lead us to God and, we, knowing God, see things in a new light; we experience this dual movement again and again, each time we become more lovingly aware of the divine presence itself and that presence in others.

To express this perspective, I use a new word, "anaphatic." From the two traditional terms, kataphatic and apophatic, I take the root, *phatic* (from *phemi,* to speak or tell) and to it append another prefix, *ana* (back or backwards; in Latin, *re-* or *retro-*), as in *anamnesis,* remembrance or remembering, or as in *anachorein,* to go back or return. The word *anaphatics* suggests the articulated perception, the "re-telling" on returning or coming back to the everyday world by one newly sensitized to the presence of God in all things. It reaffirms positively this new development: not that creatures now remind us of God, but that the memory of God reminds us of creatures. We have been there and think always of God. We think of creatures too, but of God first. We re-tell our God-experience, if only to ourselves, by using created forms; in re-telling it we re-live it—in a creaturely ambience.

An earlier chapter dealt with the presence of God in his creatures as the basis of kataphatics, the way of affirmation. Having experienced the positive no-thing, which is the fullness of Being, the mystic now looks in a diametrically different way at these same contingent or finite beings, beings that do not necessarily exist, beings that are limited imitations of the divine essence. Having so experienced the divine presence, the mystic sees all persons and things first of all as filled with the presence and perfections of God—all of them affirming their source: "In him we live and move and have our being" (Acts 17:28).

The spiritual spiral moves from kataphatics to apophatics to anaphatics; that is, from the perception of similarity to the acceptance of transcendent dissimilarity and at length to the abiding recognition of familiarity. At each repeated revolution, the spiral lifts the soul closer to God as he is in himself and as he is found in his creatures, so that God is an ever-abiding and intimately growing presence.

Let us compare these three major phases of the mystical life: (1) *Kataphatics* goes from creatures to God by means of resemblances. God is mediated by our knowing and loving of creatures. (2) *Apophatics* goes directly to God by means of negation. God is mediated by our consciousness of unrestricted openness in knowing and loving. (3) *Anaphatics* goes from God to creatures by means of presence. God is mediated by our remembrances, on seeing creatures, of the experience of knowing and loving him.

To develop the last step further: after becoming aware of God by heightened consciousness of his presence, we speak of God from a different perspective. We perceive God as being present in creatures, not just as being suggested by them. It is not that they remind us of God, but that we use creaturely perfections to express our memory of the perfections of God. It is like going back and seeing kataphatics from the divine viewpoint, kataphatics *sub specie deitatis.*

This going forth and return is most dramatically visible in the mystic's relationship to Christ and his Mystical Body. We never outgrow the need somehow to be conscious of Jesus Christ. Teresa of Avila, recognizing that we had to transcend sensible and corporeal images, asserted: "What I should like to make very clear is that Christ's most sacred humanity must not be reckoned among these corporeal objects. Let that point be clearly understood; I wish I knew how to explain it."[81] Her concern was one of method or process: "The last thing we should do is withdraw of set purpose from our greatest help and blessing, which is the most sacred Humanity of Our Lord Jesus Christ."[82] To assess exactly what she meant, we must take into account the acknowledgment a few paragraphs later, that at times we do transcend all created beings: "Sometimes the soul may go out from itself and be so full of God that it will need no created things to assist it in recollection."[83] Note that Christ's human nature is created.

Teresa of Avila distinguished the presence of Christ in the spiritual betrothal from his presence in the spiritual marriage. That difference is important in discerning the role of the humanity of Christ in the highest levels of heightened consciousness.

> What passes in the Spiritual Marriage is very different. The Lord appears in the centre of the soul, not through an imaginary, but through an intellectual vision (although this is a subtler one than that already mentioned), just as He appeared to the Apostles, without entering through the door, when He said to them: Pax vobis.[84]

The resolution of the problem is not easy. In later chapters, we shall suggest further insights into it. Suffice it here to note the perti-

nent fact, the unique role of Jesus: "There is one God and one mediator between God and man, the man Christ Jesus" (I Tim 2:5). Similarly, Jesus said of himself "I am the way the truth and the life. No one
comes to the Father but by me" (Jn 14:6).

Through the incarnation, the divine and human natures are
joined in a hypostatic union in the person of the Logos. We are thus
united to Jesus Christ in a number of ways: we have the same human
nature (a created body and a created soul); we have minds attuned to
him through faith and love; we have the indwelling Paraclete, the
Spirit of Jesus, which unites us to him. Through this grace of adoption, we are thus able to say with St. Paul: "I now no longer live, but
Christ lives in me" (Gal 2:20). In union with Christ through his Spirit,
who is the mutual Love of Father and Son, we share in the life of the
Trinity: in the Son we love the Father infinitely; and in the Son we are
loved infinitely by the Father. Obviously, this union with Christ is not
transcended in mystical consciousness however exalted.

Nonetheless, the objective need for Christ as Savior does not
mean that we must always be explicitly conscious of his humanity. As
we move from the kataphatic to the apophatic through symbols, we
open ourselves unrestrictedly to the divine. We do so conscious of the
Spirit of truth, the Spirit of Jesus that dwells within us. Moreover,
since our consciousness of God is consciousness of the created effects
realized in our soul, we experience through proper self-consciousness
a participation in the life of Jesus. This self-expansion heightens our
awareness of our union with the Body of Christ and with its Head.

In short, in the kataphatic way we focus directly on the humanity
of Jesus Christ; in the apophatic way we do so virtually by means of
the Spirit of Jesus, and in the anaphatic way, we combine the two in a
vivid awareness of the divine presence in Jesus Christ and, through
Jesus Christ, in our fellow-humans and the rest of creation. Paul revealed the promise of this consummated return: "That he might make
known to us the mystery of his will, according to his good pleasure,
which he has purposed in him, in the dispensation of the fulness of
time, to comprehend in Christ as head all things that are in heaven and
on earth in him" (Eph 1:9–10).

CONCLUSION

Apophatics responds to the incomprehensibility of God by opening the mind through unrestricted openness to knowing and loving.
Without total emptiness, the mind is cluttered with created forms;

without total love, the mind is distracted and distorted by inordinate desires. Detachment facilitates a self-transcendent openness, which is much more than the negative emptiness of false mystics. This openness depends fundamentally on wholehearted love. Only a total and self-transcendent love can make a final capitulation in the presence of a loving God. On this capitulation depends the heightened consciousness which is mysticism.

To achieve this state of mind is the explicit goal of the way of negation, the *via remotionis.* Concretely, apophatics can go in either of two directions. Negative apophatics, dealing as it does with sheer emptiness, cancels itself out as a means of union with God. In eliminating everything, it eliminates in itself the means of God-consciousness. God does not demand psychic suicide but total self-surrender; consciousness must not die but capitulate. Love makes that capitulation possible through a universal willingness, which makes the mind *capax Dei*, actively receptive of God's presence.

Positive apophatics, thus rooted in openness to Being, enables the soul to be filled with the divine. The focal point is human awareness of the divine presence. It is not an awareness of nothingness or emptiness, but of a positive and transcendent reality of limitless meaning and value. Knowing that God exists, we deepen our awareness of this infinite being, this subsistent "to be," by opening our minds unrestrictedly to the vast sea of serenity. In the very act of opening to transcendence we achieve heightened consciousness of this immanent and sacred mystery.

Since a loving faith is the operative means of union with God, it goes without saying that the Christian mysteries do not impede but rather foster the requisite openness to God. They channel the mind to the divine darkness, the light inaccessible. Inordinate longings and desires contract the mind and prevent the unrestricted openness in knowing and loving, on which mysticism depends.

The mystic, however, does not remain lost in contemplation. As long as life in this world continues, the mystic, sharing also in the life of Christ, must return to the community and the world of creatures. This return now reveals the world as an oblique theophany. The intimate experience of God so fills the soul that it sees God's presence in every creature as a continuous remembrance.

The apophatic way may intimidate the uninitiated but it invigorates the courageous and fills their hearts with joys that the world cannot give, joys that come from the intimacy that only detachment from lesser loves can bring. The cross may loom large in the apophatic path, but with darkness of death, there comes a proportionate resurrection. In the stillness and the silence, the mystic becomes conscious of God's active presence in the soul. Detachment becomes no longer a penitential deprivation but a passionate reception, a throwing off of the garments of imperfection so that the soul may be clothed in the golden garb of infinite love.

5

Heightening Techniques

✧   ✧   ✧

Any method of prayer is valid in so far as it is inspired by
Christ and leads to Christ who is the Way, the Truth, and
the Life.

John Paul II*

Theophanies of analogy (kataphatics) and negation (apophatics) having been discussed, a practical consideration becomes necessary: How can the whole person best respond to the challenge of God-consciousness, since the whole person remains, even in altered states of consciousness, an embodied spirit—not an angel?

Our bodies are so patently involved that some people assert that the body—stimulated or orientated by drugs, sex, pain, or esoteric practices—is the only door to mystical experience. A working balance, however, must be found, since the physical component, though subordinate, is unquestionably significant. Assuming the interaction of soul and body, of mind and muscle, I shall examine the place of physiological and psychological techniques in Christian mysticism.[1]

By the term "physiological" I refer to bodily functions and processes, not to anatomy or structure. Physiology includes such disparate items as muscular activity, glandular secretions, metabolism, sensations, and brain waves.[2] By the term "psychological" I refer to meanings and feelings involved in the mental operations of experiencing, understanding, judging, and deciding; they obviously depend on the brain.[2]

Finally, by the term, "techniques," I refer to the totality of psycho-physical means of bringing the subject into conscious harmony

* John Paul II, Homily in honor of St. Teresa, *Acta apostolicae sedis* 75 (1983): 257.

119

with God. The term need not imply an impersonal or mechanical activity. Traditionally, techniques of mystical prayer are good habits, sapiential and practical skills, that foster and perfect the life of grace. Such a broad description, however, would cover the whole of one's spiritual life, were it not limited here to general, physiological and psychological means to mystical experience. In short, the precise question concerning techniques—hardly academic for those seeking the face of God—is whether with the help of ordinary grace one can by voluntary mental and physical action and inaction so alter one's state of consciousness as to achieve a Christian mystical experience.

A 1989 Letter from the Congregation for the Doctrine of the Faith dealt with aspects of Christian meditation.[3] Of special relevance for this chapter is a semantic question about the terms "technique" and "method." The Letter, without defining the term "technique," rejected a place in Christian meditation for "impersonal techniques" (sec. 3) or for "any technique in the strict sense of the word" (sec. 23), but it spoke favorably of the use of methods of meditation (sec. 16–25) and even "psychological–corporal methods" (sec. 26–28).

To be able to reject with good reason "any techniques in the strict sense," one must have envisaged these techniques as actions performed with no true relation to God and grace and as clearly inconsistent with Christian mysticism—for example, actions such as merely standing on one's head, genuflecting, taking peyote or other drugs, or reciting in a purely verbal and mindless fashion the mantras, "Om" or "Maranatha." The Letter, however, is ambiguous about what is meant, for it referred to Zen, Yoga, and Transcendental Meditation as "Eastern methods" (sec. 2, n. 1), not Eastern techniques. But in this connection, it did state an important truth: "The majority of the great religions which have sought union with God in prayer have also pointed out ways to achieve it. Just as 'the Catholic Church rejects nothing of what is true and holy in these religions' [Decl. *Nostra aetate*, n. 2], neither should these ways be rejected out of hand simply because they are not Christian" (sec. 16). Indeed, the Letter noted an obvious technical fact: "Human experience shows that the position and demeanor of the body also have their influence on the recollection and dispositions of the spirit" (sec. 26). The Letter recognized the value for meditation of "the basic life functions, such as breathing or the beating of the heart," and commended the use of the mantra-like "Jesus Prayer" (sec. 27). Reference was made also to the *Exercises* [no. 258] where St. Ignatius suggested that "at each breath or respiration, he is to pray mentally, as he says one word of the 'Our Father' or any other prayer that is being recited, so that between each breath and another a single word is said" (sec. 27, n. 32). Here is a traditional technique going back over four hundred years.

In summary, although the Letter stated: "Genuine Christian mysticism has nothing to do with technique," it did so in terms of the preceding sentence which referred to "any technique in the strict sense" (sec. 23). As a point of clarification, in English, the word "technique" is hardly pejorative. *Webster's New International Dictionary* defines it thus: "Expert method in execution of the technical details of accomplishing something, especially in the creative arts." Certainly the spiritual life needs expert methods. The Letter showed a concern about dangers and excesses—such as an exclusive reliance on a "mental void" (sec. 11, n. 120), which method I have criticized earlier as "negative apophatics." Nevertheless, it acknowledged a proper role for techniques in the broader sense, as used in this chapter; that is, as expert methods of meditation grounded in faith, pursued in charity, and aimed at facilitating a return to the Father through the Son and in the Holy Spirit. The spirit of its message is well-phrased in the Introduction: "Christian prayer is at the same time always authentically personal and communitarian. It flees from impersonal techniques or from concentrating on oneself, which can create a kind of rut, imprisoning a person in spiritual privatism which is incapable of free openness to the transcendental God" (sec. 3).

In this chapter, I shall move from the old ways to the new, or if not to entirely new ways to a new understanding of the old ways. In doing so, I first indicate the traditional practices. Second, I analyze, from a contemporary perspective, the scientific basis for altering states of consciousness. Third, I consider our mystical capabilities: the difficulty in identifying empirically whether an experience is natural or mystical; the possibility that the mystical life differs from the ordinary graced life owing only to a natural component; and finally, the opening of the soul to God in faith and love as a learnable quasi-symbol of the divine presence and as the core of mystical experience. This last issue is central, for if mysticism is a normal development, then the breathtaking question arises: How is this great gift of God to be acquired?

Traditional Practices

Bodily activities do not a mystic make, but no one becomes a mystic without them, so integrated is human nature. Mystics in both the East and the West have resorted to physiological techniques to help them in their spiritual quest. Usage varies widely according to the time, the place, the culture, and the religion. Five basic categories, however, are apparent. Generally speaking, the first two give only remote conditioning for contemplation; the next two exert a more proximate influence; and the last one combines the prior practices into a well-integrated and an effective system.

Manual labor has long been considered indispensable to the contemplative life. Hindu gurus advocated karma yoga—union through work. Benedictine monks caught the twin constituents of Western monastic spirituality in the motto, *Ora et labora* ("Pray and work"). Even where technology has made life more sedentary, physical work still has its surrogates in exercise and sports.

Deliberate relaxation, as a balance to work, whether physical or intellectual, has an updated Sabbath role in fostering the calmness and tranquillity so helpful in prayer. For when the body is free from muscular tensions, both thought and emotions are more easily controlled. Although scientifically grounded relaxation programs are often geared to the spiritual life, they teach a physical or physiological skill.

Ascetical deprivation is a crude but often effective mind-changing practice. The lives of saints and mystics abound with examples of the use of vigils, fasting, mortifications (such as the hair-shirt, discipline, chains, knotted cords), and long isolation in silence and darkness, all of which have served as the prelude to extraordinary prayer experiences, if not as their necessary condition.[4] Sometimes, these penitential practices are carried by a Paul of the Cross or a Rose of Lima to apparently pathological extremes. Even when used more moderately, they may be motivated in part by a quasi-Neo-Platonic desire to do violence to the body so that the mind will be free for a higher spiritual awareness, or even in part by a latent masochism triggered by guilt or a distorted desire to expiate for sins.

Bodily regularization makes a gentler attempt to alter consciousness, one more consonant with medical prudence. Although usually presupposing an ascetical lifestyle, it relies chiefly on bodily actions, especially posturing and breathing. Let us look at them separately.

When we speak of *postures,* we immediately think of the asanas of Hatha Yoga, but most religions have their own set of sacred gestures and other bodily actions. Kneeling, bowing, prostrating, genuflecting, making the sign of the cross, raising the hands—all these can be as dispositive of inner religious conviction as sitting in the Lotus position or standing motionless on one's head. The oriental *T'ai Chi Ch'uan* adds a dynamic element as it flows from one pose to another, each barely held, reminiscent perhaps of the prophet David's dancing before the Ark or of Teresa of Avila's dancing before the altar in the company of her Carmelite sisters.

When we speak of *controlled breathing,* we often link it with the postures. The slowed down and rhythmic use of this vital function, where the voluntary and the involuntary meet, tends to relax the body, to change moods, and to calm the mind. The breathing pattern may vary: sometimes merely regular deep breathing, sometimes breathing elaborately proportioned according to its four phases: inhalation, retention, exhalation, abstention. When one concentrates on the breathing itself or when one adds a verbal or cognitive component (a mantra to be repeated in harmony with the breathing), the mind itself seems to become more easily unified and more profoundly focused.

Systematic combinations of work, relaxation, deprivation, posture, and breath control have resulted in highly refined spiritual techniques. Yogis, Zen Buddhists, Sufis, Christian Hesychasts: each group has its own contemplative procedures. Here are mind-changing techniques at their best, where physiology is put to the service of mysticism. I do not intend to analyze these systems, but I shall examine the altered state of consciousness which—however different the systems, the physical practices, and the religious vision—seems, in the early stages, to be common to them all.

Altered States

To try to make clear the physiological changes that underlie the use of the combined traditional practices, I shall discuss some of the findings that have been reported by two scientists who, from slightly different viewpoints, examine the same general area: one describes a basic meditation procedure and the resulting "wakeful metabolic state," and the other analyzes the most relevant aspect of that state, alpha-wave production. Together these studies reveal the heart of the physiological contribution that traditional practices make to mystical experience.

The Wakeful Hypometabolic State

Herbert Benson, M.D., of the Harvard Medical School, wrote a short study of what he called *The Relaxation Response.*[5] The idea for the book came from his work with experts in Transcendental Meditation, a skillfully packaged and, at the time, a highly popular form of mantra Yoga. Dr. Benson noted that the practice of TM frequently helped reduce blood pressure and produced a unified set of responses in other bodily processes. He discovered, too, that the same responses could be obtained by persons who, though untrained in TM, used a similar technique—but one without the Hindu rite of initiation, the sacred and secret mantra, and the expensive price tag. After further testing, he concluded that his technique led to a physical state of deep rest as well as to a new level of consciousness. I shall consider three main aspects of his study: the simplified technique; the physiological results; and the mystical applicability.

First, the technique is simple with no pretensions to originality. Benson acknowledged its antiquity and its universality. He stated that he merely purified it of cultural and religious overtones. In the process, he also effectively demythologized TM, his inspirational starting point. The directions are matter-of-fact: (a) Sit comfortably in a quiet environment; (b) Close the eyes and relax the body completely; (c) Say a mantra, such as "one," at each exhalation, all the while breathing consciously through the nose; (d) Continue for about twenty minutes, ignoring distractions by repeating the mantra; and (e) Remain quiet for a few minutes after finishing to adjust to a different state.[6]

Second, the physiological result of this technique is that one enters a fourth state of consciousness, called a "wakeful hypometabolic state." The other three states are sleeping, dreaming and being normally awake. What happens in the relaxation response is that after a few minutes, with the body relaxed and the mind emptied through controlled breathing and the use of a mantra, the metabolic processes of the body show a radical change of pace, under a master plan orchestrated by the hypothalamus in the brain. More specifically, there is a slowing down of the breathing and the heart rate; a lowering of the exchange rate of oxygen and carbon dioxide; a lowering of the blood pressure and the lactate level of the blood; and, of special importance, a slowing down of brain-wave frequencies with a change from beta wave to alpha wave production.

This relaxation response is the counterpart of an emergency reaction, for both are needed in coping with the environment. The emergency reaction, or fight-flight reaction, is hypermetabolic, stimulating the body to deal with threatening circumstances. The relaxation response is hypometabolic, enabling the body to reduce the stress occasioned by these conflicts. In calling both states "integrated responses," Benson meant that, given the requisite conditions, the effect is automatic and coordinated. The sympathetic nervous system is controlled by hormones from the hypothalamus, and the body changes accordingly. The responses cannot be directly willed, but they can be caused by deliberately putting oneself in the appropriate circumstances or by carefully performing the requisite procedures.

Third, any mystical applicability after this biochemical litany may seem out of the question. What has the wakeful hypometabolic state to do with mysticism? Benson's answer is his fifth chapter, of which the "chief purpose is to illustrate the age-old universality of this altered state of consciousness."[7] After a cursory survey of Hindu, Buddhist, Sufi, Taoist, Jewish, and Christian mysticism, he concluded: "We believe that people have been describing the type of thinking which elicits the Relaxation Response throughout many cultures and religions."[8]

Benson did not actually say that the wakeful hypometabolic state and mystical experience were the same. It is more a matter of mysticism by implication or, better, by association. By quoting Teresa of Avila, John Ruusbroec, and other mystics and mystical writers, he gave the impression that they are all discussing the same thing—the wakeful hypometabolic state. Clearly, he considered it to be a vehicle for transcendent experience: "This approach is not to be interpreted as viewing religion or philosophy in a mechanistic fashion. The ultimate purpose of any exercise to attain transcendent experience corresponds to the philosophy or religion in which it is used."[9] He quoted William James on this point:

> The fact is that the mystical feeling of enlargement, union and emancipation has no specific intellectual content whatever of its own. It is capable of forming matrimonial alliances with material furnished by the most diverse philosophies and theologies, provided only they can find a place in their framework for its peculiar emotional mood.[10]

Joseph Maréchal, S.J., writing some ten years after James, squarely confronted this same issue, but he made an important distinction: "From the empirical and external point of view all the isolated religious manifestations—*lower than the mystic states described as immediate union with God*—seem identical from one religion to the other; there is certainly a difference in their combination and harmonization, but not in the psychological type to which they are individually reducible."[11] Recognizing that grace is not empirically visible, Maréchal nevertheless insisted on the radical difference that it makes, "a difference of value and finality."[12]

Benson did not make this distinction, though the very first quotation that he used to illustrate his approach contains Ruusbroec's insistence on just such radical finality: "Whoever then has, in his inward exercise, an imageless and free ascent unto his God, *and means nought else but the glory of God,* must taste the goodness of God, and he must feel from within a true union with God."[13]

In later books, Benson added an explicit "Faith Factor." He used the term very broadly: "This involves eliciting the Response in the context of a deeply held set of personal, religious, or philosophical beliefs."[14] These beliefs—convictions is a better term—already involve patterns of neurotransmitters. When the mind is opened by the relaxation response, it is more easily able to develop new thought processes, skills, and disciplines.[15] Since Benson's aim was admittedly practical, he showed how strong convictions of any sort tended to enhance the Response: "The potential for this simple Relaxation-Response technique increases when it is exercised in the context of a person's belief system."[16] This became the theme of his latest book, *Your Maximum Mind,* with its two phases: first the Response to open the mind and then the development or strengthening of neuronal patterns by meditating on ideas, goals, or practices involving such areas as health, athletics, exercise, dieting, brain power, and spirituality.

Benson's progressive relaxation technique is somewhat limited even on the physiological level. A further development is needed if the technique is to be attuned to the fostering of mystical experience. Charles F. Stroebel, M.D., without adverting to mysticism, has made an important contribution with his "quieting reflex," which has benefits that go beyond his goal of eliminating stress.[17]

Stroebel's major insight focuses on the fight-or-flight response, which is at the heart of the stress-tension syndrome. He recommended that one begin to counter the effects of a threatening annoyance, anxiety, worry, or fear through the action of smiling, not a forced grimace with dead eyes, but an inner glow suffusing the features and a smile accompanied by deep breathing.

According to Dr. Stroebel, there are two gear-shift mechanisms, which are crucial in eliminating stress: the muscles of the face and those of the diaphragm.[18] Both sets of muscles are more or less under our control and yet can operate without our direction. Using them properly, we can influence our involuntary muscles and our moods. By assuming a positive and joyful expression and by breathing deeply in a slow and regular way, we change our emotional state and induce full relaxation.

William James saw emotions as sensations of bodily changes. The very act of slumping or pouting or cowering tends to make a person feel depressed or sullen or afraid; a smile which is made inwardly and lights up the face tends to dispel the adverse emotional sequelae of stressful events or untoward circumstances.

An underlying explanation for this use of the smile is its effect on the brain's limbic system, which responds to our sensations, feelings, emotional states, and stress, thus involving the fight-flight syndrome. The limbic system conveys this information to the hypothalamus which in turn regulates the immune system and, through the pituitary gland, the whole endocrine system. When the input is positive the body functions optimally, with the immune system on alert and the hormones in balance.[19]

Smiling outwardly and inwardly is a skill that can be developed even in troubled times. Of course, a lasting and convincing smile requires a basis in reality. To emphasize the good things in one's experience, to dismiss at least temporarily negative thoughts and feelings, to believe in the meaning and value of life in a moral universe—these attitudes can help liberate the psyche from environmental dependence and can enable a person to face events with a certain smiling equilibrium and to experience what Teilhard de Chardin called "the universal Smile," obviously referring to God, who protects and fosters through divine providence the good of those who love him.

In a second way, Schroebel's "quieting reflex" improved on Benson's technique by shortening the amount of time for a complete cycle and by projecting this shortened form throughout the whole day. Specifically, Schroebel recommended using not two twenty-minute periods a day but rather a six-second method to be repeated intermittently. His method involves a challenge and response. The phases of this sequence are as follows:

1. The *challenge* takes the form of a clue—some tension, annoyance, anxiety, or alteration in breathing.
2. The *response* is fourfold:
   a. Smile inwardly and with eyes and mouth, suggesting to oneself, "Alert amused mind, calm body."
   b. Breathe easily and deeply.
   c. While exhaling one's breath, let the jaw, tongue, and shoulders go; feel a wave of heaviness; and feel warmth flowing through the body to the toes.
   d. Resume normal activity.[20]

This "quieting reflex" is to be repeated 50 to 100 times throughout the day (all told, only five or ten minutes) until in four to six months it becomes an habitual reflex.[21] As a result, whenever a disquieting clue appears, one automatically goes through the phases contrary to the fight-or-flight syndrome. One lives, then, in an habitual state of mental quiet and bodily relaxation, a state conducive to prayer and contemplation.

It is enlightening here to compare the practice on a different, but in some way parallel, level which Teresa of Avila recommended: "Make fifty acts of self-oblation to God daily and make each with great fervour and desire for God."[22] Of course, she did not suggest any breathing, relaxing, or brain wave techniques. Yet it is clear that her practice was in harmony with the psychological aspects of the quieting reflex and no doubt involved some of them, at least unconsciously.

Moreover, note how short a time Teresa's self-offering takes, how it permeates the whole day, how easily it becomes habitual, how it is a peaceful acceptance of all the happenings of life, and how it responds to divine goodness with something of an inner smile. We should not overlook the fact that she, like the rest of us, had to take up her cross daily and that she experienced the fight-or-flight syndrome with its resultant tensions and stresses. It is significant that she, too, appreciated the value of a smile, saying often: "God deliver me from gloomy saints." Significantly, from a totally different religious perspective, we have the tradition of the Buddha smile, an external manifestation of the contemplative spirit, analogous to what characterized the personality of Teresa.

In short, to be successful on the psychological level these physiological techniques need to utilize higher functions of the mind. In doing so they make the whole person more receptive to the possibility of heightened consciousness. We have seen the limitations of Benson's approach and the remedy that Stroebel has suggested.

For Benson mysticism is a special alpha state, physically induced but coupled with an ideational component. Spiritually, his simplified procedure is merely a means of altering brain waves so that, while the body cooperates, the alpha state dominates in a religious reverie. But if the hypometabolic state is possibly, as suggested, an ordinary prelude to some mystical experiences, we must take a closer look at these mysterious waves to see how much they reveal of the secrets of the saints.

The Alpha-wave State

Dr. Barbara Brown, an expert in the developing field of biofeedback, has made an exhaustive study of the voluminous material on mind-body interaction in two books, *New Mind, New Body* and *Stress and the Art of Biofeedback*.[23] She brought together the advances in the biofeedback area, with special emphasis on the role of alpha waves. Using her data, we find phenomena closely paralleling some stages of mystical experience.

Convinced of the importance of alpha-wave research, Brown fought against three tendencies: mystification, oversimplification, and presumption. First of all she noted that most persons have experienced the alpha state, whether contemplatives or not. It is a standard part of our brain-wave production. To go into the alpha state is not an unusual mystical experience, but as familiar a one as daydreaming or resting. Second, there is not just one alpha state, but "perhaps almost an infinite number of alphas."[24] Great differences exist between individuals and within the same individual. Frequency, amplitude, location, variation, cause, and condition—these variables make each person's alpha profile almost unique. Third, in 1974 Brown observed that over the last forty years there have appeared more than a thousand reports on alpha waves involving more than two thousand researchers, but that "after all this work, it is surprising how little we can say about the meaning and the function of alpha."[25] She warned that "concluding anything about alpha is perilous."[26] Therefore, the relation of the mystical state and the alpha state remains an important though problematic aspect of mysticism.

Despite the limitations of scientific knowledge in this field, Brown reported some emerging generalizations on the relation of alpha waves and meditation. I shall consider just two topics suggested by her study: the role of the alpha mantra and the subjectivities of the alpha state.

The term "alpha mantra" is used only once, in a subheading, and is never fully developed. It seems, in fact, to be identified by Brown with the signal of her feedback machine. Thus she speaks of the "relaxing effect of sitting still in a quiet place with nothing more than the feedback signal of one's alpha to disturb the silence"[27] and again of "a feeling of dissolving back into the feedback signal."[28] On the assumption that her "alpha mantra" is a mechanical aid, the following reservation is well taken: "While I question the value of alpha feedback for the advanced meditator, I find nothing wrong in its use as an educational aid."[29]

Biofeedback machines aside, I think the notion of an alpha mantra can profitably be pushed further. Certainly there is—perhaps more frequently than realized—the use of the delicate alpha sensation itself to focus and stabilize consciousness, freeing it from discursiveness and the multiplicity of forms. Subtle and almost imperceptible, the alpha mantra barely fulfills the Aristotelian minimum for cognition: "The human soul is not able to know without a phantasm."[30] Consider, on the other hand, what simplicity and quiet there is when the mind focuses exclusively on its own rhythmic electrical discharges. How crude and noisy, in contrast, is the beating heart, the heaving breath, the echoing words, or the fragmenting thought, although these grosser mantras may, of course, lead to the refinement of an alpha-wave state. Here, then, is the quintessential physiologic technique, the use of one's own alpha waves as a mantra.

The second topic concerns the alpha subjectivities, with which we must familiarize ourselves before attempting to compare them with Christian mystical experiences. A fundamental characteristic can be noted: alpha states and environmental awareness are inversely proportional. "The best alpha producers are generally those who lost awareness of their environments, tending to lose all awareness of time and reporting later that their 60- or 90-minute session seemed like only a few minutes."[31] Here we have an aspect of the time-space detachment which is symptomatic of mystical experience.

Dr. Brown concluded that the alpha state and meditation give rise to very similar feelings: "Even the sensation of separation from the material universe can occur in both; a depersonalization, loss of individual identity, and a feeling of becoming aware of the unifying thread of life."[32] Or take, for example, another list of experiences reported from biofeedback sessions: "A sensation of floating, a feeling of dissolving back into the feedback signal, the loss of time perception, detachment, and other non-ordinary states and feelings."[33] These experiences were common to certain drug states, but Zen meditation also revealed similar findings.

> Many advocates, including some researchers, believe that alpha is instant Zen, instant satori, that the filling of the head with alpha waves with its accompanying divorcement from material reality is the equivalent of the Zen no-mind state. They tend to believe that the no-mind is the absence of thoughts of material attachments to the self, a dissolution of the ego. The experience is described as the ecstatic, mystical state of unity with the universe.[34]

The alpha state may be with or without content; even when content is present, it may be vaguely amorphous or vividly concrete. It may be a feeling, a picture, an idea. "Some people report the flow of considerable imagery, almost a daydreaming reverie."[35] As long as one does not focus on the contents of the alpha state intently or analyze them discursively, the state will not be interrupted. Nevertheless, awareness of contents does militate somewhat against the unification of consciousness. Here is where the mantra often proves helpful, recycling the same feeling, image, or thought, thereby focusing and simplifying mental operations.

Dr. Brown has made the alpha waves come alive as sources of somewhat familiar but largely uncharted experiences, ranging from a merely pleasant feeling to a sense of being in tune with the universe. By her research and experimentation, she has opened up new possibilities for the study of contemplative life.

In short, the work of both Benson and Brown afford us a scientific basis for understanding how consciousness can be so altered by physiologic techniques as to produce a state that characterizes in part many varieties of contemplation and mysticism—at least in their early stages. Later in this chapter, I intend to consider the effect of these alpha experiences in terms of the distinction between acquired and infused contemplation.

The Assessment

To evaluate these physiological techniques, we shall look at them both positively and negatively. First, we mention possible concerns. We have touched upon some of them in the previous chapter, so the treatment here will be brief. Then we look more thoroughly at the very real benefits that accrue from using these techniques as a means of fostering mystical experience. Let us begin then with the negative aspects.

(1) Certain theorists, as we have seen, consider all mystical states to be natural and essentially similar. Aldous Huxley's "perennial philosophy"[36] and Abraham Maslow's "peak experiences"[37] are, in their own way, part of a naturalistic reductionism that contradicts the traditions of Christian mysticism. The value of physiological techniques, however, is not diminished by the theoretical limitations of this position.

(2) Some people, with genuine spiritual aspirations may, as we have seen, easily become content with "the natural rest which the soul obtains when it is free from images and form," as John of the Cross described it,[38] without moving on to the riches of the life of grace. Ruusbroec, too, mentioned such people who are "turned in upon the barrenness of their own being"[39] and who have "unified

themselves in the blind and dark vacancy of their own being."[40] This problem may not be as frequent among the spiritually-minded today, who are aware of the many clearly secular modes of rest and relaxation.

(3) Sincere beginners in prayer, however, may be tempted to prematurely bypass both spiritual reading and discursive meditation for a spiritually flavored natural rest. They think they are mystics; Teresa of Avila called them "dolts" (bobos).[41] Having heard that contemplation involves emptiness, they stupidly spend their prayer time in a daze, their minds and hearts inoperative. Wasting precious time and energy, they deceive themselves. But this phase passes quickly in those who are truly sincere.

(4) Emptied souls, unfilled by love, may find themselves subject to unexpected evils. This is more worrisome, but relatively rare. R. C. Zaehner did warn of the return of the proverbial seven devils.[42] Elsewhere, he quoted Bernanos on how Satan counterfeits the peace that surpasses understanding: "Far higher than the pleasures that only stir your entrails, his masterpiece is a silent peace, solitary, icy, comparable only to the enjoyment of nothingness."[43] The description gives the remedy: good will is always necessary or one's personal and spiritual life becomes distorted and debased.

The benefits certainly outweigh the concerns one might have. One fact will dispel most worries about this state of physiological rest: sooner or later this state will appear if one prays regularly, quietly, and without busyness. Indeed, people experience it in many other, totally secular activities. The task, then, is not to reject it but to use it properly, for it can help lead the soul at least some of the way to union with God. Here are some positive aspects of this physiological state.

(1) Longer periods of prayer are facilitated by the removal of restlessness, the body becoming more obedient and tranquil.

(2) More attentive prayer is facilitated by the elimination of distraction, for the mind is freed from preoccupations and from its continuing dialogue with itself.

(3) More profound prayer is facilitated by transcending forms and discursiveness, for the mind learns to function on a less divided level and with a larger capacity for spiritual experience.

(4) More docile prayer open to the subtle promptings of the Spirit is possible when the mind listens in stillness and peace.

In short, the physiologically induced hypometabolic state with alpha waves helps in varying degrees to dispose a person for mystical experience by minimizing, at least in part, the impediments arising from our dual nature. It does so by gradually subjecting the senses, emotions, imagination, and discursive reason more completely to the spirit.

How necessary for the mystical life is this removal of obstacles can be seen from the purpose that John of the Cross attributed to the dark night of the senses, for him a state of infused contemplation: "The purgation of the senses is the only entrance and the beginning of contemplation leading to the purgation of the spirit, and . . . serves rather to accommodate sense to spirit than to unite spirit to God."[44] Earlier in the same treatise, he developed the point more fully: "God leads the soul into the night of sense in order to purge the sense of its lower parts and to subdue it, unite it, and bring it into conformity by setting it in darkness and causing it to cease from meditation."[45]

Note that the purpose of the night of the senses is largely natural as is the purpose of the physiological techniques—the accommodation of sense to spirit. Thus there are two complementary means of disposing the soul for the mystical experience: in the dark night of the senses the emphasis is on the radical purgation of inordinate appetite; in the physiological mind-changing process the emphasis is primarily on the elimination of forms and partly on the pacification of the body.

Although, according to John of the Cross, the soul cannot purge itself sufficiently without the passive purifications of the dark night of the spirit, he urged it to activity: "It befits the soul, in so far as it can, to contrive to labor on its own account to purge and to perfect itself, so that it may merit being taken by God into that divine care wherein it becomes healed of all things that it was unable itself to cure."[46]

It is clear that physiological techniques can lead to an altered state of consciousness called the wakeful hypometabolic state, with the body at peace and the mind in the alpha state. In itself, of course, this relaxed alpha state is certainly not supernatural and is not even essentially mystical. Moreover, for mysticism, at least normal grace and infused virtues are needed. The alpha state can facilitate, it clearly cannot cause, infused contemplation.

The precise function of this natural alpha state in mysticism is kenotic; it helps empty the imagination, dispel tensions, and restrain discursive reason, so that the soul is better disposed to open itself to God. For, as John of the Cross insisted, "Pure contemplation is to receive."[47]

Nevertheless, the crucial act of the mystic is not in emptying the mind but in loving God. John of the Cross again speaks to the point: "God communicates himself most to the soul that has progressed farthest in love; namely, that has its will in closest conformity with the will of God."[48] For the Christian, mysticism is fundamentally a loving union which, through connaturality, brings awareness of God. "We know through love" (*Per amorem cognoscimus*), said Gregory the Great.[49] There is no shortcut in mysticism other than the conformity of our wills to the will of God. No psychological or physiological technique can ever substitute for this love. Can physiological techniques lead to Christian mysticism? Yes, but only as the humble instrumentalities of a purified and intensified love of God.

Mystical Capabilities

Having examined physiological and psychological techniques, we realize that they conspire with grace to generate mystical consciousness by helping to foster unrestricted openness in knowing and loving God. The question arises: can we differentiate the roles played by nature and grace in this peak experience? The first task, primarily a descriptive one, is an attempt to determine whether it would be helpful or even possible to identify empirically these experiences as natural or graced, as acquired or infused. The second task, more theoretical, is an attempt to determine whether true mystical experience can be achieved with the help of the ordinary grace available to every person.

The Identification Puzzle

To draw lines of demarcation as we move from the physiological to the mystical is not easy. Empirical observation reveals the ambiguity of the events of the contemplative life, including such dramatic ones as ecstasy. To illustrate the abiding difficulties of discernment even in the early stages of mysticism, I shall pose some cases in which the standard subjectivities of the alpha state are operative. These considerations will highlight the empirical problem that many good people have in discerning their stage of prayer. I shall start with an historical case and follow it with two hypothetical ones.

The first case comes from an account that the poet Alfred Lord Tennyson, gave in a letter about a mantra-induced state that he had frequently experienced.

> I have never had any revelations through anaesthetics, but a kind of waking trance—this for lack of a better word—I have frequently had, quite up from boyhood, when I have been all alone. This has come upon me through repeating my own

name to myself silently, till all at once, as it were out of the intensity of the consciousness of individuality, individuality itself seemed to dissolve and fade away into boundless being, and this not a confused state but the clearest, the surest of the surest, utterly beyond words—where death was an almost laughable impossibility—the loss of personality (if so it were) seeming no extinction but the only true life.[50]

Suppose a hypothetical case in which someone, when all alone, merely repeats the name of Jesus until he, too, is no longer conscious of his own individuality. In fact, his individuality seems to fade and dissolve into boundless being—which represents God to him. He feels that he shares in the only true life and that he is immortal. What if he then applied to himself St. Paul's words, "I live, no longer I, but Christ lives in me" (Gal 2:20)? Which experience, the historical or the hypothetical, would be mystical? Perhaps, in the broadest sense, both. Which would be extraordinary? Probably neither. Traditional spiritual advisers, however, might call the hypothetical "infused." Might it not be more correct to say that the hypothetical is graced but not infused, and that in some way so is the historical?

Let us next take a parallel hypothetical case, that of a committed Christian woman with a firm and fervent faith who tries to love God wholeheartedly and conform her will to God's will, and who during the day frequently recalls the presence of God and remains faithful to her half-hour of daily mental prayer.

What happens when the woman inadvertently goes into an alpha state? Would not the standard subjective alpha experiences, which Dr. Brown reported, take on a Christian dimension? She might begin to feel detached from environmental awareness, yet with a sense of the unifying thread of life. In a confused and general way, she might easily identify this alpha feeling with the presence of God and respond to it peacefully and lovingly. Her ego might at times feel depersonalized as if she were dissolving back into the natural alpha mantra and into the presence of God. The duration of this prayerful alpha state might seem sometimes to be only a few minutes long, though a whole hour might have passed.

So we must ask, was this a "mystical" experience or merely an alpha experience elevated by ordinary faith and charity? Or to speak in more traditional terms, was the experience acquired or infused? Here the answer is easy. It was acquired contemplation, because only natural physiological responses and ordinary grace were postulated. What new evidence would show it to be infused? A brief clarification is important: sanctifying grace, the gifts of the Holy Spirit, and the supernatural virtues are all infused. So acquired contemplation involves infused graces. The point at issue is whether the grace of contemplation is an additional and extraordinary infused grace.

To restate the question: What empirical evidence distinguishes two different states of graced contemplation, one as acquired, the other as infused? John of the Cross recognized the problem, saying of the dark contemplation of the night of the senses: "This loving knowledge is apt at the beginning to be very subtle and delicate, and almost imperceptible to the senses,"[51] and elsewhere: "Although the soul be occupied therein, it can neither realize it nor perceive it."[52] John mentioned that among souls enjoying infused contemplation, beginners often think they are merely wasting time and the proficient sometimes think they are deceiving themselves. If the evidence seems to be empirically so ambiguous, is there any way to prove that the contemplation is infused?

The best indication for John of the Cross that the soul has passed into infused contemplation is from the subsequent effects: the soul is no longer able to meditate discursively as it used to do and is no longer able to get satisfaction from created things of sense or spirit, but it does have a longing for silence and solitude with an attentiveness to God in a confused, general, and loving way.[53] The subtlety of his psychological insight is seen in his asking not what mystical experiences the soul does have (often a dangerous question), but rather what experiences it does not have. He wanted to discover whether the subject can still pray in the way that he or she normally does most other things, by using imagination and discursive reason, or perforce rests in the darkness of a transitional state in which, though the mind yearns constantly for God and not his creatures, it can experience God neither on the former level of consciousness which it is leaving nor on the new level of consciousness which it is just entering. The transition unsettles the soul, beset with self-doubts and frustrations; but it is a good time, a growing time.

Of course, the criteria of John of the Cross for indicating the presence of infused contemplation focuses on experiences very different from some of the descriptions of the pure alpha reveries reported by Dr. Brown. John would have classified much of the latter as hindrances. To distinguish the alpha state by itself from the mystic state (which may involve alpha), we look to a difference in the content of the experience, using the word, content, with sufficient broadness.

John understood content apophatically: "In order to come to this essential union of love in God, the soul must have a care not to lean upon imaginary visions nor upon forms or figures of particular objects of the understanding: for they would disturb it and for this reason the soul must renounce them and strive never to have them."[54] For him, faith had a fundamental role in mystical experience. He envisaged a faith simplified in its loving awareness of God's freely given presence, not a particularized propositional theologizing. Each stage of prayer thus reveals a different depth of faith. Belief in the presence of a loving God forms the core of the faith experience, which God offers to all. Mystical experience is a heightened awareness of the dimensions of this gift of faith.

We conclude this section with a renewed emphasis on the unitary character of graced nature and with confidence that God, the author of nature and grace, will use both nature and grace to raise us to himself. As for labeling, Eckhart dismissed the attempt peremptorily:

> If I were so good and holy that they had to raise me to the altars with the saints, still people would be talking and worrying about whether this were grace or nature working in me, and puzzling themselves about it. They are all wrong in this. Leave God to work in you, let him do it and do not be upset over whether he is working with nature or above nature for nature and grace are both his.[55]

The distinction between acquired and infused contemplation seems to be nullified, at least presumptively, inasmuch as both would be empirically similar functions of a human nature elevated by grace. Theological substantiation of this position comes from pursuing a closely related issue: Is mysticism a normal development of the way to perfection for the ordinary person who seeks to know God as fully as possible through a life of prayer?

The Expectation Parameter

We shall focus here more sharply on mysticism as a normal development of a life of grace and virtue. We consider then the theological core of Christian mysticism in order to clarify the interaction of nature and grace in attaining heightened consciousness of God. We already know something crucial about mysticism from the fact that nature is graced by being made capable of sharing in the self-communication of the living God and thereby of participating in divine consciousness.

Karl Rahner grounded his Christian anthropology on this notion of the supernatural existential and concluded that there can be no intermediate stage between grace and glory or between faith and vision.

> The deification of man and the possession of uncreated grace, which Christianity grants to all the justified, cannot in any real sense be surpassed by anything which is not glory and the direct contemplation of God, but these are reserved for man's final consummation. Mystical experience cannot leave behind it the sphere of "faith" and the experience of God's spirit which faith confers, by means of a new experience which would no longer be faith at all. On the contrary mysticism can be conceived of only within the normal framework of grace and faith.[56]

This position is not totally new. Back in the thirteenth century, Aquinas said: "Grace is nothing else than a certain commencement of glory."[57] Three centuries later John of the Cross said substantially the same thing: "For such is the likeness between itself [faith] and God that there is no other difference save that which exists between seeing God and believing in him."[58]

Four centuries after John of the Cross, Rahner spoke of mysticism "as merely one mode of the experience of grace in faith."[59] He brought out the full implications of this insight as applied to mysticism by focusing on the natural component of graced nature. Following the insights of Maréchal, Rahner envisaged mystical experience as a conscious state that, for a graced person, is at least in principle, as learnable as are infused virtues. One can learn to love God more and more perfectly, and one can learn to be more and more conscious of the divine presence. Rahner wrote:

> Mystical experience must not be interpreted as something which fundamentally transcends and supersedes the supernatural experience of the Spirit in faith. That is why the "specific difference" of such experience, as distinct from the "normal" experience of the Spirit, must belong to man's natural sphere. It would consequently be the special mode of an experience of transcendence and "return" to the self which is in itself natural. This does not contradict what we have just said about mysticism as the experience of grace. *Psychologically* mystical experiences differ from normal everyday pro-

cesses in the mind, only in the natural sphere; and in so far as they are fundamentally learnable.[60]

Rahner included as "natural" such clearly natural phenomena as interior absorptions and suspension of the faculties as well as parapsychological phenomena (for him, parapsychology "covers everything which average, everyday consciousness knows nothing about"[61]) such as mind reading and faith healing. Moreover, a mystical theology does not rule out the preternatural. Incidentally, by preternatural is meant that which, although it transcends a given created nature, does not transcend all created nature. For example, what is preternatural for a human may be essentially natural for an angel. Speaking broadly Rahner wrote: "Theology as such cannot provide an answer to the question as to whether this greater personal depth of the mystical act, which is itself natural, and the greater reflectiveness and purity of the transcendent experience, which accompanies it and which is in itself also natural, although exalted by grace, are in themselves wondrous (preternatural), or naturally obtainable by practice (or possibly both according to the level at which the phenomenon occurs)."[62] For Rahner, this judgment is ultimately that of empirical psychology.

Although a natural component may characterize mysticism as such, the experience always remains a faith experience: "The dogmatic theologian can only determine that on earth there cannot be a higher experience in the theological sense than the experience of faith in the Spirit of God."[63] This statement harmonizes well with John of the Cross' description of mysticism as "illumined faith." He wrote: "The more intense is a man's faith the closer is his union with God."[64] Indeed, this union through faith brings supreme enlightenment in this life.

Rahner asked a critical question: Is mysticism necessary for Christian perfection? He assigned the test for empirical psychology to apply: Is it possible, without the suspension of the faculties and related phenomena, to achieve the requisite spiritual maturity (which would involve the radical self-discovery of the subject in unconditional surrender to the mystery called God)?[65] If such maturity is possible, mysticism is not necessary; if it is not possible, then mysticism is necessary. But always what makes the faith experience mystical is a natural though elevated component.

The role of faith is crucial here since mysticism and faith both involve consciousness. From the perspective of cognitional theory, we see that faith is our response to the gift of grace mentioned by

Paul: "The love of God is poured forth in our hearts from the Holy Spirit who is given to us" (Rom 5:5). Here we repeat Lonergan's words: "Faith is knowledge born of religious love."[66] Without love there is no faith, for faith is "the eye of religious love, an eye that can discern God's self-disclosures."[67] But the gift freely offered to all is not actually received by anyone who does not fall in love with God, however unemotional and even minimal that love is. By rejecting God's love, by refusing to live by that gift, one turns from God and is dead to God. On the other hand, if one accepts that love, one may have the grace to accept further revelations which, in the words of Hebrews 11:1, make explicit the richness of what "He is," namely trinitarian, and how he is a "rewarder of those who seek him," namely incarnate and redemptive.

Faith, which is a response to love, is in harmony with our nature and its dynamic exigence for reality. Faith perfects and elevates our powers. "This apprehension [of transcendent value] consists in the experienced fulfillment of our unrestricted thrust to self-transcendence, in our actuated orientation toward the mystery of love and awe."[68] Faith as light permeates one's whole spiritual life, superlatively so in mystical experience.

Having looked at the central role of faith and its relation to love, we can now examine more fully the normality issue.[69] Is mystical experience of God a normal development of Christian life or is it an exceptional and extraordinary event, specifically different from other forms of prayer and requiring special divine assistance? God has certainly bestowed singularly extraordinary graces in the mystical life. He acts freely in all realms. The question, however, aims at determining what freedom he has given human beings. We seek to understand the gift of grace by discovering whether or not the mystics form an elite corps due to God's special selection of them or whether they reflect the full flowering of the grace which is given to all. In short, are mystics to be imitated or only admired? Are they role models or oddities?

Now let us examine some further reasons to justify one's holding, granting always the assistance of supernatural grace, a natural rather than an extraordinary difference between the ordinary Christian life and the mystical life.

First, there are no *a priori* obstacles. Scripture and tradition do not stand in the way. Joseph Maréchal, though personally arguing for a new and qualitatively distinct element in mysticism, recognized that: "It is not forbidden to Catholics to reduce the higher mystical states to a simple quantitative increase of normal psychological potentiality and ordinary supernatural grace, or, if you will, in theological language, to a pure intensification of the infused virtues communicated at baptism."[70]

Moreover, nothing that we know about nature contradicts in principle any such working harmony. Nature remains a kind of emergent probability. Scientists, philosophers, theologians, and mystics too, keep learning more and more about what nature can actually do. In fact, the cultural "turn to the subject" has resulted in many new insights into human potentialities in the realm of the spirit.

Second, although the field is theoretically open, we should use Occam's razor to avoid unnecessary multiplicity. The reasonable presumption is that an event or experience is natural, not preternatural. A heavy burden of proof always rests on whoever appeals to the miraculous or diabolical. Unless the evidence is compelling, mysticism should not readily be attributed to a *deus ex machina,* however pious and humble such recourse may sound. If an extraordinary grace is a prerequisite, and it conceivably could be, the need must be shown positively, for the presumption favors the ordinary potentialities of graced nature.

Third, the testimony of some mystics—the major argument for an extraordinary component in mysticism—must pass careful hermeneutic scrutiny. Often their accounts have differed significantly. Fully aware of the gratuity of grace and the generosity of God from whom all good things come, mystics are not as a group either culturally or scientifically versed in the capacities of human nature. The accounts of Christian mystics or about them were written by persons with little knowledge of physiology, psychology, psychiatry, or of such specific matters as hypnosis, auto-suggestion, progressive relaxation, biofeedback, autogenics, and drugs, or of the psychic accomplishments of Yogis, Zen Buddhists, Shamans, Dervishes, Voodoo practitioners, and witch-doctors, to name but a few of the many, in and out of organized religion, who achieve remarkably altered states for themselves or others.

Fourth, mystical theologians have relied heavily on a frequent assertion of the mystics that the mystical experience was not subject to their will, that it came and went as God chose not as they would have chosen.

As a matter of fact, a large segment of our personal and even daily lives has proved to be independent of our control. For example, everyone seeks insights, but the light does not always come. Artists beseech the muse for inspiration, often without success. Authors are subject to writer's block, and then for no apparent reason the words start to flow. Sometimes, people cannot control their anger or jealousy, cannot remove distractions from their prayers or burning temptations from their imaginations. They cannot stay awake at Mass and cannot go to sleep at night.

Familiar with that lack of control, one might well expect that mystical experience would not always be present on demand. It involves levels of consciousness which transcend the ordinary multiplicity of concrete images to focus totally on the incomprehensible God. Moreover, it requires a supreme simplification and unification of the mind and a great intensity of pure love. To get everything into harmony at the same time is not easy. Regrettably, so-called "peak experiences," even when clearly secular, are not usually at our beck and call.

Fifth, despite the widespread assertion that the experience is a gift, different in kind from everything else that they have known, Christian mystics often assure those who aspire to the contemplative life that prayer and fidelity will lead them to the fountain. On the authority of the mystics, some theologians spoke of infused contemplation as being in the ordinary course of spiritual development, even to the point of insisting that infused contemplation was necessary for true holiness.[71] The reasoning was that if God commands us to be holy as he is holy, and if to achieve holiness we need the purifications of infused contemplation, the nights of the senses and spirit, then there must be a universal call to such mystic states, which are thus in the normal course of spiritual development. The emphasis was placed on divine gratuity rather than human potentiality: the grace is extraordinary, but God will normally grant it in response to prayer and good works. The line between acquired and infused contemplation becomes almost invisible.

Sixth, from a different perspective, we look at the possible linkage between holiness and mystical experience. Here we venture into the inner realm of the spirit known fully only to God. Empirically speaking, it is not clear that all holy people are mystics or that mystics are always the holiest of holy people. We are prompted to query: Why does not God give the choice graces of mysticism in proportion to a person's holiness? Thinking of mystic states as essentially "natural" suggests a possible explanation. On the "natural" level, there may be impediments to formless prayer, suspension of the faculties, trance, or heightened sense of union. Limiting factors such as genetic variations, psychoneuroses, hormonal or electrical imbalance, hyperkinetic tendencies, deep-seated traumas, resistance to interiority: these may keep very holy persons from a mystical experience or paradoxically may foster it in some who are much less holy.

On the other hand, non-mystical persons might have an implicit mystical life or a minimally perceptible infused contemplation, which muted experience might serve rather as the context of their dynamic active life than as the explicit focal point of an interior awareness of God's presence. Both types would be aware of God and both would conform to God's will, but they would experience God very differently. Perhaps one person would experience enlightenment, the other strengthening, as the Carmelite, Ruth Burrows, has suggested.[72] Both would enjoy a graced participation, but only through the prism of their unique psyches, their holiness distinguished but not limited by differences.

Seventh and finally, the advantages of recognizing a natural component in the mystical experience are significant. As a skill that can be learned and taught with great profit, as a natural operation that has been graced, it reveals the unfolding of the germinal gift that God has implanted in the human subject. Mysticism emerges not as an adventitious exception but as the divinely planned response to the universal call to realize God's self-communication. Thus mystical experience can manifest dramatically what God has done for all human beings: all have the chance to be his adopted sons and daughters, to share in the trinitarian life, to become in this life conscious of the presence of God through an intensely personal, though currently mediated, immediacy—it is the call to become a theophany.

The Symbolization Process

On the assumption that the specific difference between the ordinary and the mystical life of a Christian is a "natural" development, I shall focus now on a central and learnable process, which complements holiness in fostering states of heightened consciousness. This process is the conscious opening of the soul to God through faith and love, which opening is a quasi–symbol of the divine presence. The points to be considered are: the overall context, the symbolic core, the spiritual power, the possible misinterpretation, and the practical directives.

1. Some preliminary observations will help to put the issue in context. Human beings seek to know God, but even mystics can have no immediate knowledge of God in this life. Whoever knows God does so mediately; that means, through created effects. So a prime task is

to determine what type of created mediation will best enable a person to become fully conscious of God.

The fact that no finite creature can adequately mediate the infinite God is the underlying justification for moving from the kataphatic path to the apophatic. The vehicles of transition are one or more symbols, which capture this creaturely inadequacy and thus better convey the truth about the divine essence than do other created resemblances. But they contain the seeds of their own demise as they carry out their pedagogical function of leading the mind—more obviously in the higher reaches of prayer—to reject created forms including these very symbols. This emptying procedure characterizes the apophatic way. So we ask: Is it conceivable that anything could be introduced into that void without destroying the void?

We answer that question by asking another: What is supposed to be going on in the mind that has voided itself of created forms and inordinate desires? From our earlier examination of negative apophatics, it is clear that just being empty-headed is not enough for mystical experience; in fact, it is a major obstacle. What is required is positive apophatics with its openness to the positive nothingness that is God. Let us examine this positive apophatics more closely.

2. A clue to the solution of this elusive problem lies in scrutinizing further the function of symbols. Symbols are definitely created effects, but can any one of them or all of them together adequately mediate the divine? The very thought of introducing even one symbol into the apophatic way seems uncomfortably close to reducing the apophatic to the kataphatic. Before suggesting certain necessary distinctions, let us recall the general definition, which we developed in the chapter on kataphatics: Religious symbolization is an act of the mind using things or events analogously to produce meanings and feelings about limit situations, thereby tending to unite the person using the symbol with the being symbolized or conversely to separate the person from the non-being symbolized.

The apophatic realm is characterized by unrestricted openness in knowing and loving God. Clearly, this openness is a created effect; more significantly, it is also a means of mediation. Through consciousness of its own unrestricted openness, the subject becomes aware of the infinite presence of God. The apophatic way is a *faute de mieux* mediation of divine immediacy. For what else remains if created analogies fail, except to make a virtue of emptiness? We ask then how that empty mediation takes place. The proposed answer is that the mediation results from a special type of symbol, or better a quasi-symbol, unique to each person, namely, the mind as conscious of its own active and unrestricted openness. Through self-consciousness, the apophatic mind expands obliquely into God-consciousness, reaching an interface with the divine.

To avoid the appearance of reducing apophatics to kataphatics, we make the following observations. Kataphatics goes as far as it can in intending creatures as a means of God-consciousness. It is most successful with open-ended symbols, which are replete with finitude and suggest the insufficiency of all things as mediators of the divine. More radically, however, apophatics bypasses even these symbols in refusing to intend any creature at all as a means of God-consciousness.

What does a person intend when he prays apophatically? Only God in both his knowing and loving. He knows that his mind cannot fathom the mystery that is God, but with a kind of negative insight he eliminates from his mind everything that is not God. And he intends God alone by loving him with his whole heart. This twofold intentionality toward the divine does not of itself give heightened consciousness of God, but it is the indispensable foundation.

The next step is taken by having recourse to the quasi-symbol of which we spoke, one that differs from an ordinary symbol in that intentionality is replaced by self-consciousness. Though intending only God, the apophatic is still conscious of his own openness to God, for self-consciousness is intrinsic to all mental operations. Thus the apophatic is able to transcend all creatures including himself and remain conscious of that transcending, too. But it is a consciousness without introspection, which is a kind of intentionality and which would make the subject present to himself as an object. That is why the term quasi-symbol is more accurate and why the distinction between kataphatic and apophatic is not abrogated and why the security of the apophatic void is not violated.

3. The apophatic mind is both a knower and a mediator, a symbolizer and a symbol, and it is conscious that God, who is symbolized, is present directly and intimately but only mediately. So fundamental and intense is this inner experience that mystics speak of it as occurring at the apex of the soul, for it touches the deepest exigencies of the human spirit. This phrase does not refer to an anatomical point but to an experiential peak as transcendently lofty as the soul can reach in meeting the transcendent God. What this unrestricted openness does in fostering mystical experience is to relate powerfully and unequivocally the basic orientations or potencies of our nature to God as their fulfillment. All persons have a natural desire for the intelligible, for the real and the true, and for the good. This thrust toward the fullness

of transcendent reality becomes concretely experienced through positive apophatics. Self-consciousness of this ongoing expansion affords the best mediation of the divine. Openness in knowing and loving fashions the apophatic into both the mediating agent and the living symbol of God.

4. Unfortunately, the experiential reality may be misinterpreted. Denis the Areopagite has suggested in his distinction, which we have already seen, between similar and dissimilar symbols how this error may take place. He preferred the dissimilar symbols because they keep the mind from confusing the symbolized with the symbol, for example, by envisaging the Father as actually an old man. The sense of heightened consciousness may, however, prompt a person falsely to identify human nature with the divine. The prevalence of monistic and pantheistic interpretations of religious experience show how easily and how frequently that confusion occurs. The possibility of abuse, however, does not invalidate its proper use, but it does indicate something of the power of this inner symbol. Moreover, it also underscores the need that all involved in spirituality have for sound religious training in addition to prayer.

5. If properly understood, the open mind as a symbol of God helps explain something of the mystery of mysticism and of the overall genesis of a heightened awareness of the presence of God. Practical directives for making proper use of this quasi-symbol have already been mentioned and will just be recalled briefly. There are three basic ones. First, there must be a wholehearted love of God and conformity to his will. As a by-product inordinate desires are eliminated. Second, for full purity and scope on the cognitive level, there must be the rejection of created forms, thus facilitating the natural rest and related natural phenomena, which are to serve as a vehicle for an intensified experience of the divine. Third and concomitantly with the other two, there must be a profound sense of interiority to facilitate an expansion of consciousness, thereby making the opening of the mind experientially symbolic of the presence of God.

These directives indicate learnable skills, which normally can bring the graced subject to a heightened consciousness of the divine. Of course, this attainment presupposes that the graced man or woman has responded with faith to the love that the Spirit pours forth in their hearts. Only on a foundation of loving faith, can true mystical capabilities develop through the practice of the "natural" techniques that enable the subject to open mind and heart to God and to experience its own openness as a quasi-symbol of the divine presence bringing it into the intimacy of a mystical union.

CONCLUSION

The techniques of Christian mysticism involve the total subject, mind and body. Since mysticism is heightened consciousness, psychological operations are primary; but since mystics are embodied spirits, physiological operations, too, have an indispensable role. Of course, this mind-body unit is a graced nature, so both the psychological and the physiological participate, but differently, in the same supernatural realm.

The justification for speaking of techniques at all has been the need for disposing the subject for this more intense consciousness of God. Techniques, as suitable means for achieving goals, have long been a standard part of various traditions of spirituality. Accumulating techniques is not equivalent to forming an instruction manual for a machine, but rather to teaching conscious subjects the way through their own graced actions of authentic and fruitful living in the presence of God.

More specifically, since the distinction between the normal life of grace and the mystical life seems essentially "natural," the learning of techniques becomes part of the challenge of a life of heightened consciousness of the presence of God. The true lover seeks every means to grasp the beauty of the beloved.

6

The First Principle of Christian Mysticism

✧　　　✧　　　✧

*He that has my commandments and keeps them, he it is
that loves me; and he that loves me will be loved by my
Father and I will love him and manifest myself to him.*

Jn 14:21

Every life is structured, but not every life is well-structured. Kant
made a useful distinction between maxims and principles. Maxims are
the subjective generalizations that we live by; principles are the objective moral norms that should inspire our maxims. Since everyone
has religious maxims, negative or positive, a major spiritual task is to
discern one's personal maxims—what guidelines one actually follows
—and then if need be to bring them in harmony with true principles.

Spirituality is primarily practical; it looks to action, to love in
action. We achieve union with God by an ongoing series of decisions
that open up the mind to consciousness of the divine presence. We
are, in Albert Camus' words, the sum total of our choices. Habitual
ways of action spring from internalized maxims. The test of authentic
spirituality depends on the principles that are at work in our lives
universalizing our maxims; that is, making our maxims sure guides
which all right-minded men and women, faced with the same set of
circumstances, would obey.

Having examined the transition from kataphatics to apophatics
and having seen the techniques and methods available to heighten
consciousness of the presence of God, we need to consolidate further
our notions of mysticism.[1] A life of prayer, directed as it is to union
with God, needs a unifying principle, which will integrate theory as
well as practice. Now a principle is a beginning, a starting point from
which being or knowledge proceeds. Both aspects, the existential and
the cognitive, are operative in mystical theology, which seeks the

148

means and the meaning of divine union. In the discourse after the Last Supper, Jesus formulated just such a twofold principle:

> He that has my commandments and keeps them, he it is that loves me; and he that loves me will be loved by my Father and I will love him and manifest myself to him (Jn 14:21).[2]

This principle with a promise—obedience leads to presence—coordinates law and love and light. Law sets up the norm, love fulfills it, and light results. When asked for clarification, Jesus repeated the principle, rephrasing it slightly but without changing it substantially; for the abiding presence of the Revealer and the Revealed, Jesus and his Father, form the core of the manifestation.

> Judas, not the Iscariot, said to him, "Lord how is it that you will manifest yourself to us and not to the world?" Jesus answered and said to him, "If anyone loves me, he will keep my word, and my Father will love him and we will come to him and make our abode with him" (Jn 14:22–23).

Transcending national and sectarian boundaries, Jesus issues an invitation to everyone, but reveals the law of love as the condition of vision. He will manifest himself only to those who keep his word, his commandments—the two are synonymous here. Unfortunately, the world will not experience this manifestation, because, not believing in him, it does not do his will. Nevertheless, Jesus does not dispel the world's unbelief by an overwhelming theophany. He has given to the world all that is necessary. If it is to realize this promised manifestation it must do so the only way possible, by faith operating through love.

What I propose here is to examine the implications of the words of Jesus: "I will manifest myself to him." I shall look at three areas: first, the Johannine context, focusing on the indwelling of the Paraclete, the Spirit of Jesus, and its effects as experienced by believers; second, the mystical interpretation given by the two Carmelite Doctors of the Church, Teresa of Avila and John of the Cross; and third, the resolution of difficulties, harmonizing the mystical interpretations with the modern exegetical understanding of the text. Together, these three considerations will help us appreciate the richness of this promised manifestation and unify our response to it.

The Johannine Context

The discourse after the Last Supper (Jn 13–17) reveals the full dimensions of the promise of Jesus to manifest himself to those who love him. This manifestation is essentially the experience of oneness which results in the soul from the effects of the indwelling Paraclete, the Spirit of Jesus. In this section, we shall discuss four observations about this Johannine revelation: first, the ground is the indwelling of the Paraclete; second, love, peace, and joy are the effects of this indwelling; third, together these effects give the experience of oneness; and fourth, this unitive experience is the promised manifestation of the presence of Jesus.

The indwelling of the Paraclete enables Jesus, though he is with the Father, to be present to his disciples. The biblical testimony is straightforward. In the post-resurrectional interim, at least between the Ascension and Parousia, Jesus does not appear as visibly present to the believers. Jesus, however, has sent to them the Paraclete, that is, the Holy Spirit as his personal presence. The promise of Jesus is thus fulfilled through the indwelling of the Paraclete. Raymond Brown summarized the scriptural evidence thus:

> The one whom John calls "another Paraclete" is another Jesus. Since the Paraclete can come only when Jesus departs, the Paraclete is the presence of Jesus when Jesus is absent. Jesus' promise to dwell within his disciples is fulfilled in the Paraclete. It is no accident that the first passage containing Jesus' promise of the Paraclete (xiv 16–17) is followed immediately by the verse which says, "I am coming back to you."[3]

The effects of the indwelling, peace and joy and the love they come from, show how personal and intense this presence can be. And certainly, whether or not we call it mystical, it is a peak religious experience. Let us look, then, at three perceptible effects of the indwelling Paraclete: love, joy, and peace.

The experience of love is the root of the other two effects, but the Johannine emphasis on love as a keeping of the commandments—its truest test—should not make us think of love as only a legalistic fulfillment of duty. Fundamentally, love is a personal response to goodness. As envisaged in the Last Discourse, both loving and being loved are rich experiences to which the words, "Abide in my love" (Jn 15:9), invite us. It is a call to the kind of experience that St. Paul described to the Ephesians when he prayed that the Spirit might inwardly strengthen the believers, "that Christ may dwell in your hearts by faith, that being rooted and founded in love, you may be able to comprehend with all the saints, what is the breadth and length and height and depth, to know also the love of Christ which surpasses all understanding, that you may be filled unto the fullness of God" (Eph 3:17–19).

The experience of peace, the fruition of love, is the most obvious characteristic of mystical contemplation. For here growth in prayer is marked by a gradual pacifying of the mind, beginning with one's loving, in the appropriately named prayer of quiet. It is not surprising, therefore, that Jesus, after promising to manifest himself to those who love him, would say a few verses later, "Peace I leave with you, my peace I give unto you, not as the world gives do I give you peace. Let not your heart be troubled, nor let it be afraid" (Jn 14:27). Two chapters farther along, we read: "These things have I spoken to you that you may have peace" (Jn 16:33). This promised peace, which comes from the indwelling Paraclete, elevates, directs, and intensifies the believer's power to love. That is why it is called a peace which the world cannot give, for it rises from the depths of the love that is poured forth by the Spirit.

The experience of joy becomes gradually but intermittently more intense as love deepens and prayer progresses. Although many trials, persecutions, and dark nights may be the plight of the believer, he is assured, "Your sorrow will be turned into joy" (Jn 16:20). And this will be "a joy that no one can take from you" (Jn 16:22). Moreover, it is a fruit of prayer, "Ask and you shall receive that your joy may be full" (Jn 16:24). What must we do on our part to achieve this abundant joy? Obey with love.

> As the Father has loved me, so have I loved you. Remain on in my love. And you will remain in my love if you keep my commandments, just as I have kept my Father's commandments and remain in his love. I have said this to you that my joy may be yours and your joy may be fulfilled (Jn 15:9–11).

Together, the effects of love, peace, and joy lead to the experience of oneness. Each is a subjective sharing in the life of Jesus, and through them we become aware of his presence. He tells us, as we have seen, "remain on in my *love*," for "my *peace* I give to you," that "my *joy* may be yours." But why does he share these experiences with his followers?

That they all may be one, just as you, Father, in me and I in
you, that they may be [one] in us. Thus the world may believe
that you sent me. I have even given to them the glory which
you have given me, that they may be one, just as we are one, I
in them and you in me, that they may be brought to completion as one (Jn 17:21–23).

This passage establishes the mutual indwelling of the Father and
the Son through the Spirit as the model and the source of the unity of
Christians. So complete is the primary unity that those who see Jesus
see the Father. To bring the believers into this unity is the work of the
Paraclete, the Spirit of Jesus. By means of the indwelling of the Paraclete, the faith which operates through love brings the believer to an
awareness of his union with the Father and the Son. This process,
culminating in experiential unity, begins with foundational unity; for
only if the branches are part of the vine can they bear fruit. The Spirit
of Jesus must dwell within us before he will, in response to our love,
manifest himself.

The unitive experience is the promised manifestation: "completion as one." The intimate awareness of divine union that the indwelling Paraclete works in believers brings to a climax the self-revelation
of Jesus on earth. Conscious presence is the substance of the promise.
For Jesus promises the believer a light, a knowing, a revelation. Before saying explicitly that he will manifest himself, Jesus clearly prepares the way for a true understanding of what the promise means. He
speaks of another Paraclete, the Spirit of Truth whom the Father will
send: "You do recognize him since he remains with you and is in you"
(Jn 14:17). Jesus tells his disciples that he will go away, but will return
and that, although the world will not see him any more: "You will see
me because I have life and you will have life" (Jn 14:19). This thought
he elaborates in the next verse: "In that day, you will recognize that I
am in the Father and you are in me and I in you." (Jn 14:20).

Only after indicating the cognitive quality of the new experience,
did Jesus promise that if anyone loves him, "I will *manifest* myself to
him" (Jn 14:21). He then explains what the indwelling Paraclete will
do: "He will *teach* you everything and *remind* you of all that I told you
(Jn 14:26); and, as the Spirit of Truth, "He will *guide* you along the
way of truth . . . and will *declare* to you all the things to come"
(Jn 16:13).

The Paraclete's mission is, therefore, to complete the mission of
Jesus. Brown thus concluded: "Jesus bore God's name because he
was the revelation of God to men; the Spirit is sent in Jesus' name

because he unfolds the meaning of Jesus for men."[4] Bultmann expressed the same idea more succinctly: "The Spirit, like Jesus himself, is Revealer."[5]

In brief, Jesus removes himself from our physical presence so
that, through his Spirit, he can more perfectly communicate to us his
divine presence and thus reveal his Father. So perfect is this communication that the first disciples of Jesus have no advantage over those of
the latter days in terms of their faith relationship. "For both," Bultmann observed, "he stands the same distance away."[6] And he quoted
approvingly Kierkegaard's remark: "There is no disciple at second
hand. The first and the last are essentially on the same plane."[7] Thus
to all generations, Jesus will manifest or reveal himself, but only
through the response of faith to the self-revelation of God.

Rudolph Schnackenburg clarified the interplay between revelation and faith. "Revelation is self-disclosure on the part of God."[8] But
this communication is mediated through the prophets and above all
by the Son who is the culmination and "the final and perfect revealer."[9] In opposition to Bultmann's narrowly existential view that
revelation is not enlightenment but a happening, he stated that John
teaches that revelation includes both the fact that Jesus is sent as the
revealer and the content or message of that revelation.[10] Faith, for
Schnackenburg, is both intellectual and existential—involving "a total personal commitment to God" and not simply a naked intellectual
assent.[11] Moreover, he noted the dual character of revelation, something we considered earlier in contrasting the disciples and the world:

> Divine revelation is, therefore, "manifest" insofar as God
> potentially reveals and makes accessible to every man both
> himself and the revelation of salvation. Yet in another sense,
> it remains "hidden" insofar as it is not actually accessible to
> all men but only to those who believe.[12]

So far, from our analysis of the Johannine context, we see that the
promised manifestation of Jesus comes primarily from the indwelling
Paraclete, the Spirit of Jesus, and secondarily from the love—poured
forth in our hearts by the Spirit—which brings peace and joy culminating in the experience of oneness. The awareness of this indwelling
constitutes the fulfillment of the promise that Jesus made to manifest
himself to all who believe in him and keep his commandments. Our
next task, then, is to discover how actually manifest this divine revelation can be to those who excel in that total response which is loving
faith. We shall consider the degree of light that mystical experience

sheds on the Johannine text and the intensity of the promised manifestation.

The Mystical Interpretation

Two great Carmelite mystics, both Doctors of the Church, have commented briefly on the Johannine text. Their writings are abundantly empirical, though clearly grounded in Thomistic theology. Of the two, Teresa of Avila is the more descriptive; John of the Cross, the more abstract. We shall consider Teresa first as she reports her own experiences and then John as he discusses, also using psychological data, the more theoretical structure of Christian mysticism.

In all her writings Teresa of Avila insisted on the necessity of the law of love—conformity to the will of God. For her, love meant essentially that the wills of lovers be in harmony. Without this loving harmony, prayer is sterile; but with it, lavishly fruitful. She summed up her theology of prayer thus:

> All that the beginner in prayer has to do—and you must not forget this, for it is very important—is to labor and be resolute and prepare himself with all possible diligence to bring his will into conformity with the will of God. As I shall say later, you may be quite sure that this comprises the very greatest perfection that can be attained on the spiritual road. The more perfectly a person practices it, the more he will receive of the Lord and the greater the progress he will make on this road.[13]

What is this great spiritual attainment? For Teresa of Avila and for most Christian mystics, it is transformation in God. The year before her death, she wrote a spiritual testimony, a report to the Bishop of Osma, who had once been her confessor. By this time, she had already experienced the transforming union, or spiritual marriage as she usually called it. In treating of this consummate union and the concomitant intellectual vision of the Trinity, she referred to the Johannine promise of which her experiences were a fulfillment:

> My interior peace and the little which joys or troubles can do to deprive me permanently of this presence make it so impossible for me to doubt the presence of the three Persons that I seem clearly to be experiencing the truth of those words of

St. John, that he will make His abode with the soul [Jn 14:23]. And this not only through his grace, but because he is pleased to make the soul conscious of that presence which brings so many blessings that they cannot all be described.[14]

This awareness of presence is not merely the fruit of any act of faith. Nor does it bypass faith. Faith must last as long as life does. Rather it is illumined faith, an intensification through unifying love, peace, and joy of the faith experience. It is indicative of this affective aspect to note how, as Teresa described this intimate presence at its very apogee, she was still sensitively preoccupied with conformity to God's will:

There is no need to go in search of reflections to know that God is there. This is almost my normal state, except when I am seriously oppressed by ill-health. Sometimes it seems to be God's will that I should suffer and have no interior comfort, but never, even for a single moment, does my will swerve from the *will of God*. This submission to *his will* has such power over me that my soul desires neither death nor life save for short periods when it longs to see God. But then its realization of the presence of these three Persons becomes so vivid as to afford relief to the distress caused by its absence from God and sustains the desire to live, if such be *His will* in order that it may serve Him better.[15]

John of the Cross, in speaking of the Johannine text, complemented the interpretation given by Teresa that the promise is fulfilled by mystical experience. For both, it was applied to the same kinds of experience, the transforming union and intellectual visions; and for both, it was part of the journey in faith, the sole proximate and proportionate means to divine union.[16] Although John spoke of "the abyss of faith where the understanding must remain in darkness and must journey in darkness,"[17] he affirmed, in the same context, the paradox that Christian mysticism consisted in an illumined faith. He thus described the process of that illumination:

The Holy Spirit illumines the understanding which is recollected, and illumines it according to the manner of its recollection, and the understanding cannot find any other and greater recollection than in faith; and thus the Holy Spirit will illumine it in naught more than in faith. For the purer and the more refined in faith is the soul, the more it has of the infused charity of God; and the more charity it has, the more it is illumined and the more gifts of the Holy Spirit are communicated to it, for charity is the cause and the means whereby they are communicated to it.[18]

The direct references that John of the Cross made to the Johannine text are found in two different works. In the first, *The Ascent of Mount Carmel,* he discussed the stages that lead to the transforming union. Of special interest to us is his treatment of intellectual visions, like Teresa of Avila's vision of the Trinity, which we mentioned earlier. The function that they have in the developing life of contemplation will help to clarify the meaning of the gospel word, "manifest."

John of the Cross distinguished intellectual visions from sensory and imaginative ones, from which he would have souls detach themselves, for they easily impede union with God. But intellectual visions are a touch of divinity, an experience and a taste of God, "a part of the union towards which we are directing the soul; to which end we are teaching it to detach and strip itself of all other apprehensions."[19] Moreover, only those who have reached the state of union can have these manifestations of knowledge which "can come only to the soul that attains union with God, because they are themselves that union."[20] It is significant here that he explicitly referred this naked knowledge or intellectual vision of God to the promise of Jesus. In fact, he explained how to work for this great grace:

And the means by which God will do this must be humility and suffering for the love of God with resignation as regards all reward; for these favors are not granted to the soul which still cherishes attachments, inasmuch as they are granted through a very special love of God toward the soul which loves him likewise with great detachment. It is to this that the Son of God referred in St. John. [He quoted Jn 14:21.] Herein are included the kinds of knowledge and touches to which we are referring, which God manifests to the soul that truly loves him.[21]

John of the Cross spoke at great length of intellectual visions, which are sublime experiences of one or more attributes of God; for example, his omnipotence, fortitude, goodness, or sweetness.[22] Significantly, he later contrasted the illumination from these visions with the illumination derived from faith. He asserted: "In that illumination of truths, the Holy Spirit indeed communicates some light to the soul, yet the light given in faith—in which there is no clear understanding —is qualitatively as different from the other as is the purest gold from the basest metal, and quantitatively as is the sea from a drop of sea water."[23] God can grant extraordinary graces to whomever he chooses. But it is important to note that these visions depend on faith and are in some way a by-product of the union with God that can be achieved only through faith. We have not discussed these special graces at any great length, choosing rather to emphasize that which is most fundamental and most perfect in the heightened consciousness of union with God, namely, the dark vision of faith.

The second source of the references made by John of the Cross to the Johannine text is a book which dealt with perfection within perfection, *The Living Flame of Love*. Earlier, he had discussed at great length the transforming union, here he even surpassed himself in the depth and sublimity of his analysis. "For although in the stanzas which we expounded above [in the *Spiritual Canticle*], we spoke of the most perfect degree of perfection to which a man may attain in this life, which is transformation in God, nevertheless these stanzas [in *The Living Flame of Love*] treat of a love which is even more complete and perfected within the same state of transformation."[24] In this rarefied mystical context, the reference in his Prologue to John 14:23 dramatically reveals the implications Christ's promise had for John of the Cross:

> There is no reason for marvelling that God should grant such high and rare favors to those on whom he bestows consolations. For if we consider that he is God and that he bestows them as God, with infinite love and goodness, it will not seem to us unreasonable. For God said that the Father and the Son and the Holy Spirit would come to him that loved him and make their abode in him, and this would come to pass by his making him live and dwell in the Father and the Son and the Holy Spirit, in the life of God, as the soul explains in these stanzas.[25]

John of the Cross made two redactions of the *Flame;* in both of them the section quoted from the prologue is the same. But in the second redaction, when commenting on the first stanza of his poem, he repeated the substance of the prologue section with some minor variations and one important addition concerning the means to be used. That change is significant here, not because he spoke of purgation and charity as a prerequisite for divine union—that is his standard teaching—but because he assumed that if these are perfected, the soul will then experience, specifically as a fulfillment of Christ's promise, the mystical glories about which he was writing.

> And it must not be held incredible that in a faithful soul which has already been tried and proven in the fire of tribulations and trials, and found faithful in love, there should be fulfilled that which was promised by the Son of God— namely that if any man love him, the Holy Spirit would come within him and would abide and dwell in him.[26]

To sum up what we have seen so far of the Carmelite interpretation of the Johannine text, we can make three conclusions: that the promise of Christ issues a general invitation to the fullness of the mystical life; that the mystical life consists in illumined faith, the soul's experience of being united with God; and that this illumination depends on love which is characterized by perfect detachment from creatures and perfect conformity to the will of God.

The Resolution of Difficulties

Despite the cogency of the mystics' understanding of the promise of Jesus, some exegetes have shown a deep reluctance to admit any mystical dimension whatsoever. Even Raymond E. Brown, wide-ranging and balanced though he is, seems to share slightly in this anti-mystical bias. He is at pains to safeguard the fundamental meaning of the text from a facilely romantic or vaguely gnostic misunderstanding that the word "mystical" might suggest. And yet, authentic Christian mysticism must be grounded in the New Testament, including the Gospel of John.

We shall examine three caveat-propositions derived from Brown. A clear appreciation of them will sharpen our focus on the richness of the experience that Jesus has promised to those who love him and on the relationship of that promise to true mysticism. In general, we can agree with the prudence of these warnings without, however, having to conclude that a mystical interpretation or application of the text is unjustified. Rather we shall be able to see how harmoniously the Carmelite interpretation accords with the essential holding of modern Catholic exegesis. The three propositions are: (1) The promised manifestation is not reducible exclusively to a vertical relationship with

God; (2) The promised manifestation is not restricted to the mystic presence encountered by an ascetical elite; and, (3) The promised manifestation is not equivalent to a direct gnostic vision of the Godhead. Let us now examine each proposition separately.

First, when Brown spoke of Johannine unity, he distinguished two kinds: the horizontal which the believers have among themselves and the vertical which they have with the Father and the Son. Both kinds are, of course, made possible through the presence of the Paraclete. Brown did make clear: "Unity for John is not reducible to a mystical relationship with God."[27] But he did not reduce unity to the horizontal or communal level either. "The vertical dimension, apparent in the frequent statements about immanence in the Last Discourse . . . means that the unity is not simply human fellowship or the harmonious interaction of Christians."[28]

Certainly, Christian mystics, although they appear to emphasize the vertical relationship, are keenly aware of the horizontal requisites. No true mystic attains the desired union with Jesus Christ, unless he or she shares in this love for the members of his Body. Thus, Teresa of Avila, writing about the Fifth Mansions of *The Interior Castle,* where she discussed the prayer of simple union—in which the intellect and the interior powers are made passive, the will having already been made so in the prayer of quiet—explained the necessity of both dimensions. First, she set up the goal: "What do you suppose his will is, daughters? That we should be altogether perfect and one with him and the Father as in his Majesty's prayer" (Jn 17:21–23).[29] She then elaborated on the necessity for this twofold love for anyone who hopes to enter the Fifth Mansions and attain union:

> The Lord asks only two things of us: love for His Majesty and love for our neighbor. It is for these two virtues that we must strive, and if we attain them perfectly we are doing his will and so shall be united with him. But, as I have said, how far are we from doing these two things in the way that we ought for a God who is so great! May his Majesty be pleased to give us grace so that we may deserve to reach this state, as it is in our power to do so if we wish.[30]

Second, the recognition of the need to preserve the universal coverage of the promise—that the manifestation will be made to *everyone* who believes in Jesus and loves him—sometimes leads to an anti-mystical imbalance. Thus, for example, in writing of the promised manifestation (Jn 14:21), Brown stated that the passage is "not concerned with the presence of Jesus encountered by the mystics: the presence of Jesus is promised not to an ascetical elite, but to Christians in general."[31]

Brown understands the promise to include all believers, not just Christian ascetics. And rightly so, granted the fulfillment of the requisite condition. But what is that? Brown answers: "The condition upon which the indwelling depends: keeping Jesus' commandments and thus loving him."[32] Those who have fulfilled this condition most profoundly and wholeheartedly can be expected to experience this indwelling most fully. There is no doubt in Brown's mind that John considered presence to be proportionate to love. He states explicitly: "The presence of Jesus in the Christian stands in parallelism with the presence of love in the Christian."[33] He goes even further: "The indwelling and the recognition [of the Spirit of Truth] are coordinate. As Bengel put it, the lack of recognition rules out indwelling, while indwelling is the basis of recognition."[34] An ascetic and mystic, such as John of the Cross, would readily subscribe to this language. His own formulation is unequivocal:

> God communicates himself most to that soul that has progressed furthest in love; namely, that has its will in the closest conformity with the will of God. And the soul that has attained complete conformity and likeness of will is totally united and transformed into God supernaturally.[35]

Third, a concern over the syncretic character of much current spirituality and a lingering fear of gnostic tendencies in general has prompted Brown to take a cautious approach to "mystical" interpretations of St. John. Thus, in speaking of that great text, "That they may know you, the one true God, and Jesus Christ, the one whom you sent" (Jn 17:30), Brown called it "the most 'gnostic' statement in the Bible."[36] But he hastened to distinguish it from Gnosticism, "for it is rooted in a historic event in a way in which Gnostic thought is not."[37] He explained further, "Here 'know' means to be in a vital and intimate relationship with the Father and Jesus, and such a relationship comes through faith in Jesus and hearing his words."[38] Then he focused on a point that is crucial for us: "John never suggests that this relationship can come through ecstatic contemplation of the divinity as in the *Hermetica,* nor through a mystic vision of God, as in the mysteries."[39] To grant Brown's conclusion, however, in no way rules out a Johannine mysticism; but it does require us to specify what this mysticism involves.

A common misunderstanding of Christian mystical experience is that it affords, after heroic purification, a direct vision of the God-head. If so, the effects promised by Jesus—peace and joy and oneness —fall far short of this sublime gnosis, this face-to-face knowledge of God. But mystical experience and the beatific vision are not the same thing and John did not confuse them. After contrasting Jesus with Moses, he said: "No one has ever seen God; it is God the only Son, ever at the Father's side, who has revealed him" (Jn 1:18).[40]

In this connection, the Carmelite understanding of mystical experience proves fully in accord with scripture. Teresa of Avila stated the principle simply: "The soul recognizes the presence of God by the effects which he produces in the soul, for it is by that means that his Majesty is pleased to make his presence felt."[41] She developed this important observation more fully:

> A kind of consciousness of the presence of God . . . is often experienced, especially by those who have reached the Prayer of Union and the Prayer of Quiet. There we are on the point of beginning our prayer when we seem to know that he is hearing us by the spiritual feeling and effects of great love and faith of which we become conscious, and also by the fresh resolutions which we make with such deep emotion. This favor comes from God: and he to whom it is granted should esteem it highly for it is a very lofty form of prayer. But it is not vision.[42]

Teresa of Avila applied this same principle when she spoke of spiritual marriage in the Seventh Mansions of *The Interior Castle*. She related how her soul experienced "the greatest joy because Christ is now its life."[43] To assure herself of this special grace, she looked to the effects it produced in her soul:

> This, with the passage of time, becomes more evident through its effects; for the soul clearly understands by certain secret aspirations that it is endowed with life by God. Very often these aspirations are so vehement that what they teach cannot possibly be doubted; though they cannot be described, the soul experiences them very forcibly. One can only say that this feeling is produced at times by certain

delectable words which, it seems, the soul cannot help uttering, such as, "O life of my life and sustenance that sustains
me!" and things of that kind.[44]

John of the Cross dealt similarly with the possibility of a direct
vision of incorporeal or spiritual substances—souls, angels, God—
saying: "Although these visions of spiritual substances cannot be unveiled and be clearly seen in this life by the understanding, they can
nevertheless be perceived in the substance of the soul, with the
sweetest touches and unions, all of which belongs to spiritual feelings."[45] So, fundamentally and essentially, mysticism remains a faith
experience, not vision. "This dark, loving knowledge, which is faith,
serves as a means to Divine union in this life, even as, in the next life,
the light of glory serves as a means to the clear vision of God."[46] It is
easy to see how far this view is from any claim to gnostic immediacy
and how well it comports with the modalities of the Johannine
promise.

Finally, these three caveat-propositions which we have gathered
together from Brown's discussion—warning us against a mysticism
which is purely vertical, ascetically elitist, and presumptuously immediate—are not at variance with the Carmelite understanding of the
Johannine text, but rather, if understood fully, reinforce what is con-
stitutive of all sound Christian mysticism.

CONCLUSION

Our focus has been on the promise of Jesus to whomever loves
truly: "I will manifest myself to him." Both mystics and exegetes interpret the promised manifestation as a heightened consciousness of
union with Jesus through the indwelling of the Paraclete—the Holy
Spirit acting as the personal presence of the absent Jesus.

This promise gives a deep-seated confidence to those thirsting for
the presence of God. Such a theophany has become more than a
possibility; it is an assured probability for those who love Jesus and
keep his commandments. It is probable rather than certain, not because God does not want it, but because we may not will it purely
and perseveringly enough. God makes the offer and awaits our
acceptance.

The promised manifestation is not a direct vision of God but
rather an intimate sense of union with him through the effects of love,
joy, and peace culminating in the experience of oneness. St. John's

gospel contains explicit pledges of these effects: the Carmelite doctors use the Johannine texts to explain their own mystical experience and teaching. The highest mystical states, including the transforming union, are for them functions or fulfillments of this glorious promise.

It is not surprising that the first principle of Christian mysticism be found in St. John's gospel, which has been described as "the charter of mystics." For, as Brown observed, "The dominant interest in John is one of realized eschatology."[47] John, of course, also teaches an apocalyptic or future eschatology, but what is relevant for us is his emphasis on present actualizations: we already have eternal life; we now share in the glory which is to come; we experience through loving obedience the manifestation of Jesus himself.

Law and love and light, then, mark progressive phases in the heightening of our consciousness of God, through opening ourselves in obedience to his commands. This challenge of transcendence would clearly surpass our noblest efforts were it not for the promise and the presence of the Spirit of Jesus. Through the Paraclete, we can conform so perfectly to the will of God that—even in this life—we have a foretaste of that eternal Beauty, which alone can quiet the restless surgings of our soul.

7

Fulfillment in the Spirit

✧   ✧   ✧

Love the Love that loves you eternally.

John Ruusbroec*

The longer we study mysticism, the more clearly we see that techniques, principles, theories, even the scriptures themselves are not enough. We must do more than accept the truth, we must live the truth. Fulfillment comes to us through a process of self-transcendence, so that by our own actions elevated by grace we share consciously in divine life.

The story of personal holiness has its foundation in the Trinity as the beginning and the end of human life. It has its dynamism in its participation in the divine nature. And it has its final culmination on earth in a transforming union which reveals that the glorification of God is our sanctification. We shall examine these three aspects of human self-transcendence: its foundation, its participation, and its culmination.

The Trinitarian Foundation

Examining the role of the Trinity in mystical experience, we look at its inner life and its outer workings. Our primary focus in the intimate trinitarian realm is divine consciousness, the knowing and the loving shared by three conscious subjects. This perspective is obviously related to mysticism, which we have defined as a kind of heightened consciousness. Of special relevance is the role of the Spirit as

---

* John Ruusbroec, *Seven Steps in the Ladder of Spiritual Love*, Works, 2d. ed. rev. (Tielt: Uitgeverij Lannoo, 1944–1947), III, p. 268.

the mutual love of the Father and the Son. This mutuality is at the heart of our own experience of the triune God through the indwelling Spirit of Jesus.

The outer workings of the Trinity, the creation and elevation of humankind, reveal our destined share in divine consciousness. Through the missions of the Son and the Spirit, the Trinity enters our realm of spiritual existence in a new way. Accepting these truths in faith, we find them illumined by the mystical experience of the divine presence as truths not yet seen but already luminous.

The Inner Life

To understand what it means to be a mystic—one who is profoundly conscious of the presence of God—it is critical to note that divine consciousness is itself shared. For divine consciousness is not an entity added to each divine Person; it is identified with the divine nature, which is common to all three Persons. To be God is to be conscious. Through grace, human persons become participators in the divine nature and thus in divine consciousness. So divine Persons and human persons participate in the same divine consciousness—but very differently.

Indeed, consciousness is intrinsic to the actuality of every spiritual being. Whoever knows can know to the extent that he is; whatever is can be known to the extent that it is. As a pure act, God is supremely intelligent and intelligible, totally aware of his infinite nature and of all the ways it can be imitated.

It is important to realize that in God there is only one consciousness, though there are three subjects of consciousness; for the divine consciousness belongs to the divine nature which is participated in equally by the Father, Son, and Spirit—a unity of consciousness in a plurality of persons. Bernard Lonergan analyzed this fact from a subjective perspective:

> Where the act is one, the consciousness is one; but because there are many subjects, there are also many conscious subjects; and therefore it follows that the three subjects are conscious of one another through one consciousness which is possessed in different ways by the three.[1]

The three Persons share in the divine consciousness equally but differently. They do so differently, since they themselves are constituted by their opposed relationships; otherwise the three Persons would be one as is their nature. Using the formulation made definitive by St. Anselm, the Council of Florence in 1442 stated: "[In God] all is one, where there is no opposition of relationship" (*Omniaque sunt unum, ubi non obviat relationis oppositio*).[2] There is no need here to examine in detail the four subsistent relations; it will suffice to identify them briefly: the Father's generating of the Son is *paternity;* the Son's being generated by the Father is *filiation;* the Father's and Son's breathing forth of the Spirit is *active spiration;* and the Spirit's being so breathed forth is *passive spiration.* But only three relationships are really distinct (for active spiration does not oppose, except by a logical distinction, paternity and filiation).

As subsistent relations, these three divine Persons, though really distinct from one another, remain identified with their one conscious nature. Thus the Council of Florence stated: "On account of this unity, the Father is wholly in the Son and wholly in the Holy Spirit; the Son wholly in the Father and wholly in the Holy Spirit; the Holy Spirit is wholly in the Father and wholly in the Son."[3] Being "wholly in" one another means, as Lonergan pointed out, sharing in the same act of consciousness: "The individual Persons are really within the very consciousness of one another."[4] Without understanding fully how this takes place, we can still appreciate something of the ultimate perfection of intimacy.

The intimate self-communication of divine life through the triple participation in the one conscious nature is formulated by a concrete Greek word, *perichōresis,* a "going around." The derivation of the word is often taken to suggest a dancing around or about, as if the root were *perichoreuō.* The proper source, however, is *perichōreō,* which means to go round about, to come round to, to come to in succession. The mistake creates a felicitous image but an incorrect one.

The Greek term was translated into two Latin equivalents, first *circumincessio* and later *circuminsessio.* These words reflect a nuanced distinction: *circumincessio* (from *cedere,* to go or proceed) is closer to the Greek perspective and has a more dynamic or active emphasis, looking first at the plurality of Persons and then at their reciprocal identity with the one nature; *circuminsessio* (from *sedere,* to sit) has a more static emphasis, closer to the Latin perspective, looking first at the one nature and then at the threefold sharing in that nature. The two terms suggest movement and rest, the ebb and flow that Ruusbroec found in all creation and in the Trinity too.[5] To sum up, perichoresis is a conscious and reciprocal penetration, involving motion and rest, of the three divine Persons through their individual identity with the same divine nature.

This description will be helpful when, a little later, we discuss the human side of grace and indwelling in terms of what one might call a *participated perichoresis*—that is, a created mode of the divine reciprocity—as a means of understanding the trinitarian character of mystical consciousness, which is from the Father through the Son and in the Spirit. So far, we have been looking mainly at the inner trinitarian life (the immanent Trinity) and not at the Trinity in its relationship to human subjects (the economic Trinity).

Before returning to a more explicit analysis of mysticism, I must mention an aspect of the immanent Trinity that will also prove to be of fundamental importance to an understanding of the Spirit's mission, namely, the Spirit as the mutual bond of love uniting the Father and the Son.

This insight, which has its deepest roots in the central definition of God as love (1 Jn 4:16), has a long theological history; it has been used by Augustine, Hilary, Anselm, Richard of St. Victor, William of St. Thierry, Bonaventure, Aquinas, and others. Mystics, understandably, have found the notion immensely enlightening and strengthening, for it enables them to appreciate the indwelling of the Spirit and its connection with mystical consciousness. However, it also has a romantically memorable quality, which makes it vulnerable to anthropomorphic misunderstanding.

The Nicene-Constantinopolitan Creed speaks of the Spirit as the one "who proceeds from the Father and the Son" (*ex patre filioque procedit*).[6] The phrase, *filioque,* later added to the conciliar statement by the Latin church, occasioned an unresolved controversy between the Latins and the Greeks. Latin theologians have traditionally understood this procession as the hypostasizing of the love that the Father has for the Son and the Son has for the Father. The basis for thus speaking of the Spirit as the bond of mutual love is that what appears to be two acts of love is really one. The Father and the Son share the same conscious nature and love the same infinite goodness in one another; they do so by one act—for all their acts are identified with the one nature—the only difference is that they are two opposed centers of consciousness. The mutual love of the divine Goodness results in a third mutually opposed, subsistent relationship—the Spirit as the personification of this infinite and mutual loving.

William Hill, in countering Rahner's denial of mutual love between the Father and the Son on the grounds that "this would presuppose two acts," gave a fuller explanation of what we have been considering.

> But why could it not be the one act of two persons—in which the fullness of love demands not only lover and beloved (subject and object, agent and patient), but two who love and are loved in a single self-identical act of loving? If so then the Father loves as Father (i.e., paternally) and the Son loves as Son (i.e., filially), with the distinction being entirely on the level of that relationality. . . . And indeed, in the divine instance, the loving relationality would issue forth into a third person, the personification of that very love. . . . Rahner's view appears to confuse essential love in God with notional love. The former is activity and so a prerogative of the essence, the latter is a pure "regarding" that brings one into the realm of personal distinctions.[7]

Pertinent also is the clarification that Matthias Scheeben made, piercing through the ambiguity of words. He contrasted the Word of God (the Son) with the knowledge of God (the nature); similarly, he contrasted the Sigh of God (the Spirit) with the love of God (the nature).

> Since, as is always the case with God, no real composition is conceivable between the expression and the knowledge reflected in it, between the sigh and the love surging in it, the Word must really be the knowledge itself and the Sigh must really be the love itself. Then Word and the Sigh as such are produced, whereas the knowledge and the love as such are not produced.[8]

More pointedly, generation is the uttering of the Word, spiration is the outpouring of love. The infinite communication of the Word is a Person; the infinite communication of the love is a Person. All three Persons are identified with the wisdom and the goodness of God, with the act of knowing and the act of loving, but because of the opposition of their relationships, they are different centers of consciousness, different Persons.

The Outer Workings

The triune God also acts outside the Godhead; that is, acts *ad extra*. Generally speaking, these actions are common to all three Persons, not only in giving creatures existence but also in disposing them to participate in the divine. This elevation requires grace. Uncreated grace is primary and refers to the self-communication of God, by which we become participators in the divine life. Uncreated grace brings with it the created grace which actually empowers us to know and love God intimately. The Spirit is sent by the Father and the Son for a full trinitarian communication. The reference to created grace tells us that although the Spirit dwells personally within us, it is not through a hypostatic union but through a hypostatic presence; that is, we do not become God substantially, but we are related intimately to the divine Persons in our knowing and loving.

To understand these outer workings we shall look separately at two related notions, exemplarity and mission. The one looks more at nature, the other more at grace, but both are integrated existentially in graced nature.

1. *Exemplarity.* Many theologians—Bernard, Eckhart, Ruusbroec, and others—have made the notion of divine exemplars central to their spirituality in a profound effort to understand such words of revelation as: "God created man in his own image and likeness" (Gn 1:26–27); and Christ is "the image of the invisible God, the first born of every creature. For in him were all things created in heaven and on earth, visible and invisible" (Col 1:15–16).

Briefly, exemplarity means that from all eternity God is conscious of each one of his creatures and from all eternity decrees their existence and proper operations. These divine ideas are identified with the divine essence, in accordance with the principle of Aquinas: "Whatever is in God is God."[9] So each human being has been in God as an exemplar from all eternity. This truth does not mean that God loses his simplicity, but it does reflect his knowing and willing of what happens in time.

To the extent that we are aware of ourselves in our conformity with God's will, we can be conscious of these eternal exemplars and eternal norms as manifested in our concrete lives. We catch a glimpse of this reality by reason; moreover, we find through revelation that we are eternally destined to share in the divine life and consciousness.

Bernard of Clairvaux used the notion of exemplarity to explain the Genesis text about God's creating human beings in his own image and likeness. A human is eternally the image of God; over this similarity he has no control; it is his very nature, whether he is saint or sinner, blessed or damned. But being free, he can by his choices make his nature either upright (*recta*) or curved (*curva*); that is, either he freely reaches up to God or inordinately turns to creatures.[10] In other words, though the image stays the same, the likeness may vary.

For Bernard, the love of God alone perfects the likeness of those who begin their return to God from the realm of dissimilarity, *regio dissimilitudinis*.[11] To overcome this unlikeness, Bernard said, perfect love was needed: "The reason for loving God is God himself, the way is to love without measure (*modus sine modo diligere*)."[12] When the true divine likeness is perfectly restored, then the soul, like the Bride in the Canticle, achieves the answer to her cry, "Let him kiss me with the kiss of his lips" (Ct 1:1). The mystical marriage results from the out-pouring of the Spirit which unites the soul with God.[13] As Bernard wrote: "Such conformity joins the soul in marriage to the Word, when, being already like him in nature, she shows herself no less like unto him in will, loving as she is loved. If then she loves perfectly, she has become his bride."[14]

Exemplarity thus occasions a multileveled love: we love ourselves and others as ourselves, first of all because of the imperishable dignity of all human beings in their archetypal beauty. In fact, the radical dignity of all creatures forms a universal theophany urging the receptive mind to a total love of God. Whatever we or others have done or failed to do, we all remain fundamentally and eternally lovable. Sin alone engenders the sadness of diminished destinies.

Ruusbroec wrote perceptively of the power of sin to harm the unity of the spirit in itself and in its union with God. For sin is in conflict with the exemplar or archetype. Ruusbroec, in a way similar to Bernard's, explained this conflict by referring to the relationship between the soul's essence and its powers: the essence—the exemplar in existence—passively receives God without interruption; the powers of the soul, however, actively determine personal holiness or sinfulness. True unity occurs when the essence and powers are in harmony. The created spirit has an exigency for total unity. But, as Ruusbroec stated, sin prevents it: "Sin builds up a barrier, and gives rise to such darkness and such unlikeness between the powers and the essence in which God lives, that the spirit cannot be united with its proper essence; which would be its own and its eternal rest did not sin impede it."[15] Through knowing and loving in the Spirit, the subject achieves full integrity and thence full union with the Father and the Son.

The perfection of this conformity completes the circle by returning us to God through approximating the way that, in terms of exemplarity, things once were and radically still are. For exemplarity is not a static notion; it is the dynamic core of man's relation to God as Origin and End. Exemplarity may conjure up the image of God's taking these eternal archetypes and hurling a universe into existence only to draw them back into a divine embrace. Ruusbroec used the gentler and more accurate image of the ebb and flow within the Trinity and within the individual soul. Of the latter, he wrote: "The essential union of our spirit with God does not exist in itself, but it dwells in God and it flows forth from God and it depends upon God and it returns to God as its Eternal Origin."[16]

2. *Missions.* In bringing about this return of the soul, God acts also in ways not common to the three Persons. For grace depends on two divine actions called missions (from *mittere,* to send), each one consisting of a procession and a presence. Since mysticism is heightened consciousness of the loving presence of God, the two missions—motivated by love and resulting in presence—form the very heart of mysticism.

Let us examine the missions separately: first, the Son is generated by the Father and is sent by the Father to be present in the created world as its incarnate redeemer; second, the Spirit is spirated by the Father and the Son and is sent by the Father and Son to be present in human beings so that they can share in divine life. The processions of generation and spiration result in a special divine presence through the incarnation of the Son and the indwelling of the Spirit.

The missions are not actions done in common and merely appropriated to the Son and the Spirit, but are proper to each one. They are personal. As William Hill explained, "It is not the doing of something in the order of efficient causality, but is an actualization in the order of personal being."[17] Moreover, the change that takes place occurs in creatures, not in God. Bernard Lonergan stated: "A mission of a divine person is so constituted by a divine relation of origin that it requires by means of a condition consequent a fitting *ad extra* term."[18] What results is a contingent effect fittingly related to a particular divine Person, Son or Spirit. Essentially the missions bring human nature into a hypostatic union with the Son and bring human beings into participated union through the Spirit.

Moreover, both missions manifest a love presence: the Son is the self-revelation of the Father, who is the origin of love, and the Spirit is the mutual love of Father and Son. The Spirit by indwelling in us enables us to share in that mutual love. Aquinas described the central role of the Spirit: "As the Father utters himself and every creature by the Word he begets . . . so also he loves himself and every creature by the Holy Spirit in as much as the Holy Spirit proceeds as love for that primal goodness according to which the Father loves himself and every creature."[19]

The Spirit, as the *nexus duorum,* the bond between Father and

Son, brings this mutual love into our souls. "The love of God is poured forth in our hearts by the Holy Spirit who is given to us" (Rom 5:5). Only through the Spirit can we address the Father as "Abba" (Rom 8:14; Gal 4:6) and Jesus as "Lord" (I Cor 12:3). Through the Spirit, we are brought into the trinitarian life, for the Spirit shares with humans this twofold love, which our incorporation into Christ by adoption through the Spirit makes possible. We share in the Father's love of the Son and the Son's love of the Father. The graced subject is caught up in love both actively and passively, through aspiration and surrender. In the Spirit are the words of Jesus realized: "That they may be one, just as you Father in me and I in you, that they may be one in us" (Jn 17:21). The missions, that of the incarnate Son and the indwelling Spirit, perfect a unity in humans, for it is the Spirit as Paraclete, as the Spirit of Jesus, who dwells within the graced subjects, making them part of the Body of Jesus.[20]

What takes place in the graced subject is, as I suggested earlier, a participated perichoresis: the eternal and reciprocal penetration by the divine Persons is participated in by graced human beings. This sublime intimacy is implied in the very idea of the divine indwelling. First of all, through the indwelling of the Spirit, we are made participators in the divine nature, which is the focal point of perichoresis. We do not participate by nature but by adoption and grace, but we do participate—with the three Persons. Second, we are one with the Spirit, who is the mutual love of Father and Son.

As the divine Persons differ from one another through the opposition of relations, so human persons too share in an opposition as creatures. More significantly, through union with the Spirit, they share in the Spirit's mutual relationships and enjoy a truly perichoretic role in the life of the Trinity. To the extent that the soul, though not identified with the divine nature, participates in it, it shares in the immanent life of God. It loves and is loved, it knows and is known, not as an outsider looking in, but as a participant in the intimate exchange which makes the divine *koinonia,* a fellowship of love.

The graced subject thus realizes in a created mode a participated perichoresis; he or she participates in the divine nature and through the Spirit is consciously one with the whole Trinity enjoying proportionately the mutual inherence of the divine Persons. Moreover, this adoptive fellowship with the divine includes the whole community of graced subjects who form in the Spirit the Body of Christ. Yves Congar spoke of perichoresis, the trinitarian "*interiorité réciproque*," as "the theological concept which accounts, first for the theology of the local Churches and their relations with the universal Church, second for the rapport between the *ecclesia*—local or universal—and its pastor or head."[21] An internalizing of the social dimension of the mission of the Spirit is essential to an integral and truly Christlike spirituality.

This perichoretic intimacy, as we shall see, both affords the dynamic means of mystical prayer and characterizes its fulfillment. It is the living out of the two great commandments of love. Aquinas related the notions of creation and return to the trinitarian life: "Just as the processions of the Persons explain the production of creatures from the first principle, so the same process explains their return thereto as to their destiny."[22] This procession and return, the fulfillment of exemplarity through the divine missions, finds its full actualization in participated perichoresis as we shall see more clearly in examining two major aspects of conscious participation in divine life.

Conscious Participation

To discuss the Trinity is to be concerned with consciousness. But theological convictions, even about the indwelling of the Spirit, are not necessarily lived experiences. To learn how a person can become fully responsive to the truths of faith, we shall examine two necessary but sometimes overlooked operations of a true mystic: connaturality (fully attuning the mind to the concrete good that is God) and epectasy (continuously opening the mind to that same divine good).

Connaturality

The quest of the human spirit for oneness in itself and in God has roots in exemplarity and bears fruit in connaturality. Acknowledging the existence of our divine exemplar does not suffice to make us fully conscious of God. This knowledge must be perfected by love, so that we can experience God through a kind of kinship, congeniality, or connaturality. Lonergan wrote: "God's gift of his love is the cause of our knowledge of God by connaturality."[23] Let us see how this connaturality—which is found in art and decision making, in friendship and love—can operate in mysticism.

Connaturality attunes the mind to the concrete; its special function is to make possible intellectual consciousness of singular or individual beings. The term concrete, of course, includes both the material and the spiritual. We get to know all reality, including the divine, through some kind of union with it. The reason why connatural knowledge is necessary is that the mind does not have immediate contact with concrete reality but must mediate it by experiencing, understanding, and judging. So the mind is once-removed from the concrete. The good, however, is always concrete and singular. We desire to experience the good that we love. "The lover," Aquinas wrote, "is not content with a superficial knowledge but strives to enter into everything that belongs to the beloved; he does not rest with an external and superficial attachment, but craves a perfect and intimate expression."[24]

The process of connaturality operates in this way: the intellect pushed by the senses, feelings, emotions, and various forms of love goes beyond the abstract to an experience of the concrete individual. The push comes from the fact that intensely loving the good brings our mind into harmony with that good's singular existence. Since we have a unitary consciousness which tends toward full reality, this loving affects our knowing and attunes that knowing more perfectly to its target. If strong enough and pure enough, love can push our minds to an extraordinary awareness of the presence of the loved object. John of St. Thomas, though evidencing some naive realism, summed up the function of connaturality thus:

> The appetite passes into the very condition of the object in as much as the object by this experiential affection is rendered more conformably proportioned, united, and delightful to the subject. The mind reaches out and really feels its object as something that really penetrates it. In this way love acts on the mind as a formal cause.[25]

Underlying the connatural is the moral. The perfection of connaturality—the mutual interaction of knowing and loving as the condition for intellectual consciousness of the concrete good—depends more or less on moral authenticity; the higher the good, the greater the authenticity needed. The artist working in colors or sounds needs less, the truly prudent and equitable counselor needs more, the apophatic contemplative needs most.

The first law of morality is that there be consistency between knowing and doing. That one acts in accordance with one's lights is the condition for human integrity. Otherwise the mind is a house divided against itself, and so divided, it never has the psychic strength required for true mystical experience. Without a high degree of this inner moral harmony, a true connatural experience of God is not normally possible. Traditionally, holiness is the test of the authenticity of mystical experience. It is not that God cannot so endow the unauthentic, but that unauthenticity itself usually impedes connaturality. How can one become conscious of the utterly pure and simple God, if one's mind is torn apart by inordinate desires, even if it has eliminated forms and figures and images of creatures?

In perfecting our consciousness of the divine through connaturality, we seek to bring into harmony these two fundamental desires: the desire for meaning (ultimately the infinite mystery) and the desire for value (ultimately the supreme good). Do they combine to form a natural desire for God? A natural desire for happiness, yes; but not necessarily a natural desire for God. Most people recognize in themselves a desire for happiness. But some deny any desire for God, and many find the desire minimal. Objectively, we cannot be happy without God, but until that fact is known and acted upon, human desires remain frustrated. In short, the natural desire to know seeks the meaning of the infinite mystery; the natural desire for value seeks the presence of the supreme good; true wisdom grasps the identity in God of these two sought-after objects; and mystical consciousness reflects the profound fulfillment of these desires through union with God, who alone brings us happiness.

To experience God immediately as our final end is not possible in this life. Whatever experiences of God we have here are mediate, and the connection between God and happiness is not psychologically compelling. Although we may hold through reason and faith that to know God face to face is our destiny, we do not experience that reality or the final rest that it affords. On earth, God remains the transcendent unknown. William O'Connor wrote: "No object even God can take the place of happiness in general and become the object of a necessary tendency of the will toward its connatural end, until it is seen and recognized as the absolute and perfect good."[26] Growth in the spiritual life is a deepening awareness of the necessary connection between happiness and union with God, asserted in faith, approximated in mysticism, realized in the beatific vision.

Not all who are convinced that God alone can make them happy and who lead good and prayerful lives have heightened consciousness of the divine presence. Reaching divine union requires: first, the gradual strengthening of the linkage between the desire for ultimate reality and the recognition that God is infinite mystery and goodness; and second, the identification of God exclusively as the sufficient and necessary object of the human desire for happiness. For the mind to be able to transcend the world of its experience and to achieve intimate consciousness of God, it needs to have the full power of its most fundamental desires brought to concentrated attention on God as its own unique fulfillment and on God as supremely intelligible and lovable in himself. Let us examine the dimensions of the return to God through an expanding openness to infinite truth and goodness.

Epectasy

Through exemplarity and connaturality, men and women may achieve a deepening intimacy with God. Loving openness prepares their minds for divine consciousness. To describe the mystical approach to God, I use a strange, even awkward word, epectasy (*epektasis* from *epekteinein,* to stretch or expand), which was used in the Greek church at least by the fourth century and which has its scriptural roots in Paul's letter to the Philippians: "I do not count myself to have arrived, but one thing I do: forgetting the things that are behind and stretching forth to those that are before (*emprosthen epekteinomenos*), I press toward the mark, to the prize of the heavenly calling of God in Christ Jesus" (Phil 3:13–14).

The Greek Fathers found in the notion of epectasy a great spiritual insight. Gregory of Nyssa (330–95) in his allegorical *Life of Moses* compared bodies moved by gravity to the soul free of attachments moved by the desire of heavenly things, using the text from Philippians as his theme.[27] His argument was that worldly desires can be satiated at least for a time, but the desire for God increases exponentially. The more we love God the more we desire him. Gregory thematized this notion of continuous growth: "The one limit of perfection is the fact that it has no limit."[28] He illustrated this point by reference to Moses: "Once having set foot on the ladder which God set up (as Jacob says), he continually climbed to the step above and never ceased to rise higher, because he always found a step higher than the one he had attained."[29] And farther on he wrote: "What Moses yearned for is satisfied by the very things which leave his desire unsatisfied."[30] Elsewhere in a homily on the Canticle, Gregory used the word epectasy to describe the soul's search for God:

> The actual good, even if it appears the greatest and the most perfect possible, is never anything but the beginning of a superior good. Consequently, here also is verified the word of the apostle that, by epectasy towards what is ahead, the things which had formerly appeared fall into oblivion.[31]

Earthly appetites are satisfied temporarily because finite desires can be satisfied by finite objects, but the desire for God is insatiable because of the infinite capacity of man and the infinite reality of God. In seeking creatures, we are caught up in a circle of desire and satisfaction and renewed desire for the same old satisfactions. Seeking in the Spirit, the soul's very satisfaction leads not to satiation but to an invigorated and expanded desire. St. Maximus the Confessor, the seventh-century mystic and martyr, phrased it thus: "He [God] sets in movement in us an insatiable desire for himself, who is the Bread of Life, wisdom, knowledge and justice."[32]

The notion of epectasy can be further clarified by comparing it with two other terms used to describe mystical activity. The first and most familiar is *ecstasy,* and it connotes a going out of oneself with a loss of sense awareness. The second is *enstasy,* as used by Mircea Eliade, and it denotes a going into oneself to the exclusion of all else; it is a centering action.[33] The third is *epectasy,* and it denotes an opening of the mind and heart, a stretching and expanding toward meaning and value.

All three have their role. But *ecstasy,* generally an involuntary experience, is phased out of the mystical life with the transforming union, if not before. *Enstasy,* though within one's powers, may at times prove too narrow and isolative for an incarnational religion. *Epectasy,* however, encompasses but ever transcends forms and desires. It is a receptivity of the mind, a going beyond creaturely limits in knowing and loving God. It is not a hubristic leaping of boundaries, but a humble opening of the mind to the infinitely mysterious and lovable God.

The spiritual path should be one of continuous progress. This going forward, whether fully experienced or not, is the fruit of a twofold openness: an unrestricted desire to know God and a universal acceptance of his will. Indeed, this openness is reflected in the Pauline distinction between the spirit and the flesh (not to be equated with soul and body). As we saw in the first chapter, the spirit comprises all human realities, body and soul, open to the Spirit of God; the flesh, the same realities closed to the Spirit of God.[34]

If we remove all forms and images from our minds so that we seem to have opened ourselves to God, we have not yet fully expanded our minds; we have merely emptied them as far as knowing is concerned. An intelligent mind can arrive at the conviction that God transcends its capability for knowing, and can reject the use of created forms and images. It can even go farther by being aware of this transcending through a conscious opening of the mind—not just rejecting a concept or image but going beyond them, beyond the very notion of the created. But this is only a necessary step in the right direction; the unitive strength comes from loving. There is no true mysticism without love.

In one of his letters, John of the Cross commented briefly on the words, "Open your mouth and I will fill it" (*Dilata os tuum et implebo illud*) (Ps 80:11). "The appetite is the mouth of the will. It is opened wide when it is not encumbered or centered upon any mouthful of pleasure. When the appetite is centered upon something, it becomes narrow by this very fact, since outside of God everything is narrow."[35] This expanding of love is harder to perfect than the emptying of the mind.

To rectify one's loving involves great sacrifice and suffering—a taking up of the cross of Christ. To follow the injunction: "Open your mouth and I will fill it," means a painful stretching of the mind, a tearing loose from creaturely adhesions. This operation becomes bearable in proportion to the greatness of our love. And love can achieve such a victory, "for love is strong as death" (Ct 8:6). The complete opening of the mind means a death to much that we previously called our life, but with each partial death there comes a resurrection to a new life as we are filled with God.

The instructions that John of the Cross gave to beginners illustrate the need for openness in both knowing and loving. Speaking of an early stage of contemplation, the prayer of quiet, he described the soul as "attentively loving God and refraining from the desire to see or feel anything."[36] What is necessary is the purifying and voiding oneself of all forms and apprehensible images.[37] In a later work, he emphasized even more strongly this need for complete openness in knowing and loving:

> Pay no attention, neither partially nor entirely to anything which your faculties can grasp. I mean that you should never desire satisfaction in what you understand about God but in what you do not understand about him. Never stop with loving and delighting in your understanding and experience of God, but love and delight in what is neither understandable nor perceptible. Such is the way, as we have said, of seeking him in faith.[38]

To appreciate this advice, which may seem unduly restrictive, we should recall the essence of this heightened awareness which is mystical experience. It is not, as we might tend to suspect from John's words about what is neither understandable nor perceptible, a mindless vacuity. Despite the thorough purification of created forms—

concepts and images, even of God—the mind possesses a loving watchfulness in responding to God's presence through faith, hope, and charity. The mind knows and trusts and loves, but it does so with faith in the infinite mystery of awe and love.

The soul, though unsatisfied, learns to be properly content with an obscure but loving presence; it does not inordinately desire to see and feel God, because it realizes that what it would see and feel would not be God but a created veil. When it does understand and experience God, it stretches forward beyond those limited lights and feelings toward what is neither understandable nor perceptible, because this experience of not knowing brings the mind closer to knowing God as he is.

To sustain this continuing purification, the soul needs a foundation of pervading humility: the acknowledgment of one's limits and the recognition of one's sinful unworthiness. The soul, though discouraged by the frailties of its nature and of its actions, does not lose heart, because it is empowered by the Holy Spirit. Accompanying the humility, there is great joy in the luminous and loving darkness.

More technically, this venture into the void is sustained and completed through connaturality, by which, as we have seen, exemplarity achieves existential fruition. The question arises: How can connaturality prove adequate in the face of this infinite challenge to know and love God? How can anyone expect to know the infinitely true and to love the infinitely good? On the other hand, how can God really love us? Humility helps us accept in reverential fear what our patent contingency forces us to admit: as creatures we are radically distanced from God. And yet we have learned from revelation—with the crucified Savior as our pledge—that we can be "participators in the divine nature" and that we are destined to be "brought to completion as one" and "to see God face to face."

The role of the Holy Spirit is to do what is impossible for human beings to do. "This strength lies in the Holy Spirit in whom the soul is there transformed," as John of the Cross wrote, adding that both in the transformation of glory and the transformation of the spiritual marriage, "He supplies what is lacking in it."[39] What is supplied more than makes up for the limitations of the soul; it fulfils the desire for reciprocal love. "The soul's aim is a love equal to God's. She always desired this equality, naturally and supernaturally, for a lover cannot be satisfied if he fails to feel that he loves as much as he is loved."[40] The Spirit makes possible the realization of this equality.

The indwelling Spirit, as the Spirit of Jesus, lifts the humble soul to a participation in the love of the Father for the Son and in the love of the Son for the Father. This reciprocity gives a divine character to human love. The human subject is aware, through the power of the Spirit, of being loved infinitely and of loving totally. Indeed, since it is the Spirit at work in the "deified" soul, the mystic in some way participates in the infinite love of the Spirit. In this ebb and flow of divine love, the soul confidently opens itself with a loving transcendence to the plenitude of being and opens itself, with humble acceptance, to the fullness of love. Empowered by the Spirit, the soul expands unendingly in giving and receiving, in opening and being filled, in seeking transcendence and in finding immanence.

The realization of this obscure though loving presence of God faces a last barrier—the overcoming of the subject-object separation. John of the Cross used an analogy to express the divine communication that the Spirit gives to the soul. "By his divine breath-like spiration, the Holy Spirit elevates the soul sublimely and informs her and makes her capable of breathing in God the same spiration of love that the Father breathes in the Son and the Son in the Father, which is the Holy Spirit himself, who in the Father and the Son breathes out to her in this transformation, in order to unite her to himself."[41] The result is this: "The soul united and transformed in God breathes out in God to God the very divine spiration which God—she being transformed in him—breathes out in Himself to her."[42] This is the participated perichoresis that we spoke of earlier in the chapter. The Spirit, as the mutual love, brings about this perfection of union, this harmony of opposites, this completion as one.

The Final Stages

Heightened consciousness reaches its apogee through what has been called technically a transforming union, more poetically a mystical marriage, and most radically a deification. Each term highlights aspects of this major theophany, whereby consciousness is transformed, divine life is shared, and two are made one.

The mind of even the greatest mystic begins as a blank page upon which nothing is written.[43] We all begin without innate ideas, even ideas of God. To speak of the mind as a *tabula rasa* does not mean that the mind is inert. The mind is alive and ready to function: it ever seeks reality—to know it and to love it. This potentiality, this dynamic openness to reality, makes it possible for us to achieve mystical consciousness of God. To receive the divine gift of love, which the Spirit pours forth in our hearts, requires a capacity to love or what

Basil the Great called "an agapetic power."[44] A stone or an animal cannot become conscious of God or receive his grace because it has no capacity. Humans begin with blank and undifferentiated minds, but they can, through the eros of the spirit and with the help of God, share in divine consciousness. We have already seen something of that development. Let us look now at its major stages.

The transforming union is part of a continuum, although the process varies owing to individual differences in psyches, experiences, and graces. Without getting bogged down in the complexities of various theories of mystical growth, we can sketch out in sequence the major steps to transformation. Unfortunately, the use of a faculty psychology has impeded to some extent the understanding of spiritual development. This does not mean, of course, that the great mystics, lacking a complete cognitional theory, were false guides, but only that their insights can sometimes profitably be translated into more accurate language.

We look then at a traditional division of the stages of infused contemplation according to the Carmelite school, as exemplified by Teresa of Avila and John of the Cross. They analyzed mystical development in terms of a growing passivity of mental faculties: the will, the intellect, and the senses. It might seem that one should proceed in the reverse order, beginning with the senses. But because freedom is a matter of choosing, we find that we can control our loving more easily than we can control our knowing. Established in love, the rest of the mind and the senses, too, gradually share peacefully in the divine presence. Only then is the whole psyche one with God. We shall consider these stages separately.

Partial Union. Through loving, the mind achieves an obscure but real awareness of the divine presence. Transcending, though only imperfectly, created forms and inordinate desires, the mind dwells lovingly on God, despite occasional dryness and distractions. Teresa of Avila spoke of passive recollection, as a transition to the prayer of quiet or as an early stage of it. It retains traces of the vocal prayer and meditation that characterizes active recollection but manifests a new peacefulness owing to a faith-inspired love, which day by day grows stronger and more meaningful. This knowing, while remaining unsatisfactorily thin and diaphanous, affords the beginner a firm foundation. For the darkness of faith is a positive darkness filled with the mysterious but loving presence of God.

Simple Union. Through deepening contemplation, the mind now experiences vividly a connatural union with God. Knowing and loving intensely, the mystic is no longer distracted by thoughts or desires. Temporarily locked into this intense consciousness of God's loving presence, he or she remains well-oriented in terms of time and place, but the senses, though still functioning, do not impede this union.

Sometimes, however, due to the intensity of this focused attention, the senses are temporarily phased out. This loss of contact with one's surroundings (alienation of the senses or suspension of the faculties) may be called ecstasy or rapture, depending on whether it happens gradually or suddenly. For these transports occur when the strength of the attention overwhelms the weakness of the psyche. Some persons cannot bear the highly concentrated experience of simple union without losing sense consciousness; others with apparently equal stimulation do not succumb; so too, on a purely natural level, individuals differ about crying, screaming, or fainting, in the face of emotionally charged situations.

Symeon the New Theologian (950–1022), one of the greatest of the Byzantine mystics, said that ecstasy pertains to novices and beginners, not to those accustomed to the uncreated light.[45] He compared the ecstatic to a prisoner who had never experienced anything but the dimmest light, but who unexpectedly looked through a crack and saw a scene in bright sunshine. Eventually he would find it normal, but in the beginning would be overwhelmed. This effect recalls Plato's Cave parable.

Although non-mystics may consider ecstasy to be an essential characteristic of mystical experience—and certainly for the outsider it is a dramatically memorable one—both the Eastern and Western churches recognize that it is not a phase which everyone goes through and that it is only a passing phase for ecstatics who go on to the heights of mysticism.

Transforming Union.   Simple union brought to perfection becomes a transforming union. In the process, the loving consciousness of the divine presence has become habitual. The psyche has been strengthened so that it does not suffer ecstatic alienation of the senses. The mind has been so radically confirmed in grace that it can say truly, "But we have the mind of Christ" (I Cor 2:16). Usually there is present an intellectual vision of the Trinity. This latter grace is not just a special bonus, but rather, through connaturality, reflects a functional articulation of the trinitarian structure of mystical experience, which is always from the Father through Christ in the Spirit.

To speak of the transforming union as a mystical marriage helps bring to our attention four important aspects: the love, the oneness, the fruitfulness, the normality. First, the term recalls the role of love, both in reaching and enjoying this divine union: "God is love" (I Jn 4:8). Second, the term suggests the union that takes place: "He who is joined to the Lord is one spirit" (I Cor 6:17). Third, the term indicates the productivity in good works that results: "If anyone love me, he will keep my word" (Jn 14:23). Fourth, the term suggests the normality of the state: "Doing the truth in love, we reach full growth in all things toward him who is the head, Christ" (Eph 4:15).

More concretely, as we have noted in chapter four when speaking of the anaphatic return, the one who has been transformed in love and has finally attained spiritual maturity manifests that achievement through an abundance of works. At the same time, such a one still enjoys a deep consciousness of the divine presence, the soul's having been united with the rest of Trinity through the Holy Spirit. Just as an earthly marriage marks a loving and productive union, so the mystical marriage begins a new stage of love and productivity in union with God. This perfection does not necessarily come only at the end of life; ideally, it should be realized early so that it could characterize one's whole life. In this respect, it would be chronologically more like the sacrament of marriage than like the last rites. Although it does prepare one for heaven, it certainly fits one for living fully on earth the divine mystery.

The transforming union is, in a word, regenerative, for it actualizes the potentials of graced nature and revitalizes the mystic in whom Christ is continuously born anew. But this final stage is only incidentally, if at all, a life of visions and ecstacies, miracles and preternatural wonders. The main purpose of the transforming union is to bring integrated and elevated subjects to a heightened consciousness of God so that through their love "they may be brought to completion as one" (Jn 17:23).

Despite their spiritual rebirth in Christ, mystics inhabit a world warped by sin. The cross and the recurring sequence of death and resurrection remain for them an ever-present reality. The transformation begins a period of fulfillment, but it is not yet a state of ultimate perfection. Seeking union with God, the mystic can say with Paul: "For me to live is Christ and to die is gain" (Phil 1:21), since this life, however enhanced, cannot be compared to the life of love that is to come.

The transforming union gives the lie to the allegation that the mystical life is a diminished and truncated one that renders a person unfit for fully human functioning. On the contrary, this revitalization means that Christ now lives in the mystic, who has the mind of Christ and who experiences an ordered harmony of heightened consciousness and a god-like potentiation of knowing and loving through the indwelling Spirit of Christ.

The word "deification" is often used to describe the transforming union or mystical marriage and some of their non-Catholic or even non-Christian counterparts. For the Christian, the *locus classicus* is one we have seen: "He has given us most great and precious promises, that by these you may be made sharers of the divine nature" (I Pet 1:4). This text, coupled with the Johannine promises of the indwelling Trinity and of completion as one, together with many Pauline texts, has led Christian mystics and Doctors of the Church to speak clearly of a deification, *theosis*. The tradition is a long one, which is given special emphasis by the Greek Church, but is not rejected by the Roman Church.

The fundamental question is: What does deification imply? In what sense can a creature be deified and made one with God? John Damascene (675–749), recognized by both Greeks and Latins, distinguished clearly between enlightenment and substance in speaking of the goal of the mystery, which is that "one is deified through an inclination toward God, but deified by a share in the divine effulgence, and not transformed into the divine being."[46] The inclination that he speaks of involves the expanding operation of epectasy.

At this point, it is important to recall that openness to God in knowing and love is a quasi-symbol of the divine presence even in the apophatic way. Through self-consciousness, the mystic becomes aware of himself as a subject of ever-expanding openness to God. God is, as it were, directly symbolized by the response of the mind to his presence. Of course, every stage of the mystical life, even the transforming union, is a created effect of God's love, however "natural" the means used to achieve it. Every stage is a function of the intensity of love, the perfection of openness, and the depth of self-consciousness. Through this intimate union of shared consciousness, there arises an experience of deification.

Christian mystics reject a substantial identification with God; there can be no true monistic, pantheistic, or advaitic non-duality. Yet mystics often speak the language of deification and unity. For example, Ruusbroec saw this conscious return or deification as "a union without difference" and "beyond distinction." Yet he explicitly contrasted conscious identity, a oneness in enjoyment and beatitude, to a substantial oneness in nature and being. With reference to the text of John 17:23, he wrote:

Christ prayed the highest prayer, namely, that all his beloved might be made perfectly one, even as he is one with the Father—not in the way that he is one single substance with the Father, for that is impossible for us, but in the sense of being in the same unity in which he, without distinction, is one enjoyment and one beatitude with the Father in essential love.[47]

John of the Cross, some 800 years after John Damascene and about 100 years after John Ruusbroec, wrote similarly about union of the soul with God:

When God grants this supernatural favor to the soul, so great a union is caused that all the things of both God and the soul become one in participant transformation, and the soul appears to be God more than a soul. Indeed it is God by participation. Yet truly, its being (even though transformed) is naturally as distinct from God's as it was before, just as the window, although illumined by the ray, has an existence distinct from the ray.[48]

This mystical participation is essentially a sharing in the consciousness of God: I am conscious of myself; I am conscious of God; I am conscious of God's being conscious of me. Adverting to the notions of connaturality, exemplarity, and epectasy, I realize how intimately personal that conscious union is: I am conscious of being, in my essence, one with God for all eternity and thus I am conscious of my capacity to love God with expanding openness throughout all eternity and in return to be loved proportionately by him. I am conscious also of having been given existence and of now returning through love to that original oneness in the bosom of the Trinity.

Does this knowledge suffice for the transforming union? Of course not. More than ideas and propositions, more than the trust and beliefs of faith are necessary. These facets reveal but also fragment what is absolutely simple. A pure and intense love alone can approximate the divine, not by fusing together the facets as if mystical experience were like a stained-glass window, but by a transcending that in comparison seems to move into the realm of light itself. Human consciousness illumined by faith must be heightened by charity, so that a person becomes one spirit with God, not substantially but consciously—knowing and loving God in some marvelous way as he knows and loves himself.

Openness, this quasi-symbol, thus manifests its role: it makes way for the uncreated Being. God alone can fill the void that the openness of mind and heart makes. Having cleared the mind of created forms and having removed all inordinate desires, we seek in open-endedness, the loving presence which is the face of God. The Spirit of love not only binds together Father and Son, but brings humans into that same unity of consciousness. This heightened state which is mysticism is an awareness of the eternal mystery: "For we, beholding the glory of the Lord with unveiled [open] face, are transformed into the same image from glory to glory as by the Spirit of the Lord" (II Cor 3:18).

CONCLUSION

In this last chapter, we have discussed in its fullness the heightened consciousness of the loving presence of the triune God. This spiritual experience can be summed up in three points: its culmination is in participated perichoresis; its mediation is by the indwelling Spirit; and its implementation is through connaturality and epectasy.

The focus of the *culmination* is the conscious inner life of the Trinity, as characterized by the operation of periochoresis. The three Persons have a relationship of opposition to one another; each is identified with the divine nature, which is a conscious nature; and all three, by reciprocally sharing in the same conscious nature, interpenetrate with infinite intimacy.

The culmination of human consciousness occurs through what I have called a participated periochoresis, namely, a reciprocal sharing through grace and glory with the three Persons in the conscious nature of God.

The *mediation* of this human participation is accomplished by the indwelling Spirit of Jesus, who is the personification of the mutual love uniting Father and Son. The Spirit brings the graced subject into a special relation with all three Persons. Grace enables humans to share in the divine nature; the indwelling reveals the tri-personal dimension of that participation.

The human *implementation* of this sharing in trinitarian consciousness comes through the operations of connaturality and epectasy. Through connaturality, the subject experiences its participation in the divine nature as if it were second nature to it; the clarity of this intimacy reveals its dynamic relationship with the Persons of the Trinity. Through epectasy, that same participation which is open-ended in this life is ever-increasing in the next, the symbol subsumed by the fullness of reality. Together connaturality and epectasy elevated by the indwelling Spirit ensure that the sharing in divine consciousness which envisages a transforming union here, also encompasses there an eternity of bliss in an infinitely expanding horizon.

Epilogue: The Emerging Light

✧   ✧   ✧

In an attempt to reflect the unity of Christian mysticism in terms of the heightened consciousness of the loving presence of God, I shall summarize my findings by means of a sacred and universal metaphor —light. A consistent theme throughout the Bible, it reached its most straightforward expression in John: "God is light, and in him there is no darkness at all" (I Jn 1:5). This symbol, with its primitive roots and its psychological fruitfulness, speaks to us of consciousness, divine and human. As a light that dispels the darkness, the divine light transcends the boundaries and limits of created nature and opens the mind to the fullness of God. "In your light, we shall see light" (Ps 36:9). The mystical way is openness to the light, a growing participation in divine consciousness.

The sequence of chapters follows the process of enlightenment from mystical potentiality to mystical fulfillment. God calls all men and women to the fullness of light. I shall review the steps to this heightened consciousness.

Chapter One. *The capacity for enlightenment,* with which we all begin, is our subjectivity: we are conscious persons with a need to be open to the whole of reality—the true, the good, and the beautiful. As subjects we have a potentiality, under God, to be elevated beyond our purely natural, created limits and to be made existential participants in the divine realm. God enlightens us beyond our "natural" competence and our present comprehension. Indeed, by his eternal decree, he has already graced our nature, inviting us to share his intimate triune consciousness.

Chapter Two. *Divine illumination* does occur. Theophanies, both pre-mystical and mystical, shed God's light into our minds. We become conscious of the Transcendent through mediated immediacy although not, in this life, through direct vision. In truly seeking divine light, we must preserve an awareness of God as both our origin and

188

our destiny, our creative source and our ultimate end. He makes us, elevates us, empowers us, and then communicates himself in order to fulfil us in love. Our minds become luminous as we reflect his light; we are not radiant in ourselves, but we receive light from Jesus, the Word of God, "the true light, who gives light to every one" (Jn 1:9).

Chapter Three. *God as refracted light* communicates himself through creation, shining forth in the multiplicity of things he has made. Knowing God kataphatically leads logically to a realization of the intrinsic limits of even the most beautiful traces and images of God, just as perceiving the colors of a rainbow suggests but does not capture the purity and intensity of the primary, white light of the sun. Symbols distil this openness to reality, and we yearn profoundly not just for God's artifacts but for infinite Beauty itself. Moreover, even flawed creatures and actions, evil or sinful though they may be, still reflect the sun as if behind clouds. The mystery of death and resurrection brings to a painfully sharp focus the presence of a compassionate and providential God. Suffering allows the clear light of divine love to flood the soul who willingly bears the cross yet still seeks the face of this tremendous lover.

Chapter Four. *God as pure light* is the focus of the second major way of enlightenment. Transcending God's many-splendored creatures, we move by the negative path of purification to face God, "who dwells in light inaccessible" (I Tim 6:1). This apophatic approach requires putting aside created forms and inordinate desires. The created mind cannot yet comprehend this pure light, which it perceives to be darkness. But this very darkness becomes luminous in proportion to one's detachment and love, and there emerges a growing awareness of the loving and infinitely real presence of God.

Chapter Five. *Ways of removing natural veils* are necessary whatever one's mystic bent. By learning to control the senses, the emotions, and the mind on the "natural" level, an embodied spirit removes obstacles so that prayer can flower in peace. The physiological and psychological opening of the psyche lets light pour into the mind. These many skills make operative the natural functions which bring the normal life of grace to the level of mystical consciousness.

Chapter Six. Hope in *the promised manifestation* of infinite meaning and value strengthens the spirit, so that it may endure the painful emptiness and suffering that precedes divine illumination. Jesus Christ promised that he would indeed manifest himself through his Spirit to those who love him and keep his commandments. He established the sequence from law to love to light: law sets up the norm; love fulfils it; and light reveals its source. Jesus guaranteed this result: "I will love him and will manifest myself to him" (Jn 14:21). All light radiates from the manifestation of the One who is himself the Light.

Chapter Seven. The *luminous event,* the promised participation in the light, is achieved by union with the Trinity through the Spirit of Jesus. This indwelling, with its reciprocal (perichoretic) sharing in divine consciousness, facilitates the response of connaturality (a loving harmony with light) and of epectasy (an ongoing openness to light). This openness of mind, consciously appropriated, symbolizes the efficacious presence of the triune God. Thus it is that the mystic, with a faith that operates through love, shares consciously in the divine embrace that, with many stages of intimacy, leads luminously to heightened consciousness—the mystical difference that love alone can make.

Notes

✧　　✧　　✧

CHAPTER 1

1. Augustine, *Soliloquies,* II, 1 (J.-P. Migne, *Patrologia Latina,* 32: 886): "Deus semper idem; noverim me, noverim te." Migne hereafter cited as *PL* or *PG* (*Patrologia Graeca*).

2. Ibid., *Confessions,* I, 1 (*PL* 32:661): "Fecistis nos ad te, et inquietum est cor nostrum, donec requiescat in te."

3. Teresa of Avila, *The Complete Works,* trans. and ed. E. Allison Peers, vol. 2: *The Interior Castle* (London: Sheed and Ward, 1972), p. 201.

4. Ibid., p. 350. The translation has been changed slightly to reflect the Spanish *le ganaréis,* which Peers translated more loosely in the third person.

5. Ibid., p. 218.

6. Bernard J. F. Lonergan, S.J., *Method in Theology,* 2d ed. (New York: Herder and Herder, 1972), p. 8. His theory of conscious intentionality has proved helpful in my analysis of mysticism.

7. Blessed Marie de l'Incarnation, *Relation autobiographique de 1645* (Sablé-sur-Sarthe, France: Abbaye de Solesmes, 1976), ch. 52, p. 100.

8. Thomas Aquinas, *Summa theologiae,* I, a. 59, q. 4, c. See also *Tractatus de substantiis separatis,* ed. F. J. Lescoe (West Hartford, Conn.: St. Joseph College, 1962).

9. John Henry Newman, *A Grammar of Assent* (New York: Longmans, Green, 1947), ch. 4, pp. 29–74.

10. Teresa of Avila, *Interior Castle,* p. 300. An alembic is used to distil liquids. On feelings, see Lonergan, *Method,* pp. 30–34.

11. Antonio T. de Nicolás, *Powers of Imagining: Saint Ignatius,* with a translation and analysis of his collected works (Albany: State University of New York Press, 1986), p. 57. *The Spiritual Diary* is found on pages 189–217.

12. Ibid., II–II, a. 27, a. 4, ad 3: "Caritas est quae, diligendo, animam immediate Deo conjungit spiritualis vinculo unionis."

13. Jean Pierre de Caussade, S. J., *Abandonment to Divine Providence,* trans. E. J. Strictland (Exeter, England: Sidney Lee, 1921), p. 7 and passim.

14. John Ruusbroec, *The Book of Supreme Truth* in *John of Ruys-*

191

broeck, trans. C. A. Wynschenk (London: John M. Watkins, 1951), pp. 233–34. An excellent translation, more recent and more available, is that of James Wiseman, *John Ruusbroec: The Spiritual Espousals and Other Works* (New York: Paulist, 1985), pp. 257–58, where it is entitled, *The Little Book of Clarification.* I use the more accurate spelling, Ruusbroec.

15. Ignatius of Loyola, *The Spiritual Exercises*, sec. 313. The section refers to the standard marginal numbers. The translation used is that of Antonio T. de Nicolás, with some adjustments from the text and translation of Joseph Rickaby, S. J., *The Spiritual Exercises of St. Ignatius of Loyola* (New York: Benziger, 1923).

16. Ibid., sec. 316.

17. Ibid., sec. 317.

18. Ibid., sec. 331.

19. Ibid., sec. 332.

20. Ibid., sec. 330: "Solo es de Dios dar consolación al anima sin causa precedente." It is also found in sec. 336. For an excellent analysis (according to the thought of Karl Rahner) of this "consolation without previous cause" see Harvey Egan, S.J., *The Spiritual Exercises and the Ignatian Mystical Horizon* (St. Louis: Institute of Jesuit Sources, 1976).

21. Erich Przywara, S.J., *Deus Semper Maior*, 3 vols (Freiburg, i. B., 1938–39), vol. 1, pp. 250–51.

22. Karl Rahner, S. J., *The Dynamic Element in the Church*, trans. W. J. O'Hara (New York: Herder and Herder, 1964), p. 149.

23. Ibid., p. 156.

24. Ibid., pp. 155–56.

25. Ibid., pp. 150–57, n. 35. Rahner recognized that "there is a peace and harmony with oneself which is a sign of the good spirit," but he sought a deeper assurance that would clearly eliminate self-deception. Ignatius sought certainty.

26. Ibid., p. 156.

27. Raymond E. Brown, *The Gospel According to John*, Anchor Bible, 2 vols. (Garden City, N.Y.: Doubleday, 1970), vol. 1, p. 141.

28. J.-M. Déchanet, *Yoga and God* (St. Meinrad, Ind.: Abbey Press, 1975), p. 35. See also Joseph A. Fitzmyer, S.J., *Paul and His Theology*, 2d ed. (Englewood Cliffs, N.J.: Prentice-Hall, 1989), pp. 82–83.

29. Ignatius, *Exercises*, sec. 47.

30. Ibid., sec. 121.

31. Joseph Rickaby, S.J., *The Spiritual Exercises*, p. 89.

32. Ignatius, *Exercises*, Rickaby translation, sec. 65.

33. Ibid., sec. 66–70, first week, fifth exercise.

34. Teresa, *Life*, in *Complete Works*, vol. I, ch. 9, p. 55.

35. Ignatius, *Exercises*, sec. 47.

36. M. E. Humphrey and O. L. Zangwill, "Cessation of Dreaming after Brain Injury," *Journal of Neurology, Neurosurgery and Psychiatry* 14 (1951):322.

37. *New York Times*, Aug. 12, 1986, p. C1, quoting Stephen Kosslyn. See his book *Visual Cognition* (Boston: M.I.T. Press, 1986). Aldous Huxley

wrote: "I am and, for as long as I can remember, I have always been a poor visualizer." *The Doors of Perception* (New York: Harper Colophon Books, 1963), p. 15. Barbara Brown, in a book on biofeedback, briefly noted her own lack of visual imagination: "I close my eyes and I see gray. All I see is gray." *New Mind, New Body* (New York: Harper and Row, 1974), p. 23.

38. Bernard J. F. Lonergan, S.J., "The Subject," *A Second Collection,* ed. W. F. J. Ryan and B. J. Tyrrell (Philadelphia: Westminster, 1974), p. 77.

39. Aquinas, *Summa theologiae,* I, q. 29, a. 3 c.

40. Ibid., 2c.

41. Bernard J. F. Lonergan, S.J., *De Deo Trino* (Rome: Gregorian University Press, 1963), vol. 1, p. 178.

42. Aristotle, *Metaphysics,* 1074a 33–8, a text used by Aquinas in attributing a separate species to each angel.

43. Eric Voegelin, *Order and History,* vol. 4: *The Ecumenic Age* (Baton Rouge: Louisiana State University Press, 1974), p. 320.

44. Ibid., p. 326.

45. Idem, *Anamnesis,* trans. G. Niemeyer (Notre Dame, Ind.: Notre Dame University Press, 1978), p. 95.

46. Idem, *The Ecumenic Age,* p. 186.

47. Idem, *Anamnesis,* p. 96.

48. Idem, *Conversations with Eric Voegelin,* ed. Eric O'Connor (Montreal: Thomas More Institute, 1980), p. 23. Moreover, in *Anamnesis,* p. 98, he wrote: "Reason is openness of existence raised to consciousness." Note also that the human subject through the obediential potency and grace can be raised to consciousness of infinite existence and a participation in the life of God.

49. Idem, *The Ecumenic Age,* p. 330.

50. Ibid. Moreover, the non-specificity of the Question makes possible a range of formulations: "The Question remains the same, but the modes of asking the Question change."

51. Ibid., p. 242.

52. Idem, *Anamnesis,* p. 96.

53. Idem, *The Ecumenic Age,* p. 246. For a description of the content of Paul's theophany, namely, the Incarnation and the Resurrection, see p. 242.

54. Ibid., p. 242. See also *Anamnesis,* p. 98: "If reason is existential *philia,* if it is the openness of existence raised to consciousness, then the closure of existence, or any obstruction to openness will affect the rational structure of the psyche adversely."

55. Idem, *Order and History,* vol. 1: *Israel and Revelation* (1956), p. 1.

56. Idem, *Order and History,* vol. 5: *In Search of Order* (1987), p. 107.

CHAPTER 2

1. John Paul II, Apostolic Exhortation, *Redemptionis donum* (1984); English translation, *The Gift of Redemption* (Washington: United States Catholic Conference, 1984), p. 7.

2. The usual definition of theophany is that of a wondrous manifestation of Yahweh in power and glory. Often accompanied by earthquakes, storms, and fire, it also has other modalities, even the gentle breeze of I Kings 19:11–13, a more intimate presence approaching mystical consciousness. So my broader understanding, focused on the presence of God—the heart of all theophanies—involves the individual immediately through a kind of realized theophany crowning a realized eschatology.

3. Karl Rahner, S.J., *Foundations of Christian Faith* (New York: Seabury, 1978): "the original experience of God," p. 54, and "the original experience of transcendence," pp. 60, 63.

4. Bernard J. F. Lonergan, S.J., *Method in Theology*, 2d ed. (New York: Herder and Herder, 1972), p. 295: "In the primary sources a distinction is to be drawn between the doctrine of the original message and, on the other hand, doctrines about this doctrine."

5. Eric Voegelin, *Anamnesis*, trans. G. Niemeyer (Notre Dame, Ind.: Notre Dame University Press, 1978), p. 95–96.

6. Plato, *Laws*, 644D. See Voegelin, *Anamnesis*, p. 105, and his *Plato and Aristotle*, vol. III of *Order and History* (Baton Rouge, La.: Louisiana State University Press, 1957), pp. 231–36.

7. Bernard J. F. Lonergan, S.J., *Third Collection* (New York: Paulist Press, 1985), p. 195.

8. Karl Rahner, *Foundations*, p. 33.

9. Ibid., p. 65: "the term of transcendence as the Holy Mystery."

10. Bernard Lonergan, *Method*, p. 114: "For its [religious utterance's] source and core is the experience of the mystery of love and awe, and that pertains to the realm of transcendence"; and p. 119: "In the measure that experience is genuine it is related to the mystery of love and awe."

11. Ibid., p. 107.

12. Ibid., p. 106.

13. Idem., *Second Collection*, ed. W. F. J. Ryan and B. J. Tyrrell (Philadelphia: Westminster Press, 1974), p. 229–30.

14. For further studies on conversion, see Robert M. Doran, S.J., *Subject and Psyche* (Washington: University Press of America, 1979) and Walter E. Conn, *Conversion* (Birmingham: Religious Education Press, 1981).

15. Bernard Lonergan, *Method*, p. 105.

16. Ibid., p. 106.

17. Charles Davis, "Religion and the Sense of the Sacred," *Proceedings of the Catholic Theological Society of America*, 31 (1976): 87–105, 97.

18. Vatican II, *Dei Verbum*, art. 6, *The Documents of Vatican II*, ed. Walter M. Abbot. (New York: Guild Press, 1966), p. 114.

19. See Avery Dulles, S.J., *Models of Revelation* (Garden City, N.Y.: Doubleday, 1983), Chapter IX, "Symbolic Mediation," pp. 131–41.

20. Idem, "The Problem of Revelation," *Proceedings of the Catholic Theological Society of America*, 29 (1974): 100.

21. Vatican II, *Gaudium et spes*, art. 62, pp. 268–70. See also Sacred

Congregation for the Doctrine of the Faith, *Mysterium ecclesiae, Acta apostolicae sedis* 65 (1973), 396–408, art. 5.

22. See David Tracy, *Plurality and Ambiguity* (San Francisco: Harper and Row, 1987). From the perspective of post-modern theology, Tracy takes a negative, though avowedly hopeful position on religious certitude, finding in religion an inevitable plurality because of the multitude of languages and an inevitable ambiguity because of the historical conditioning of these languages.

23. For the distinction between Rahner's transcendental and predicamental revelation see his "Revelation, B. Theological Interpretation," *Sacramentum Mundi,* ed. K. Rahner, 6 vols. (New York: Herder and Herder, 1968), 5: 348–53.

24. Idem, "Mysticism," *Encyclopedia of Theology: The Concise Sacramentum Mundi* (New York: Seabury, 1975), p. 1010.

25. Avery Dulles, *Models of Revelation,* p. 149.

26. William James, *The Varieties of Religious Experience* (New York: Modern Library, 1902, 1929), p. 399, n. 2. James identified four marks of mystical experiences: ineffability, noetic quality, transience, and passivity. See pages 371–72. Applied to Christian mystical states, they are vague and partially inaccurate. Indeed, James concluded: "The subdivisions and names which we find in the Catholic books [he read both Teresa of Avila and John of the Cross] seem to me to represent nothing objectively distinct" (p. 399). He admitted, however: "My own constitution shuts me out from their enjoyment almost entirely, and I am speaking only at second hand" (p. 370).

27. Ibid., p. 371.

28. Joseph Maréchal, S.J., "On the Feeling of Presence in Mystics and Non-mystics," in *Studies in the Psychology of Mystics,* trans. A. Thorold (London: Burns Oates and Washbourne, 1927: reprint ed. Albany: Magi Books, 1964), p. 103.

29. Reginald Garrigou-LaGrange, O.P., *Christian Perfection and Contemplation,* trans. M. T. Doyle, O.P. (St. Louis: Herder, 1937), p. 128.

30. Thomas Aquinas, *Summa theologiae,* I, q. 8, a. 3 c.

31. Ibid., I, q. 12, a. 12 c.

32. Ibid., I, q. 12, a. 13 c.

33. Ibid., I, q. 8, a. 3, ad 4.

34. Ibid., I, q. 12, a. 5, ad 2.

35. John Ruusbroec, *Book of Supreme Truth* in *John of Ruysbroeck,* trans. C. A. Wynschenck (London: Watkins, 1951), p. 237. I use the more accurate spelling of the name, Ruusbroec.

36. Ibid.

37. Aldous Huxley, *The Perennial Philosophy* (New York: Harpers, 1945), Introduction, pp. vii–xi.

38. Huston Smith, "Is There a Perennial Philosophy?" *Journal of the American Academy of Religion* 55 (1987): 564.

39. Steven T. Katz, "Language, Epistemology, and Mysticism," *Mysti-*

cism and Philosophical Analysis, ed. S. T. Katz (New York: Oxford University Press, 1978), p. 26.

40. Ibid., p. 22.

41. See R. C. Zaehner, *Mysticism Sacred and Profane* (New York: Oxford University Press, 1961).

42. Katz, "Language," p. 65.

43. H. Smith, "Perennial Philosophy," p. 554.

44. S. T. Katz, "The Conservative Character of Mystical Experience," *Mysticism and Religious Traditions,* ed. S. T. Katz (New York: Oxford University Press, 1983), p. 33.

45. See James R. Price, "The Objectivity of Mystical Truth Claims," *Thomist* 49 (January 1985): 81–98.

46. Ibid., p. 98.

47. John Ruusbroec, *The Spiritual Espousals* in *John Ruusbroec,* trans. J. A. Wiseman (New York: Paulist, 1985), p. 146.

48. Antonio T. de Nicolás, trans. and ed., *Powers of Imagining: Ignatius de Loyola* (Albany: State University of New York Press, 1986), p. 180.

49. David Knowles, *The English Mystical Tradition* (New York: Harper, 1961), p. 147.

50. Ibid., p. 148.

51. Julian of Norwich, *Revelations of Divine Love,* trans. C. Wolters (Middlesex, England: Penguin, 1973), p. 187.

52. Ibid., pp. 184–85.

53. Ibid., p. 186.

54. Ibid., p. 187.

55. Frederick Copleston, S. J., *Religion and the One* (New York: Crossroad, 1982), p. 200.

56. See ibid., pp. 196, 203.

CHAPTER 3

1. These first two sections are based on my earlier articles: "Beauty, Sadness, and the Gift of Knowledge," *The American Ecclesiastical Review,* 134 (1956): 304–12; and "Man's Response to Tragedy," ibid. 150 (1964): 241–50.

2. Edgar Allan Poe, *Works,* 5 vols. (New York: P. F. Collier and Son, 1903), 5:182–83.

3. Henry Wadsworth Longfellow, "The Day Is Done," *The Complete Poetical Works of Henry Wadsworth Longfellow,* ed. H. E. Scudder (Boston: Houghton Mifflin, 1983), p. 64.

4. Poe, *Works,* 5:176.

5. Ibid.

6. Augustine, *Confessions,* trans. F. J. Sheed (New York: Sheed and Ward, 1941), bk. I, ch. 1, p. 3.

7. Poe, *Works,* 5:176.

8. Jacques Maritain, *Creative Intuition in Art and Poetry,* Bollingen Series XXXV-1 (New York: Pantheon Books, 1953), p. 164. See also Charles A. Hart, *Thomistic Metaphysics* (Englewood Cliffs, N.J.: Prentice Hall, Inc., 1959), ch. 16, "The Integration of the Transcendentals in Beauty," pp. 386–403.

9. Søren Kierkegaard, *Either/Or,* trans. Walter Lowrie, revised by H. A. Johnson, 2 vols. (Princeton: Princeton University Press, 1944), 2:207–08.

10. Ibid., p. 208.

11. Thomas Aquinas, *Summa theologiae,* I–II, q. 2, a. 8 c.

12. Ibid.

13. Idem, *In libris de divinis nominibus.* c. IV, lect. 5.

14. Augustine, *Confessions,* bk. 10, ch. 27, p. 192.

15. Aquinas, *Summa theologiae,* I–I, q. 34, a. 2, ad 2: "Delectatio non quaeritur propter aliud, quia est quies in finem."

16. Ibid., q. 23, a. 4 c: "Cum adeptum fuerit bonum, dat appetibus quietationem quandam in ipso bono adepto, et hoc pertinet ad delectationem vel gaudium. Cui opponitur ex parte mali dolor vel tristitia."

17. Jean Mouroux, *The Christian Experience,* trans. George Lamb (New York: Sheed and Ward, 1954), p. 239.

18. Gregory the Great, *Liber Moralium,* Lib. 1, c. XXV in cap. 1 Job, n. 35 (*PL* 75:545): "Intuendum quoque est quam nullus dolor mentis sit in actione praecipitationis."

19. Leo the Great, *Sermo* 95 (*PL* 54:463).

20. Augustine, *De Sermone Domini in Monte sec. Matt.,* Lib. I, c. 2, 5 (*PL* 34:1232).

21. Aquinas, *Summa theologiae,* I–II, q. 60, a. 3, ad 3.

22. Ibid., II–II, q. 10, a. 4 c.

23. John of St. Thomas, O.P., *The Gifts of the Holy Spirit,* trans. Dominic Hughes, O.P. (New York: Sheed and Ward, 1951), p. 15.

24. Ibid.

25. Ibid., p. 152.

26. Ibid., p. 151.

27. Aquinas, *Summa theologiae,* II–II, q. 10, a. 1 c.

28. Charles Baudelaire, *Oeuvres complètes,* ed. Claude Pichois (Paris: Gallimard, 1976), *Études sur Poe,* p. 334.

29. John of St. Thomas, *Gifts,* p. 125.

30. See Augustine, *Confessions,* bk. 7, chaps. 12–13, pp. 118–19.

31. Aquinas, *De malo,* q. 1, a. 1.

32. C. S. Lewis, *The Problem of Pain* (New York: Macmillan, 1940), p. 93.

33. Mark Pontifex, "The Value of Pain," *The Downside Review* 76 (1958): 345.

34. Ibid., p. 362.

35. Viktor E. Frankl, *The Doctor and the Soul* (New York: Alfred A. Knopf, 1957).

36. Ibid., p. 62.

37. Idem, *Man's Search for Meaning* (New York: Washington Square Press, 1963), p. 156. This book gives an excellent account of his experiences and theory.

38. The description of the three types of values are pieced together from Frankl's *The Doctor and the Soul*, pp. xii, 121–22.

39. Idem, *Man's Search for Meaning*, p. 183.

40. Idem, *The Doctor and the Soul*, p. xii.

41. Ibid., p. 129.

42. Ibid., p. 73.

43. Ibid., p. 75.

44. Ibid., p. 73–74.

45. Ibid., p. 75.

46. Ibid., p. 74–75.

47. Idem, *The Unconscious God* (New York: Simon and Schuster, 1975), p. 13.

48. Ibid., pp. 15–16.

49. *DS.* 3003. Concerning freedom, note the statement of the Council of Trent: "If anyone says that it is not in the power of man to make his ways evil but that God works evil things as he does good things, not only permissively, but also properly and *per se,* so that, therefore, the betrayal of Judas is as much his own work as the calling of Paul, let him be anathema." *DS* 1556. However, all evils other than sins are willed by God indirectly and *per accidens;* that is, they are consequent on God's *per se* willing of some good.

50. On the absence of chance, Aquinas wrote: "It must be said that those things which happen here by accident, whether in natural things or in the affairs of men, are reduced to some pre-ordained cause, which is Divine Providence" (*Summa theologiae*, I, q. 116, a. 1 c). Also: "Something is said to be fortuitous in things in the order of particular causes, outside the order of which they occur. But inasmuch as it pertains to Divine Providence, nothing in the world occurs by chance" (Ibid., I, q. 103, a. 7, ad 2).

51. Idem, *De potentia*, q. 3, a. 6, ad 4.

52. See J. A. Fitzmyer, S.J., *Jerome Biblical Commentary* (Englewood Cliffs, N.J.: Prentice-Hall, 1968), vol II, 53:91, p. 317. Depending on the manuscripts followed and their interpretation, however, at least two other readings from the Greek text, with slightly different emphases, are possible. But they only make explicit what is implicit in my text, which is from the Vulgate and is the one usually found in mystical writings of the past.

53. Ibid.

54. See Pseudo-Dionysius, *The Complete Works,* trans. Colm Luibheid and ed. R. Roques (New York: Paulist, 1987): *Mystical Theology,* III (1032D–1033D), pp. 138–40; and *Celestial Hierarchy,* (II 136D–145C), pp. 147–53.

55. Pseudo-Dionysius, *Celestial Hierarchy,* II (141A), p. 150.

56. The Scholastics used the analogies of proportionality and of attribution.

57. Paul Ricoeur, *The Conflict of Interpretations,* ed. D. Ihde (Evanston, Illinois: Northwestern University Press, 1974), pp. 12–13.

58. Idem, *Symbolism of Evil*, trans. E. Buchanan (Boston: Beacon Press, 1969), p. 14.

59. Ibid., p. 351.

60. Bernard J. F. Lonergan, S.J., *Method*, 2d ed. (New York: Herder and Herder, 1972), p. 64.

61. Ibid., p. 67.

62. Ibid., p. 341.

63. Idem, *The Third Collection* (New York: Paulist Press, 1985), p. 115.

64. Mircea Eliade, *Images and Symbols*, trans. P. Mairet (New York: Sheed and Ward, 1961), p. 178.

65. Ibid., p. 177 and *The Two and the One*, trans. J. M. Cohen (New York: Harper Torchbooks, 1969), p. 205.

66. Bernard J. F. Lonergan, S.J., *Insight* (New York: Philosophical Library, 1958), p. 533.

67. Eliade, *Images and Symbols*, p. 176.

68. Idem, *The Two and the One*, p. 207.

69. Idem, *Images and Symbols*, p. 176.

70. Ibid., p. 174.

71. Idem, *The Two and the One*, p. 297.

72. Idem, *Images and Symbols*, p. 33.

73. Karl Rahner, S.J., "The Theology of the Symbol," *Theological Investigations*, trans. K. Smith (Baltimore: Helicon Press, 1966), IV, p. 244.

74. Ibid., p. 252.

75. Ibid., p. 231.

76. Ibid., p. 252.

77. Paul Ricoeur, *The Symbolism of Evil*, esp. ch. I "Defilement", pp. 25–46.

78. Fourth Lateran Council (1215) Cap. II: "Inter creatorem et creaturam non potest similitudo notari, quin inter eos maior sit dissimilitudo notanda" *DS* 806.

79. Hans Urs von Balthasar, *The Glory of the Lord*, vol. 1: *Seeing the Form* (San Francisco: Ignatius Press, 1982), p. 125.

CHAPTER 4

1. Vatican I, *Enchiridion symbolorum, definitionum et declarationum de rebus fidei et morum*, edited by H. Denzinger; 36th ed., revised by A. Schönmetzer (Freiburg im Breisgau: Herder, 1973), 3016. (Hereafter cited as *DS*.)

2. Aquinas, *Summa theologiae*, I, q. 12, a. 13, c.

3. Ibid.

4. Vatican I, *DS* 3004.

5. Vatican I, *DS* 3026.

6. Karl Barth, *Church Dogmatics*, trans. G. W. Bromiley (Edinburgh: T.

and T. Clark, 1957), Vol. II, 1, pp. 65, 69, 75–84. For a different Protestant challenge to natural theology, see Emil Brunner, *Dogmatics*, vol. i, *The Christian Doctrine of God* (London: Lutterworth Press, 1949), esp. ch. IX.

7. These words are found in the *Brihad-Aranyyaka Upanishad* (2,3,5), which calls them the only suitable description of Brahman; thus Shankara in his commentary on it defines Brahman by eliminating all determinations.

8. Aquinas, *Summa theol.*, I, q. 12, a. 2, c. (Italics supplied.)

9. Idem, I *Sententiae.* d. 8, q. 1, a. 1, ad 4.

10. Ibid.

11. Idem, *Summa theol.*, I, q. 13, a. 11, c.

12. Ibid. Note also: "The things seen in the essence of God by those who see it are not seen through any likeness but through the essence of God itself in their minds." Ibid., q. 12, a. 9, c.

13. Bernard J. F. Lonergan, S.J., *Understanding and Being*, ed. by E. and M. Morelli (New York: Edwin Mellen Press, 1980), p. 211. See also *Insight* (London: Longmans, Green, 1957; New York: Philosophical Library, 1958), ch. XIII.

14. See idem, *Method in Theology* 2d ed. (New York: Herder and Herder, 1972), pp. 340–44, where Lonergan examines the appropriateness of calling God an object.

15. Ibid., p. 342.

16. Idem, *Understanding and Being*, p. 125.

17. See *Insight*, p. 251.

18. Aquinas, *De Potentia*, VII, 5, ad 4.

19. John of the Cross, *Ascent of Mount Carmel*, bk. II, ch. 15, 4, p. 149. In *The Living Flame of Love,* John of the Cross used a different metaphor to illustrate the same process: "God, like the sun, stands above souls ready to communicate himself" (Ibid., Stanza 3, 47, p. 628). God's response will be proportionate to our efforts: "As the sun rises in the morning and shines upon your house so that its light may enter if you open the shutters, so God, who in watching over Israel does not doze, nor still less sleep, will enter the soul that is empty and fill it with divine goods" (ibid., 46, pp. 627–28).

20. Patanjali, author of a classic text on yoga, in his second sutra stated that for union (yoga) with Brahman, it is necessary to suppress all movements or modifications of the mind: *Yoga chitta vritti nirodhah.* See Swami Hariharanda Aranya, ed., *Yoga Philosophy of Patanjali* (Albany: State University of New York Press, 1983), pp. 6–11.

21. David Knowles spoke of a Neo-Platonic contamination of Christian mysticism in *The English Mystical Tradition* (New York: Harper and Bros., 1961), p. 16. He noted (see p. 111) four characteristics of Neo-Platonism which Western Catholic mystical theology adopted: (1) the apophatic *via remotionis;* (2) the brief and ecstatic character of mystical illumination; (3) the readiness of divine light to flood the soul if obstacles are removed; and (4) the openness of mystical experience to all. More recently, Andrew Louth, arguing against contamination, acknowledged the influence of Neo-Platonism on the Greek Fathers but pointed to the radical opposition between them.

The former is individualistic; its God is impersonal; it gives no role to grace; and, above all, it does not envisage love between God and man. See his *The Origins of the Christian Mystical Tradition: From Plato to Denys* (Oxford: Clarendon Press, 1983): chapter 3 on Plotinus (his conclusion is on p. 51) and chapter 10, the first section of which (pp. 191–99) is on Platonism and mysticism.

22. Eckhart, Blakney translation, p. 121.

23. John Tauler, O.P., *Spiritual Conferences*, trans. and ed. E. Colledge and M. Jane (St. Louis: B. Herder, 1961), p. 157.

24. Ibid., pp. 157–70.

25. Eckhart, Blakney translation, p. 123.

26. John of the Cross, *Collected Works*, ed. and trans. E. A. Peers (Westminster, Md.: Newman Press, 1949), vol. 3, *Spiritual Canticle* (2nd Redaction), 30, 6, p. 354.

27. Augustine, *The Lord's Sermon on the Mount, De sermone Domini in monte sec. Matt.*, II, 3, 14 (*PL.* 34:1275).

28. See Lonergan, *Insight*, pp. 431–37.

29. John of the Cross, *Ascent*, ed. Peers, vol. 1, I, 14, 11, p. 63.

30. Eckhart, Blakney translation, sermon 6, p. 131.

31. John Damascene, *De fide orthodoxa*, I, III, c. 24 (*PG* 94:1090).

32. Anonymous, *The Cloud of Unknowing*, trans. Clifton Wolters (Baltimore: Penguin Books, 1971), p. 128.

33. Ibid., p. 124.

34. John Ruysbroeck, *The Sparkling Stone*, trans. C. A. Wynschenk (London: Watkins, 1951), p. 186. In the text, I use the more accurate spelling, Ruusbroec.

35. Aquinas, *Summa theologiae*, II–II, q. 179, a. 1, ad 1.

36. G. K. Chesterton, *Varied Types* (New York: Dodd and Mead, 1903), p. 59.

37. On the use of these two terms see: Reiner Shürmann, *Meister Eckhart: Translation with Commentary* (Bloomington, Ind.: Indiana University Press, 1978), pp. 12–18, 84–85; and Richard Woods, O.P., *Eckhart's Way* (Wilmington, Delaware: Michael Glazier, 1986), p. 130.

38. Eckhart, *Counsels on Discernment, Meister Eckhart*, trans. E. Colledge and B. McGinn (New York: Paulist Press, 1981), pp. 250, 258.

39. Eckhart, Sermon, "Proclaim the Word," ed. Shürmann, p. 185.

40. John of the Cross, *The Dark Night*, ed. Peers, vol. 1, II, 7, 4, p. 342.

41. St. Gregory of Sinai made this *mneme theou* the heart of his teaching: "Mental prayer or remembrance of God is higher than all other works" (*Instructions to Hesychasts* in *Writings from the Philokalia*, trans. E. Kadloubovsky and G. E. H. Palmer [London: Faber and Faber, 1967], p. 80). Again, "Watch with care and intelligence, you lover of God" (p. 90). Note also in the Western church, St. Benedict's injunction: *Oblivionem omnino fugiat* ("Flee all forgetfulness") (*Regula*, VII).

42. John of the Cross, *Ascent*, ed. Peers, vol. 1, III, 2, 14, p. 233.

43. Ibid.

44. Ibid., III, 15, 1, p. 257.

45. Ibid.

46. Eckhart, *Meister Eckhart*, trans. E. Colledge and B. McGinn (New York: Paulist Press, 1981), p. 288.

47. See Carl Jung, *Memories, Dreams, Reflections*, ed. A. Jaffé, trans. R. and C. Winston (New York: Vantage Books, 1963), pp. 398–99.

48. Ibid., p. 219.

49. John of the Cross, *Ascent*, ed. Peers, vol. 1, I, 1, p. 17, the last line of first stanza. The effects of inordinate desires are described in chapters 6 through 10.

50. Ibid., III, 13, 1, p. 249.

51. Ruusbroek, *Divine Espousals* (Wynschenk trans.) p. 155.

52. Ibid.

53. Ruusbroeck, *Book of Supreme Truth*, (Wynschenk trans.), p. 232.

54. Ibid., pp. 229–30.

55. Tauler, *Conferences*, p. 233.

56. Ruusbroeck, *Book of Supreme Truth*, p. 231.

57. Tauler, *Conferences*, p. 230.

58. Ibid., p. 212.

59. Molinos, *DS*, 1222. This is among the errors of Molinos condemned in 1687 in the constitution *Coelestis pastor* of Innocent XI.

60. Ruusbroeck, *Espousals*, p. 155.

61. Bernard Lonergan, *Method*, p. 8.

62. Vernon Gregson, *Lonergan, Spirituality, and the Meeting of Religions* (Lanham, Md.: University Press of America, 1985), p. 80. A good introduction to Lonerganian spirituality.

63. John Cassian, *Conferences*, trans. Colm Luibheid (New York: Paulist Press, 1985), p. 120.

64. See A. Louth, *Origins*, pp. 43–44, 48, 49.

65. Plotinus, *Enneads*, VI, 9. 4.

66. Ibid., VI, 9. 3.

67. See Carl Jung concerning individuation, *Memories*, pp. 395–96.

68. Bernard Lonergan, *Method*, p. 105.

69. Ibid., p. 106.

70. Plato, *Republic*, 514–17.

71. Ibid., 520c.

72. Ibid., 218d.

73. John of the Cross, *Spiritual Canticle*, ed. Kavanaugh, stanzas 14 and 15, p. 462.

74. Ibid., no. 2, p. 463.

75. Ibid., no. 5, p. 464.

76. Ibid.

77. Ibid. (Italics supplied.)

78. Ibid., stanza 39, no. 12, p. 561.

79. Ibid., stanza 36, nos. 6 and 7, pp. 547–48.

80. Ibid., no. 5, p. 546.

81. Teresa of Avila, Life, *The Complete Works*, ed. E. Allison Peers, vol. 1: *Life* (London: Sheed and Ward, 1972), ch. 22, p. 40.

82. Ibid., vol. 2: *Mansions*, 6th ch. vii, p. 305.

83. Ibid., vol. 1: *Life.* ch. 22, p. 140.

84. Ibid., vol. 2: *Mansions*, 7th, ch. 2, pp. 334–35.

CHAPTER 5

1. The first two sections of this chapter are based on my article, "Can Physiological Techniques Lead to Christian Mysticism?" Catholic Theological Society of America, *Proceedings of the Thirty-Third Annual Convention* (Milwaukee, Wisconsin, 1978), pp 97–109.

2. Although brain functions have a biochemical base, I shall not consider states induced by mind-changing drugs such as alcohol, marijuana, cocaine, mescaline, LSD, or psilocybin, despite the frequent but mistaken claims that such states are similar to and even identical with mystical states.

3. Congregation for the Doctrine of Faith, *Letter on Some Aspects of Christian Meditation* (October 15, 1989), *Origins*, December 28, 1989, vol. 19, no. 30: 492–98.

4. Some suggest that one reason why ascetical practices foster a heightened consciousness is the change in body chemistry and body rhythms that they induce. See R.E.L. Masters and Jean Houston, *The Varieties of Psychedelic Experience* (New York: Holt, Rinehart and Winston, 1966), p. 248.

5. Herbert Benson, M.D., *The Relaxation Response* (New York: William Morrow and Co., 1975).

6. See ibid., chap. 7, especially pp. 114–15.

7. Ibid., p. 76.

8. Ibid., pp. 97–98.

9. Ibid., p. 76.

10. Ibid., p. 77.

11. Joseph Maréchal, S.J., "On the Feeling of Presence in Mystics and Non-mystics," *Studies in the Psychology of the Mystics*, trans. A. Thorold (London: Burns Oates and Washbourne, 1927; Albany, N.Y.: Magi Books, 1964), p. 199. Italics supplied.

12. Ibid.

13. H. Benson, *The Relaxation Response*, p. 76. Italics supplied.

14. H. Benson, with William Proctor, *Your Maximum Mind* (New York: Times Books, 1987), pp. 6–7.

15. Ibid., p. 40.

16. H. Benson, with William Proctor, *Beyond the Relaxation Response* (New York: Times Books, 1985; Berkley Books, 1985), p. 105.

17. Charles F. Stroebel, M.D., *QR: The Quieting Reflex* (New York: Putnam's, 1982; Berkley Books, 1983).

18. Ibid., p. 114.

19. See a report on some substantiating authorities, "A Feel-Good Theory: A Smile Affects Mood," *New York Times,* Science News, July 18, 1989, p. C1. For an application of the mind-body role of the limbic system and hypothalamus in cancer therapy, see S. M. Simonton, O. C. Simonton, and J. L. Creighton, *Getting Well Again* (New York: Bantam Books, 1980), chapter 7.

20. Stroebel, *The Quieting Reflex,* pp. 119–23.

21. Ibid., p. 115.

22. Teresa of Avila, "Maxims," no. 30, *Complete Works,* ed. E. Allison Peers, 3 vols. (London: Sheed & Ward, 1972), 3:257.

23. Barbara Brown, *New Mind: New Body* (New York: Harper and Row, 1974; Bantam Edition, 1975). See also her *Stress and the Art of Biofeedback* (New York: Harper and Row, 1977; Bantam edition, 1979). These books give a sound basis for a comparison between biofeedback experiences and mystical experiences. They have excellent bibliographies.

24. Idem, *New Mind: New Body,* p. 355.

25. Ibid., p. 363.

26. Ibid., p. 371; see also *Stress and the Art of Biofeedback,* pp. 222–23, where Brown asserts that even in contemplation there is not (as Benson seems to hold) a uniform alpha state in meditation: "The information to date . . . suggests that slow alpha may indicate one type of internal focus of attention, possibly that of the passive observers, where as fast EEG activity, as found during yogic meditation and ecstasy, may indicate mental involvement in the perception of mental processes." Earlier she quoted on this point, Gopi Krishna, *The Awakening of Kundalini* (New York: Dutton, 1975).

27. Ibid., p. 386.

28. Ibid., p. 426.

29. Ibid., p. 384.

30. Aristotle, *On the Soul,* II, 7.

31. Brown, p. 379.

32. Ibid., p. 383.

33. Ibid., p. 426.

34. Ibid., pp. 383–84.

35. Ibid., p. 379.

36. Aldous Huxley, *The Perennial Philosophy* (New York: Harper and Row, 1945). See also the response of Martin D'Arcy, S.J., *The Meeting of Love and Knowledge* (New York: Harper and Row, 1957).

37. Abraham Maslow, *Religion, Values, and Peak-Experiences* (Columbus: Ohio State University Press, 1964; New York: Penguin Books, 1976).

38. John of the Cross, *The Ascent of Mount Carmel, The Complete Works,* trans. and ed. E. Allison Peers, 3 vols. (Westminster, Md., The Newman Press, 1949), vol. 1, III, 13, 1, p. 249.

39. John Ruusbroec, *John of Ruysbroec,* trans. C. A. Wynschenk, ed. E. Underhill (London: John M. Watkins, 1951), *The Book of Supreme Truth,* p. 229.

40. Ibid., p. 231.

41. Teresa of Avila, *Obras,* ed. P. Silverio (Burgos: Tipographia de 'El

Monte Carmelo,' 1935), *Castillo Interior,* Cuartas Moradas, c. III, no. 5, p. 532.

42. R. C. Zaehner, *Mysticism Sacred and Profane* (Oxford: Oxford University Press, 1957; Galaxy Books, 1961), p. 173.

43. Georges Bernanos, *Sous le soleil de Satan* (Paris: Gallimard, 1961), p. 154, quoted in R. C. Zaehner, *Zen, Drugs, and Mysticism* (New York: Pantheon Books, 1972), p. 147.

44. John of the Cross, *Works,* vol. 1, *Dark Night,* II, 2, 1, p. 400.

45. Ibid., I, 11, 3, p. 382.

46. Ibid., I, 3, 3, p. 358.

47. Ibid., vol. III, *The Living Flame* (2d redaction), III, 36.

48. Idem, *Ascent,* II, 5, 4, pp. 80–81.

49. Gregory the Great, *Moralia,* X, 8, 13.

50. Alfred Tennyson, quoted in William James, *Varieties of Religious Experience* (New York: University Books, 1963), pp. 383–84, n. 2.

51. John of the Cross, *Ascent,* II, 13, 7, p. 117.

52. Ibid., II, 14, 8, pp. 121–22.

53. For a full discussion of these criteria see John of the Cross: *Ascent,* II, 13; *Dark Night,* I, 9; and *Points of Love,* no. 40.

54. Ibid., *Ascent,* II, 16, 10, p. 134.

55. Meister Eckhart, "Counsels on Discernment," *Meister Eckhart,* trans. E. Colledge and B. McGinn (New York: Paulist, 1981), p. 284.

56. Karl Rahner, *Theological Investigations,* trans. M. Kohl (New York: Crossroad, 1981), XVII: 93–94.

57. Aquinas, *Summa theologiae,* II–II, q. 24, a. 3, ad 2.

58. John of the Cross, *Ascent,* II, 9, 1, p. 98.

59. Ibid., p. 94. See also: "Mysticism occurs, on the contrary, within the framework of normal grace and within the experience of faith. To this extent, those who insist that mystical experience is not specifically different from the ordinary life of grace (as such) are certainly right." *Encyclopedia of Theology,* ed. Karl Rahner (New York: Seabury, 1975), pp. 1010–11.

60. Rahner, *Theological Investigations,* ibid., 95.

61. Ibid., p. 94.

62. Idem, "Mysticism," *Encyclopedia of Theology: The Concise Sacramentum Mundi* (New York: Seabury, 1975), p. 1011.

63. Ibid., p. 95.

64. John of the Cross, *Ascent,* II, 9, 1, p. 98.

65. Rahner, *Theological Investigations,* pp. 98–99.

66. Bernard J. F. Lonergan, S.J., *Method in Theology,* 2d ed. (New York: Herder and Herder, 1972), p. 115.

67. Ibid., p. 119.

68. Ibid., p. 115.

69. The word "normal" is used in two ways: the one, meaning ordinary, is in contrast with mystical; the other, meaning proper or conformed to a norm, includes mystical, as it does here.

70. Joseph Maréchal, *Psychology of the Mystics,* p. 200.

71. See Reginald Garrigou-LaGrange, O.P., *Christian Perfection and Contemplation,* trans. Sr. M. T. Doyle, O.P. (St. Louis: Herder, 1958).

72. See Ruth Burrows, *Guidelines to Mystical Prayer* (Denville, N.J.: Dimension Books, 1980).

CHAPTER 6

1. This chapter has been based on my article with the same title in *Carmelite Studies* 1 (1980): 213–30.

2. The critical word, *emfaniso,* has been translated variously but not conflictingly: Raymond Brown in the *Anchor Bible* and Ronald Knox in his own translation used "reveal"; the *Jerusalem Bible* and the University of Chicago (Goodspeed) Bible used "show"; and the Douai-Rheims (Challoner) Bible used "manifest." The latter reflects the Vulgate's *manifestabo* and was familiar to most of the mystics of the Latin Church, including St. Teresa and St. John of the Cross. Therefore, I use the older translation for the text of John 14:21–23, but elsewhere in this chapter I usually follow the Anchor Bible translation by Raymond E. Brown, *The Gospel According to John* (New York: Doubleday, 1966 and 1967), Vols. 29 and 29A in *Anchor Bible* series.

3. Brown, *Gospel,* p. 1141.

4. Ibid., p. 653.

5. Rudolf Bultmann, *The Gospel of John,* trans. G. R. Beasley-Murray (Philadelphia: Westminster Press, 1971), p. 570.

6. Ibid., p. 559. Note the similar statement by Brown, p. 1142: "The later Christian is no further removed from the ministry of Jesus than was the earlier Christian, for the Paraclete dwells within him as he dwelt within the eyewitnesses. And by recalling and giving new meaning to what Jesus said, the Paraclete guides every generation in facing new situations; he declares the things to come (xvi 13)."

7. Bultmann, p. 559, n. 2, referring to Kierkegaard, *Philosophical Fragments,* ed. and trans. H. and E. Hong (Princeton: Princeton University Press, 1985), pp. 104–105.

8. Rudolph Schnackenburg, *The Truth Will Make You Free,* trans. R. Albrecht (New York: Herder and Herder, 1966), p. 94.

9. Ibid., p. 99.

10. Ibid., pp. 102–3.

11. Ibid., p. 117. He referred to Vatican I: "Since man is totally dependent upon God as upon his Creator and Lord, and since created reason is wholly subject to uncreated truth, we are bound to give to the revealing God, in faith, full obedience of intellect and will" (*DS* 3008).

12. Ibid., p. 113.

13. Teresa of Avila, *The Complete Works,* trans. and ed. by E. Allison Peers (London: Sheed and Ward, 1972), vol. 2: *The Interior Castle,* Second Mansions, ch. 1, 8, pp. 216–17.

14. Ibid., vol. 1: *Spiritual Relations*, Relation VI, p. 336.

15. Ibid., p. 337. Italics added.

16. See John of the Cross, *The Complete Works*, trans. and ed. E. Allison Peers (Westminster, Md.: The Newman Press, 1949), vol. 1: *The Ascent of Mount Carmel*, II, 9, 1, p. 98.

17. Ibid., II, 29, 5, p. 211.

18. Ibid., II, 29, 6, p. 211.

19. Ibid., II, 26, 10, p. 197.

20. Ibid., II, 26, 5, p. 196.

21. Ibid., II, 26, 10, pp. 197–98.

22. See ibid., II, 26, 3, p. 194.

23. Ibid., II, 29, 6, pp. 211–12. But here I use the translation by K. Kavanaugh and O. Rodriquez, *Collected Works* (Washington: Institute of Carmelite Studies, 1979), p. 205.

24. Ibid., vol. 3: *The Living Flame of Love* (second redaction), Prologue, 3, p. 115.

25. Ibid., Prologue, 2, p. 115.

26. Ibid., Stanza I, 15, pp. 125–26.

27. Brown, *Gospel*, p. 776.

28. Ibid.

29. Teresa, vol. 2: *The Interior Castle*, Fifth Mansions, 3, 7, p. 261.

30. Ibid.

31. Brown, *Gospel*, p. 646.

32. Ibid.

33. Ibid., p. 781.

34. Ibid., p. 639.

35. John of the Cross, vol. 1: *Ascent*, II, 5, 4, pp. 80–81.

36. Brown, *Gospel*, p. 507.

37. Ibid., pp. 507–08.

38. Ibid., p. 508.

39. Ibid.

40. See ibid., Brown's commentary on verse 18, pp. 17–18, 35–36. See also Jn 4:12 and I Jn 3:2.

41. Teresa, vol. 1: *Life*, 27, 4, p. 171.

42. Ibid.

43. Ibid., vol. 3, *Interior Castle*, Seventh Mansions, VII, 2, 5, p. 336.

44. Ibid.

45. John of the Cross, vol. 1, *Ascent*, II, 24, 4, p. 189.

46. Ibid., pp. 189–90.

47. Brown, *Gospel*, p. 507.

CHAPTER 7

1. Bernard J. F. Lonergan, S.J., *De Deo Trino* (Rome: Gregorian University Press, 1964), vol. 2, p. 193.

2. Council of Florence, DS 1330.

3. Ibid., *DS* 1331; see Aquinas, *Summa theologiae*, 1, q. 42, a. 5.

4. Bernard Lonergan, *De Deo Trino*, vol. 2, p. 205.

5. See Walter Kasper, *The God of Jesus Christ* (New York: Crossroad, 1984), p. 284.

6. *DS* 150.

7. William Hill, O.P., *The Three-Personed God* (Washington: Catholic University of America Press, 1982), pp. 223–24. (The statement that he is discussing is found in Karl Rahner, *The Trinity* [New York: Herder and Herder, 1970], p. 106.) Hill stated also: "He [the Spirit] is himself the union of Father and Son and so if given to men makes them to be, by his very personal presence, sharers in divine trinitarian life (p. 292); and "As the Spirit unites the eternal Son and the Father so does he unite adoptive sons to the Father, through the only begotten Son, in the freedom of love" (p. 302).

8. Matthias J. Scheeben, *Mysteries of Christianity* (St. Louis: Herder, 1946), p. 66; and see also p. 67: "In God, however, the love of the first two persons is really identical with the goodness of the essence which they love in each other and which they both possess. Hence in consummating their mutual love and making it fruitful in an inner product, they can and must, together with and in their love, pour forth and incorporate in this product, as in a real pledge, their mutual or rather their common good, their essence."

9. Aquinas, *Omnia Opera* (Parma: Fiaccadori, 1852–73), vol. 16: *Compendium theologiae*, nos. 37 and 41.

10. See Etienne Gilson, *The Mystical Theology of St. Bernard* (London: Sheed and Ward, 1940), chap. 2, pp. 52–54.

11. Ibid., p. 224, n. 43, and 234, n. 109. Bernard took this term from Augustine (*Confessions*, bk. VII, ch. 10, n. 16), who took it from Plato (*Statesman*, 273 D).

12. Bernard of Clairvaux, *De Diligendo Deo*, chap. I, from *Saint Bernard on the Love of God*, ed. and trans. T. L. Connolly (Techny, Illinois: Mission Press, 1943), p. 4.

13. See Etienne Gilson, *The Mystical Theology of St. Bernard*, p. 112.

14. Bernard, *Sermons on the Canticle of Canticles*, ch. 47, ed. Connelly, p. 196.

15. John of Ruysbroeck, *The Adornment of the Spiritual Marriage*, trans, C. Wynschenk (London: Watkins, 1951), p. 131.

16. Ibid., p. 127.

17. William Hill, *Three-Personed God*, pp. 284–86.

18. Bernard Lonergan, *De Deo Trino*, vol. 2, p. 226. For example, God knows Paul through divine knowledge not by means of Paul, but Paul is required not before or after but concomitantly.

19. Aquinas, *Summa theologiae*, I, q. 37, a. 2, ad 3; see also William Hill, *Three-Personed God*, p. 273.

20. See William Hill, *Three-Personed God*, p. 288.

21. Yves Congar, O.P., "Autonomie et pouvoir central dans l'Eglise," *Irénikon* 43 (1980): 302. Robert Kress also elaborated this perichoretic di-

mension of the church in "The Church as Communio: Trinity and Incarnation as the Foundation of Ecclesiology," *Jurist* 36 (1976): 140f.

22. Aquinas, I *Sententiae*, 1, d. 14, q. 2, a. 2; see also *Summa theologiae*, I, q. 32, a. 2, ad 3.

23. Bernard Lonergan, S.J., *A Third Collection*, ed. F. E. Crowe (New York: Paulist, 1985), p. 250.

24. Aquinas, *Summa theologiae*, I–II, q. 28, a. 2c.

25. John of St. Thomas, *Cursus Theologicus*, in Iam IIae, 70.18.4.11.

26. William R. O'Connor, *The Eternal Quest* (New York: Longmans, Green, 1947), p. 179.

27. Gregory of Nyssa, *The Life of Moses*, trans. and ed. Abraham J. Malherbe and Everett Ferguson (New York: Paulist, 1978), bk. I, no. 5, p. 30 and bk. II, no. 225, p. 113.

28. Ibid., bk. I, no. 5, p. 30.

29. Ibid., bk. II, no. 227, p. 113–14.

30. Ibid., bk. II, no. 235, p. 115.

31. Idem, *Sixth Homily on the Canticle* (*PG* 44:885A–888A), cited in Louis Bouyer, *The Spirituality of the New Testament and the Fathers*, trans. Mary P. Ryan (New York: Desclée, 1963), vol. I, pp. 364–65.

32. St. Maximus the Confessor, *Writings*, trans. George C. Berthold (New York: Paulist, 1985), p. 118.

33. Mircea Eliade, *Patanjali and Yoga*, trans. C. L. Markmann (New York: Schocken Books, 1975), pp. 90–93.

34. See the discussion in Chapter One, Section II, on the distinction between spirit and flesh. The words of J.-M. Déchanet are pertinent here.

35. John of the Cross, *The Collected Works*, trans. K. Kavanaugh and O. Rodríguez (Washington: ICS Publications, 1979), Letter no. 12, p. 694; and see letter no. 6, p. 688. Note also, Hans von Balthasar, *The Glory of the Lord*, vol. III, *Studies in Theological Styles* (San Francisco: Ignatius Press, 1986), p. 134: "In loving and hoping faith the soul looks out into openness, indeed she can become that openness, the open mouth that God alone can fill."

36. Ibid., *Ascent* II, 15, 2, p. 148.

37. Ibid., II, 15, no. 4, p. 149.

38. Ibid., *Spiritual Canticle*, stanza 1, 12, p. 420.

39. Ibid., stanza 38, no. 3, p. 554.

40. Ibid., p. 553.

41. Ibid., stanza 39, 3, p. 558.

42. Ibid.

43. See Aristotle, *On the Soul*, III, 4. 429b29; and Aquinas, *Summa theologiae*, I, a. 79, q. 2 c.

44. See Vladimir Lossky, *The Mystical Theology of the Eastern Church* (London: James Clarke, 1957), p. 214.

45. Ibid., p. 209.

46. John Damascene, *De fide orthodoxa*, bk. II, 12 (*PG* 94: 924A).

47. John Ruusbroec, *Little Book of Clarification*, p. 267.

48. John of the Cross, *Ascent* II, 5, 7, pp. 117–18.

Name Index

✧   ✧   ✧

Subject Index

✧　　　✧　　　✧